Illumination

Discourses With Master Teacher

1998 Illumination - Discourses With Master Teacher
Printed, September 1998
Library of Congress Catalog Card Number: 97-90345
International Standard Book Number (ISBN) 1-890648-00-0

Published By:
Endeavor Academy
P.O. Box 206
Lake Delton, Wisconsin 53965
U. S. A.
Tel: +1 (608) 254-4431
Fax: +1 (608) 253-2892
www.endeavoracademy.com
Email: publishing@endeavoracademy.com

Contents

Foreword 9
The Initiation 11
The Mechanism of The Miracle 27
Bubbles 43
Black Holes: Time and Eternity 59
A Masters' Academy 83
Mrs. Brown, Red Rock and Rover 113
Dream A Light Dream 149
Freemasonry 165
Be My Valentine 189
The Bright Lights Are Heaven 211
Faith, Crop Circles & Chapter 17 263
Christian Enlightenment 309

Foreword

    The discourses in this volume are transcripts of revelatory talks given by the Master Teacher. They discuss and demonstrate the dynamics of the transformation of human consciousness as prescribed by the illuminate teachings of Jesus Christ in A Course In Miracles and the New Testament. Elucidating these teachings, the Master Teacher speaks with both the authority and the insight of enlightenment.

    These powerful communications are intended to serve as catalysts and stimulants to your own awakening. You will notice that the Master Teacher's talks are extemporaneous and are published intentionally with little editing, in the hope of maintaining and conveying the spontaneity, immediacy and spiritual continuity.

    Read them in open-mindedness and receptivity and experience a new joyous bright mindfulness as these celestial seeds begin to bear true fruit.

    Herein lies our individual discovery of the Peace of God and the passion of resurrection which is both our natural divine inheritance and the fulfillment of the mission of A Course In Miracles.

Today it will be given you to feel a touch of Heaven, though you will return to paths of learning. Yet you have come far enough along the way to alter time sufficiently to rise above its laws, and walk into eternity a while.

CHAPTER ONE

The Initiation

Good morning. We're at the kitchen table at God's Country Place. I was ruminating within my own mind and musing about how an awakened consciousness of my nature, my awakened mind, can express the impossible; that is, to encapsulate my revelation as to the certainty of God or Wholeness into a single talk, into a single catechism of reality, what method that I could use, perhaps within the Christian vernacular, in the statement that Wholeness can be reached through the transformation of the split mind. This is an attempt to bring it together in a single statement. The statement involves this: there is no philosophy or religion of the world that has ever been or will ever be anything but a declaration that a human mind, as configurated, has the capacity of knowledge. That is to say, it has within it the possibility of coming to a Whole Self. I look at you and I say, "Yes, this new consciousness now that has come here has within it, by whatever means, the possibility of recognition of a wholeness – a statement of its Whole Self."

The difficulty is not so much in this declaration because throughout history exoterically are all the admissions of the search of split mind – the declaration: "I don't know who I am; I must find this answer," – to the reality of the enlightenment or coming to Whole. Ultimately and directly this is the sole purpose of all religions, the folding back of the mind, the return of the mind, the remembering of the mind of its previous associations with Wholeness which was Heaven. Any teaching that doesn't direct itself to the transformation of your mind, that is as you associate yourself, ultimately is going to be meaningless. If we were to go to the *Course In Miracles*, which is the greatest exposé of this teaching that obviously has ever come historically within any framework that you could think of, the *Course In Miracles* is a directive and encapsulation of all of the statements of what you term "mystical Christianity," of the initiation process, of the coming to your Christhood, of the perfection of your mind in association with God. For goodness sake! Those of you who for ten years have been doing the *Course In Miracles*: it is a direct intercession of a Whole Mind, of the identity of Jesus Christ, into the chaotic perceptual mind. If you just start with that premise, it would be an infinite benefit to you. The premise being what? "I will bring this about through the transformation of my mind." Then, you won't have to do silliness like, "I've got to forgive my neighbor," or, "I'm working on the idea of establishing relationships on earth and formulating new churches." And by silliness I don't mean that they may not have value within the framework – I'm talking about a statement of the truth of the necessity for the transformation.

Now, we'll begin with this: There is no question, as Jesus Christ says in the *Course*, that all I ever teach is forgiveness and love or Wholeness in association with my mind which is a conglomerate of memory about the schism. Then the fundamental teaching very easily can become, the confrontation

CHAPTER ONE: The Initiation

will be, between what I think I am or how I am established, and the truth of what I really must be. This is really what? Shall we do it in Christianity? This is the coming up out of Egypt, originally, the crossing of the Red Sea, the coming ultimately into Jerusalem and the reenactment of the entire passion of awakening. The idea that the crucifixion and resurrection of Christ as an historic event has no value, because our teachings must be to your transformation, and that, at best, all historical events are nothing but allegories of the statement of the passion of your awakening. That's a fact, my brothers. This is the teaching of the *Course*, not more, and not less than this.

The *Course In Miracles*, as expressed in perhaps mystical Christianity, is nothing but the search for the Holy Grail. It is nothing but that. The whole idea of the purification of you through service and forgiving is to do nothing but bring your perceptual mind together to formulate a new reality, which is the Grail. If you would begin to look at the mystical teachings of Christianity in the transformation process and incorporate those into the workings of the *Course In Miracles*, it would be of great benefit to you. The problem that you have is that always the idea of individual transformation has been expurgated from the established church, which maintains that salvation comes through a mutual association of mind, rather than the coming through transformation to a Whole Mind. But all you would have to do is begin to look historically at Christianity, and it would be very obvious to you that the heretics are the statements of Jesus Christ, and are persecuted by the establishment which is a denial of the transformation of Jesus Christ. For goodness sake!

In the early 13th century the wages, the slaughter, the burning at the stake of the Cathars, the Gnostic teachings, Brothers of the Free Spirit – the teachings of any consecrated endeavor to enlightenment of the mind have always been sought out and vigorously attacked. By what? By perceptual mind. We'll do it once more: The statement of Jesus that, "If you can find

Whole Mind, you'll kill it," is the statement of perception in the conflict that it is experiencing with its own ideas. What we are saying, then, is that enlightenment or the teaching of the *Course*, is nothing but the bringing together of opposites. This is the whole Socratic teaching of the *Course In Miracles*. Take your opposites, take your perception, and through the welding or the bringing of them together in your mind, you can see your Whole Self.

Is this a mystical talk? Yes. Christian! Christianity, as in the *Course*, is a statement that you are the only living Son of God, or are an emanation from a single whole consciousness, and can come to know that through the relinquishment of your perceptual mind. The whole teaching of Jesus, in the *Course*, is that there is no thought outside of you, so that you can direct your attention to that splitness, to the initiation process of the purgation, or the relinquishment of your previous historic frames of reference. This is exactly what the *Course In Miracles* is. Nothing more and nothing less than this.

Where are these teachings being taught? They are very fearful teachings. If you present the consciousness with the necessity of relinquishment – the whole beginning process is to give up your worldly things. You're not going to do that. Jesus provides what He terms a middle road, that you can begin to practice in the Workbook, beginning with the statements, "I don't know what anything is. My mind is split. I am really nothing." Through this meditative technique, if you will, he can relinquish himself and fall into his surrender to God, which is nothing but prayer – the mystical identification of reunion with something that appears to be outside of you. Is the acknowledgment that it is outside of you valuable? Of course. If this isn't Heaven, like Jesus says, when you look around you, where do you think you are but in your perceptual evaluation of yourself, which *has* to be hell. My declaration to you that this must be individual is met with a great deal of resistance from you. You would much

CHAPTER ONE: The Initiation

prefer to believe that you can gather cohesive evidence and present it to your perceptual mind in a manner in which you can maturate or be enlightened to God. Of course you can't. It's impossible. It cannot be done. The coming of the Holy Spirit or the Third Eye or the Philosopher's Stone or the Holy Grail or the reaching Jerusalem and on and on and on... If you guys would begin to look at the frame of reference from which Master Jesus teaches in the *Course*, you would become very excited, because directly beneath the surface of all so-called exoteric teachings lies the certainty of the necessity of initiation. Jesus teaches nothing but this.

I declare to you through the process of my own initiation that this is the only manner that you will get it. Now you can attack me for that if you wish, but as Jesus does in the *Course*, I am laying the direct responsibility for the coming about of this in the power of your mind. Will the power of your mind lead you to the certainty of the necessity for the relinquishment of yourself? Of course. There are some lovely statements in the *Course* that direct you directly to that: Your sole responsibility is not to take responsibility. The only necessity you have is to relinquish the idea that you have a necessity. I don't know how you teach that, but that's our statement. That will bring about what? The actual transformation of your body/mind associations. And if you think that we are not concerned about the enlightenment of the whole self, you're wrong. The initiation process must include the coming to Light of your physiological associations. If you think the *Course* doesn't teach this, you're wrong. It teaches only that you may become a vehicle of love and communication through this process of enlightenment.

Now, the consciousnesses who have been directly associated with ideas of enlightenment or spiritual paths will often reach a point of the admission of the necessity for the transformation of their own mind, or the giving up of their previous value systems, at which time they simply turn away.

We are going to begin at this jumping-off place. My whole teachings to you, and the teachings of the brothers who are going to come among you – not in secret this time, not in separate cells, but rather in the open, as in the *Course In Miracles*, teaching you love – will be to your individual transformation. This will make you very happy if you look at it. Why? Many of you who have been doing the *Course* – the ideas of the relinquishment of guilt, the ideas that sin and death are impossible, the ideas that the earth is not real – have encountered a great deal of difficulty simply because you, in your own thinking, have brought together some lucid thoughts that are immediately contradicted by everything around you. We want to encourage you that our whole teaching is to bring about this transformation and, in fact, to include all of the phenomena of the change of your mind. It is important that you begin to look at the teachings of Jesus that will make statements as in say the text of Chapter 22, where He says that your eyes were never designed to see. Your body's eyes are designed explicitly to be perceptual – not to see. And it's the Holy Spirit, or the bringing together of this male and female aspect of you (wow, is that mystical!), the bringing together of the potential of you, the activation within the cellular construction of your body. This is kind of a mystical talk, but for goodness sake, there is no tradition that doesn't deal with enlightenment.

The *Course In Miracles* is a course in Whole-mindedness. Now that can start to be a lot of fun and happy for you if you will what? Direct your attention in an increasing manner to a determination that there is another condition of consciousness of which the earth is not, and is not aware. This is the Workbook. Can this be practiced? Sure. This is what we want you to do. When you begin to experience the real transformation of your mind, we want to validate that for you. We want you to come to us and address us and say, "Teacher, I'm beginning to undergo some changes! I'm beginning to think differently than I used to. Everything seems the same to me, but it's entirely different in my mind. I am bringing together these thoughts. I am atoning. I am becoming enlightened." These are the people we want to hear from. We know what's happening. And we know that it is being denied by group therapy in order to force you back into the mold of perceptual falsity. Are we attacking society? No. We don't care. The statements of Jesus are that the world isn't real. Everyone must come to know that. Obviously you are going to attack that. But that's okay. Finally you are going to feel the frustration of your attempts to make the earth real, and your ludicrous attempts to associate this intense love and passion that you have, with sickness and death. You are very determined to bring them together. The whole teaching of the *Course* is: Stop doing that! That's insane! The whole teaching would be that there is only love and that there is no conflict, and that, through a change of your mind, you will change the world because the world is only your construct in your dream. Wow, is this easy!

Do you really want to look at the idea that you are the cause of the world? That the world is literally you? Of course not. But the whole teachings of initiation are to the direction that you are body/world or body/mind, or wholeness contained within yourself. What fun it becomes then. Why? As you see these things happen, you say, "Yes! I'm changing. My mind is going to be enlightened. It can happen to me." Then, when you read the stories of Rosicrucians and Masonry and all of the lovely mystical elements; the original formulations of all established religions contain elements of enlightenment – the frenzy of Damascus, or the Pentecost, or the Methodist, the vision, the activation of the potential, the shrine of reality, the grail, the hermetic idea of the formulation of the energies of the body, the awakening of the kundalini, the coming together of the yin and yang – Come on! What do you think the *Course In Miracles* is! Do I dare let it out on this tape? Will you say, "Don't tell me that Jesus is teaching bodily transformation." What do you think the resurrection is if it's not enlightenment? There are some sentences in the *Course* that have to be assiduously avoided. Things like: you can depart this world now in a blaze of Light if you so wish; this isn't real and all the other things that go with it. I suppose in that sense this is an advanced talk, but the opening statement of the *Course In Miracles* is that anything that is fearful is not real, and this is a fearful place; therefore it is not real. If you would somehow start with that premise, you could search within your own perceptual dream of falsity back to the moment of fear, the moment that you refused to go into, which is what the initiation process is, at which time you cross the veil. You bring together the opposites, you become singular perception, whole perception, true perception, through the awakening of the ajna, the Third Eye – Initiation. You become a Perfect, a New Mind. Does that become common in the statement of relationalship history? Sure. I am a definition of it. I am a perfect definition of it in Whole-mindedness. I teach nothing but give up and love. Obviously I will be judged falsely and I will be accused of perceptual evaluation, of motivation. Our whole teaching is that all motivation is false because it is contained within perceptual mind.

Will you be attacked if you teach relinquishment? Hey, brother! Why? Relinquishment is love, relinquishment is giving, which is as close as you can get to creating here – the giving of yourself. But if mind is split, mind cannot become whole except by the extension of itself, or the admission of the necessity for the nondefense of itself in association with the images that it has projected outside of it. That's what the process is and that's what you are teaching.

Will I include all of the happenstances of phenomena that go along with this – the visions and the miracles in perception? Of course. You are free to change your mind this very moment and come to see the value of the teachings of the *Course*, for example that time is not sequential, that you have simply organized in your perceptual mind associate ideas that have no

CHAPTER ONE: *The Initiation*

value whatever. Know you can become whole and realize that you are indeed the single emanation from Whole Mind or as Jesus would say, the only living Son of God. Take a big bite of that. You'll start to feel real good about it. Certainly we're going to have to get into the idea of the coming together in the temple of worship with the necessity of the transformation, the Pentecost. Without that, you will just spin and die.

I'm going to make an admission here. At the very beginning of the *Course*, Master Jesus says, and I will reiterate to you, that we are dealing with an impossible situation. All situations, or the idea of space/time, are really impossible. They are statements of the possibility of location – the idea that there really was a rage in Heaven and that there really was a schism, and that somehow something evil came out of something good, and now you have the impossible task of trying to determine within your perception which is good and which is evil. This is not what I have come to tell you. My statement is this: Nothing really happened. At the apparent moment of this apparent loss of communication, this disassociation, the repair of it – the Atonement, the at-one-ment of it – was instantaneous. The distance between the idea of the possibility of separation and the return to Wholeness is what space/time is.

You may pose the question as often as you wish, and certainly established Christianity, religion, do. "Well, if that's so, what is the purpose for me? If what you say is real, I must have something evil outside of myself, or I must accept the responsibility that I am the schism." This is my teaching. You are going to pose the question, "What am I doing here?" "You are giving me validation here in order to assert that I can come to the truth." You will be mistaken finally if you believe that I'm doing that. My indication in this is for you to see that you really have no choice in this. The idea that you could make a legitimate choice to be separate from Wholeness and then come Whole is absurd and insane. That being said, I direct you to the only release there ever could be, and that would have to be the acknowledgment of the unreality of sickness, sin and death. It literally cannot be done any other way. That, then, conversely, must involve the coming together of your Whole Mind thoughts in association with this schism which is established in your mind. That's what the initiation is, isn't it?

Hermetically, it is the activation of the *I Ching*, the genetic potential of you, with the certainty of the emanation of the single reality in the creative endeavor. Is that a real thing? Yes. Dear teacher, if you are potential, there is a necessity for your activation. In the mystical experience, as long as this is a mystical talk, "In the beginning, God created Heaven and earth," God is feminine plural in the translation. If you would like to retranslate that, "In the beginning a group of seven sisters or seven females created Heaven and earth," you would be very close to the truth. Is that okay if I put this in here? Obviously we are going to take the centers of your potential or your female or your churches, as expressed in the Apocalypse – boy this is really getting mystical – and activate them through the insertion of a male reality, as you would call it. Isn't that something? People complain about Master Jesus not having gender in the *Course*, and I notice how quickly they'll take it and say, "Brothers and sisters." We don't do that. The necessity for "sister" or female obviously is the demand of earth associations or potential with the reality of the impregnation of the male. There's a great necessity to acknowledge the female. Without the female, there would be no necessity for the male. "You are telling me that the female is evil?" The association or the idea that potential is evil is a statement of time or possibility – that is, evil in the sense that it contains notations of a distraction in regard to possibility, in regard that anything could occur that has not already been totally fulfilled within the framework of reality.

Our teaching, of course, is to come back from the black hole – to return. The going out and the coming back of you is

CHAPTER ONE: The Initiation

the maturity of the center of your body configuration, the activation of it. These are things that as you come more and more into your own enlightened mind you will use as validations, allegorically or in simile or in metaphor, and finally in the subtraction of the symbol itself in the simple statement that everything that you are doing is holy. There are some lovely teachings in the *Course* where Jesus says that nothing is symbolic; form is not real, nothing represents anything. Wholemindedness would see immediately then that what we are doing at this moment is all that there is; we are in a divine meditation or notation of the parable of our passion to reality. That's fun to do. Those of you who are alone or in a group – you can discuss this if you wish – but I assure you that the solace, the peace, will come in your own temple. The peace will come when you go into the closet and do a direct confrontation with the fear that you experience over the message that I am presenting you with now. It's a very fearful thing to you. Why? The only thing the earth is, is fear of God. Is that conflict real? That's absurd. What would Truth know of falsity? What are you going to bring to God and to Truth that He doesn't know? This is really what the *Course In Miracles* says. Truth is true and nothing else is true. So why are you concerned? All you'd need do in this forgiveness teaching is bring your whole mind together in a nonjudgmental relationship with yourself, and the miracle occurs automatically because you have removed the conflict of perceptual observation. This is the *Course In Miracles*. This is the initiation process.

Historically it can involve a lot more than just listening to a single talk. What else would be included? Well first of all, and without getting into it, there is a necessity for the purgation of the physical body. Does that involve a variance in the previous assimilations that the body underwent, to bring about a more refined excrement, the possibility of celibacy, the dealing with the association of sexuality? Of course. All of these things pertain. This talk is not designed to necessarily direct to a discipline to this, but rather to assert that as your mind comes more and more to this, the necessity for that purgation, or for that purification, will become a more and more gentle discipline.

You will find that you begin to disassociate from your previous conceptions and association to what you thought you were. That would include the family, occupation and all the other things that go with exchange in your mind. But Master Jesus would teach it that this can be brought about gently by the continuing relinquishment. We would encourage you not to tarry with this. You have always compromised it up until now. And you think that by examining your previous associations you are going to arrive at where you are in the advancement of your own spiritual acumen. I assure you that you are false.

Although I allow for progress, progress has no reality outside of time and only reality is outside of time, and on we go.

I have said that the *Course In Miracles* is a course in direct contact with God. I am astonished people say, "Well, I've been studying the *Course* for ten years," or, "I just completed a year of *Course*." That's fine, and stay with it guys, but finally every lesson of the *Course* contains all of the elements for the complete transformation because it literally teaches that the initiation must occur now, not in some historic framework. It teaches that you have never been right, and once you are, you won't be here and the world will be gone. But that is a direction of initiation or the possibility of an actual vision or illumination. I'm going to do for you Lesson 157, without much interpretation. I'm going to read it to you. You remember that this is how we teach the *Course*. We teach that if you'll do this, you will begin to have these experiences.

This is a day of silence and of trust. This day. Today. Now. *It is a special time of promise in your calendar of days. It is a time Heaven has set apart to shine upon, and cast a timeless light upon this day, where echoes of eternity are heard. This day is holy, for it ushers in a new experience;*

CHAPTER ONE: *The Initiation*

a different kind of feeling and awareness. You have spent long days and nights in celebrating death. Today you learn to feel the joy of life.

This is another crucial turning point in the curriculum. We add a new dimension now; a fresh experience that sheds a light on all that we have learned already, and prepares us for what we have yet to learn. It brings us to the door where learning ceases, and we catch a glimpse of what lies past the highest reaches it can possibly attain. It lies past the highest reaches of our perception, doesn't it? It is initiation. *It leaves us here an instant, and we go beyond it, sure of our direction and our only goal.*

Today it will be given you to feel a touch of Heaven, though you will return to paths of learning. Yet you have come far enough along the way to alter time sufficiently to rise above its laws, and walk into eternity a while. You think we're not teaching initiation? You listen to this: We will alter time! *This you will learn to do increasingly, as every lesson, faithfully rehearsed, brings you more swiftly to this holy place and leaves you, for a moment, to your Self.*

Your Self *will direct your practicing today, for what you ask for now is what He wills. And having joined your will with His this day, what you are asking must be given you. Nothing is needed but today's idea to light your mind, and let it rest in still anticipation and in quiet joy, wherein you quickly leave the world behind.*

And the Lesson is: *Into His Presence would I enter now.* Are you ready for this? *From this day forth, your ministry takes on a genuine devotion, and a glow that travels from your fingertips to those you touch, and blesses those you look upon. A vision reaches everyone you meet, and everyone you think of, or who thinks of you. For your experience today will so transform your mind that it becomes the touchstone for the holy Thoughts of God.*

Your body will be sanctified today, its only purpose being now to bring the vision of what you experience this day to light the world. We cannot give experience like this directly. Yet it leaves a vision in our eyes which we can offer everyone, that he may come the sooner to the same experience in which the world is quietly forgot, and Heaven is remembered for a while.

As this experience increases and all goals but this become of little worth, the world to which you will return becomes a little closer to the end of time; a little more like Heaven in its ways; a little nearer its deliverance. And you who bring it light will come to see the light more sure; the vision more distinct. The time will come when you will not return in the same form in which you now appear, for you will have no need of it. Yet now – the sanctification of your body *– has a purpose, and will serve it well.*

Today we will embark upon a course you have not dreamed of. Brother, listen: *But the Holy One, the Giver of the happy dreams of life, Translator of perception into truth, the holy Guide to Heaven given you, has dreamed for you this journey which you make and start today, with the experience this day holds out to you to be your own.*

Into Christ's Presence will we enter now, serenely unaware of everything except His shining face and perfect Love. The vision of His face will stay with you, but there will be an instant which transcends all vision, even this, the holiest. This you will never teach, for you attained it not through learning. Yet the vision speaks of your remembrance of what you knew in that instant, and will surely know again.

This is the highest statement that has ever been made in any vernacular of the certainty of the transformation of your mind through the application of this *Course* through the relinquishment of yourself. This is the moment of the glory of

CHAPTER ONE: The Initiation

the parting of the veil. This is our declaration to you that it has happened and can happen to you. This is our only statement. Everything else, then, through this Light, through this awakening, will change about you as you see this little place that you have constructed in the sickness of your separation has no reality. It is a hatching out, isn't it? It is a birth. It is a coming out of the tomb. It is a rolling back of the stone. It is the awakening of you to the Light that is all around you, dreamer of death dreams. You have experienced death enough now, teacher of God. Come here with us and experience Life Eternal. How very lovely; we'll see you soon.

Isn't that lovely? Into His Presence I would enter now. Let's make this contact together, this union that has become. You use, then, the energies of this enlightenment. Use this talk. Join together now in this brotherhood, this contact with God. Feel it. Open your hearts and open your minds and part the veil. Come to the Light. That's it! Into His Presence will I enter now. This is the only purpose that I came for now – to awaken. I am here now. Transfiguration. No other purpose, no other desire. Nothing can stop you in this incredible metamorphosis. It is all new.

> Ye have heard that it hath been said,
> An eye for an eye, and a tooth for a tooth:
> But I say unto you, That ye resist not evil:
> but whosoever shall smite thee on thy right cheek,
> turn to him the other also.

CHAPTER TWO

The Mechanism of the Miracle

So if you begin with the certainty that all of your thoughts are false and not real and that there is no sickness, pain and death, it will be very beneficent to you.

Indeed this is scripture, indeed this is new Christianity, indeed this is a statement of uncompromising love which was declared by Jesus Christ 2000 years ago. It is absolutely not different than that. But since we were more disassociated in that time framework, through the communicative devices that have been inaugurated in this later time period, we are able to express this in a higher frequency of reality. Yes, it is lovely to listen to that and hear what I say, but you remember this, this remains your mind construct. This is your Atonement. This is the statement of your reality in the declaration of the unreality of death. That's your assignment, dear teacher.

I want you to understand me clearly here when I express the unbound gratitude that I feel for our dear brother Jesus Christ and for you in your determination to make this repair, to bring about this repentance. There is no possibility that I could have inaugurated this or completed this great endeavor, this great purpose of Light, without you. Sometimes it appears that as a Whole Mind, I make dogmatic statements about my own association. On the contrary, the method by which I came to know this was the annihilation of my thought forms in association with the value systems that were previously a part of my dream.

This is the way that I teach it: forgive and love. If you will do that you'll begin to sense the reality of these images and thought forms that are now coming into your mind and those that we share out of time, rather than in this apparent sequential relationship of thoughts. I love you more than anything else in the universe for you are a part of me, and we are together in this final endeavor. We share that certainty of Almighty God, don't we – of a single Creator, of a single Source. How could it be conflictual? How could there be a problem, except in our continued defiance and denial of our own wholeness and perfection? And I declare to you that you are whole and perfect. That is my statement to you. If you believe me, you will be with me in this endeavor. Is it true? Of course it's true. All the message that Master Jesus, or you now, as you become an advanced teacher will ever declare, is that Heaven is real and that hell is an illusion of death. Begin to teach that now, teacher, and watch what happens. Watch the miracle that will occur as you begin to make this declaration. Why? It is a statement of Truth and it is contained within your own mind, and through the practice of it, it will come about in you despite the reservations that you still entertain. You listen, we will always be with you.

We're at the kitchen of God's Country Place. It is Tuesday before resurrection day. Sometimes when I am going to elucidate or define, I will sit for a few minutes and attempt at an admittedly different condition of consciousness to formulate the wholeness of my mind in an attempt to communicate to you definitions that will inaugurate in you a new framework of your self-

CHAPTER TWO: *The Mechanism Of The Miracle*

association. What I was doing before I turned on the tape was formulating in my mind what we mean by *A Course In Miracles*, or more directly what a miracle is. We will begin with a sentence that Jesus uses in the *Course*. Are you ready: Time has been adjusted to bring about the Atonement in you. Now that does not mean particularly that time has been adjusted within your absolute definition of yourself genetically. That remains as it was. But within this what you would call continuum, if you would look at time as a fabric of thought consciousness, there has been an intrusion or an indication of the mechanistic possibility of a speed up in your direction of sequential or linear time. And this probably would best define the miracle of my awakening which was nothing but an absolute insertion of Light that carried me to the Omega point from which I speak in association with my thoughts. Now, while I may sequence them momentarily for you, they are at a different pitch of reality; they emanate from a different what you might call "position" within the space/time continuum.

Here's how a miracle works: I direct you, or the *Course In Miracles*, which is the insertion of this energy, directs you to take your perceptual mind continuity – these are all the thoughts that you have which are in association with sequentiality, aren't they? This is the indication that you, within your framework of thought, genetically, each moment have already derived a conclusion to your present association of thought patterns. I am going to change that. That obviously would be a miracle. If you're walking down the street and suddenly are going to develop cancer... When I say, "suddenly develop cancer," it's because my mind would take you through the idea of cancer and the whole so-called attempted remedy unto death and it would be over and done and you will be perfectly healed in just a moment, although you don't process it that way. You're walking down the street, and as you have configurated yourself within your associations – for some of you getting cancer is absolutely inevitable, because you are designed by your own congruity of thought to terminate yourself in your associations that you are presented with, as you constitute yourself. Now suddenly you come upon me. This does not have to do with your observation of the miracle, unless you are determined that it does. My mechanisms of healing will shift your mind in relationship to itself. When you walk around as a healed teacher, this is happening all the time. This is the notation of Jesus that the miracle is going on all the time. Of course. This is what I do.

Now, is it necessary that the miracle be noted by the consciousness? To be defined as a miracle, the phenomena of the recovery, the phenomena of the increase in happiness by a reassociation of the mind, can be very important to the consciousness. The nature of my awakening precluded the happening of miracles, except in retrospect, because it was a dramatic insertion that caused enlightenment. We are now teaching to the point where you may utilize this shift in time that has occurred to do what? Bring about a shift in your time mind! Isn't that what we are going to do? If you made a decision right at this moment for the perfect miracle of your enlightened awakenment, I positively guarantee you that not only would it occur, but that it did occur!

Jesus calls this a holy instant and this is the progress of perceptual observation of itself in its journey to the Light. It feels this aha moment, this moment when there is a shift in consciousness. Much more happens at that time than the consciousness, who is perhaps fearful of this occurrence, wants to admit happens. As a matter of fact, at that moment he literally steps out of time, reconfigurates everything in his perceptual association, and returns to a new world but he doesn't know it. He continues to hold on to himself in his relationship with his disease. He need not do that, need he, if he will listen to these directions. There is a sentence in the *Course* where Jesus says: You may live in the Holy Instant from now until the end of time, which will be just a moment, won't it? Isn't that lovely?

CHAPTER TWO: *The Mechanism Of The Miracle*

This does however require first, the admission of the miracle and second, becoming miracle-minded, in order to allow the natural result of whole mindedness to appear before you in the new vision of your reality. Now you've got all these unhealed teachers, and by unhealed, I mean attempting to heal. Early in the *Course* Jesus says that if you're not healed, you shouldn't try to heal. Of course everybody does because they try to repair their minds within the framework of their own perceptual observations. That being said, it is sad to watch consciousnesses utilizing the *Course In Miracles* within the framework of their consciousnesses, formulating it in their limited perceptual observations and literally preventing the miracle from occurring, and using sentences like, "The *Course* evolves self-reliance." Ha! As a matter of fact, it is exactly the opposite of that. It involves God-reliance. Tota ly. And the moment one would become totally reliant, he would spring into Heaven, wouldn't he? Inevitably, an unhealed teacher will end up teaching exactly the opposite of what the *Course* teaches and of course, he must. Why? Because he's in a limited, perceptual evaluation of himself in his time associations.

Is it possible then for you to read this and see the difference in your relationalship thoughts that are occurring in your mind? Of course. This is the miracle of the Atonement, the changing of your mind in association with the perceptions that are all about you. Now, let's look at the difficulty you're having. I proclaim to you that you are dreaming and that the images you see about you are just reflections of thoughts that are changing each moment. The power or the decision of your mind to change this I declare to you to be absolutely inviolate, since all of the power of the universe is contained in your mind. Your decision to work miracles inevitably has been connected with your decision to retain the limited self in a time framework. Now, isn't it time that you looked at the result of the miracle of the power of your mind that is happening to you within your limited genetic time framework? You literally condemn yourself to death. You obliviate yourself within the narrowness of your perceptual observation. And I'm going to try to widen that for you. I want you to see – we'll start here: there is no death. Time is a method that you have invented and are employing to associate yourself with yourself in denial of your own reality.

Now, the Workbook will direct you to start practicing that, and as you walk down the street, why don't you begin to practice stopping time? I watch consciousnesses that are asleep within the framework of their own cause and effect. The only thing that can possibly happen is the direction of their own causal mind; the results at that frequency are built into the fabric of that association of time, don't you see? We are directing you, then, to utilize this new Light energy to stimulate, to ignite the genetic response that is possible within the framework of your symbiotic relationship of body response.

What did he say? What did he say?! I don't know. But now, here's the advantage of it: more and more teachers are going to evolve that, and are teaching whole mindedness. It is more than a teaching in the sense of the exchange. It is a declaration by the healed teacher, by the advanced teacher, that he is whole-minded, and does not associate in his mind with partiality. He literally is in a different framework of time, and this is what I say to you. The miracle then, will be that occurrence in your relationship with yourself through the propinquity, through the ancillary involvement of yourself in association with this mechanism. I positively guarantee you this is true.

When I make the declaration, and have made to you, that you cannot die – obviously if you can't die and there is no death, there's no need for you to be sick; sickness is just a little death – certainly there would be no need for you to get old, would there? Why would you want to get old, except that you've associated with this genetic pattern of aging. Many of you who have come now to God's Country Place notice this new vitality

CHAPTER TWO: *The Mechanism Of The Miracle*

that is enveloping you, this new Light energy, as you make the declaration, "I'm not going to die." Of course. It would be inevitable. Why? Because the cellular response of your own memories is always to eternity, inevitably because survival, longevity – total longevity – would be the closest you can get to eternity. And if you eliminate the possibility of extermination or time, you will get an automatic cellular response to your own enlightenment.

I don't know how clear this is, but we need the demonstrations of it, teachers, through the declarations of you that it is in fact happening. These will be the miracles. Will there be specific miracles or actual shifts in time? Of course! Remember that in the over-all picture of all of the perceptions of this quadrant of time, time facilitation has already occurred, and you may join with it at the highest level of the elimination of the necessity for perceptual self-evaluation. Those of you who are walking along now and suddenly these miracles are beginning to happen around you, I want to verify that and say, "Yes, that's true, these things are happening and it would be important that you see that it is just your mind." There isn't any sense in you being critical of other consciousnesses that you have constructed around you to assist you in the denial of your own reality. Jesus calls this forgiveness, teacher. There isn't any sense in you laying the blame or sharing the guilt for what you term "sickness and death" with these other mind forces or mind thoughts that are contained within your limited identity with yourself in this time framework. Stop doing it. This is a course in coming to know yourself, and this requires the admission that the thoughts that you have had, and the ones that keep cropping up, are all just part of this time continuum in your own mind associations. Can the miracle happen? Dear teacher, the miracle is happening perfectly right now. Of course! It would be possible, since you invented time, for you to simply make a decision to step out of it, and awaken to the truth and glory of the Light that is shining all about you. Isn't that lovely? He is risen. He is risen indeed! The graphic demonstration of that, that appears within your so-called historic memory is the resurrection – reconfiguration of the single whole body which has to be you. It cannot not be, because you have that thought. It is impossible that you cannot use this as a vehicle to wake up. We encourage you to do so now.

We're here at God's Country Place talking about the resurrection, the enlightenment, the wholeness of you in association with all universal consciousness. We are here talking about healing again, and everybody says, "Yes, well, why doesn't the teacher then teach that death is an opinion, and that sickness is an opinion that you have about yourself?" The application of so-called nostrums of healing are nothing but attempts to hold yourself in your own tension, in your own sickness framework. Then the healing must occur. You say, "Is it necessary that I believe you, teacher, in order for the miracle to occur?" I assure you that if you believe me absolutely and unqualifyingly, that the phrase that Master Jesus uses, "Your faith has made you whole," will positively work. Of course! It could not not work, because these are declarations of the truth of the wholeness of you.

I watch these teachers out trying to heal, and they don't like the word 'faith' and they are very fearful of the healing actually occurring. Did you know that? It is their own fear that keeps the miracle from happening, because it would be the admission that their responsibility is only to the Truth of God, rather than to themselves and their determination to formulate the process of the wholeness of the mind. Jesus calls that magic. He says you do successfully, momentarily in time, continue to change the images that are about you through the magic of the power of your mind. It is fun to watch all the so-called abundance cults in the teachings of limited prayer that cause changes in the phenomenological association to perceptual mind. And indeed they do. But where do they lead but to death, because the

CHAPTER TWO: *The Mechanism Of The Miracle*

consciousness is limiting himself within that framework of his pre-determined annihilation. This is what I am trying to take away from you. And this, if you would like to hear this, is what we've succeeded in doing.

I assure you that it is impossible for you to be reading this, or to be in association with this new mind without having resurrected. This is the major admission that's required of you. This will lead you directly to the determination that this is already over and happened (or didn't happen), coming with the admission that it is already all over.

Out of time I promise you that you, at this moment, have the absolute capacity to determine through the power of your mind that all of this is not so. Now, you are looking at it in terms of some sort of sacrifice because you believe that it is possible for you to exchange your ideas about yourself with Wholeness or God's idea about you. I assure you that is not possible. I am teaching the relinquishment or the death of self: know ye not, Nicodemus, that you must be born again? (John 3:3) And this is what's coming about now. Remember that this is a physical transaction. You are in this bodily association, and the enlightenment of your whole cellular relationship is the requirement for the absolute miracle.

Boy are we happy that we finally are beginning to work this new Light energy in you, and we are grateful to the planners of this in our mutual minds. They heard this call for help emanating at the maturation point in time and have done a direct insertion to aid in the recall of this colony of desolation that is operating in the "netherland" of despair. So come join with me now in this Light association that has come directly into your mind.

What's going to occur to you, as this miracle of the new mind or the enlightenment occurs in you, is the absurdity of perceptual associate evaluation – that the thought forms that you construct, and those include the ideas of linear association, are only formulated within themselves as you have constructed your mind. This will amaze you. In regard to time, in Time magazine this week is the statement that the Big Bang, the beginning of space/time, in a fiery affirmation of energy, occurred 15,000 million years ago. 15,000 million years! Now I would direct the consciousnesses that are held in their perceptual observations of relative time, that is, somewhere they must be, to come up with a figure like that, to tell me exactly what the difference between 15,000 million years is, and a million years or 100 years or one year, or 10 minutes, except within the association of their thought form.

What we declare to you, and you hear this now, is that the distance between the cause and the effect, which is the thought of your mind and its subsequent result, will be exactly as far apart as where you have matured in your own self-declarations of the extension of your mind – your creative capacity. Not more and not less. We are going to begin then with the assumption that the miracle occurs when cause and effect are brought together, and that if you have a thought of happiness and wholeness, it must extend from you and include all of the previous projections of your mind that are in some sort of past or future framework of reference. I declare to you that this is a fact and that this is actually happening all around you, but that you, individually in your own limited perception, refuse to acknowledge it for fear of losing your self-associations – even unto the death of yourself, or the annihilation of yourself as you have made yourself in linear time. Isn't this so?

Now the resistance to this is enormous, because it is a statement that you must include the philosophy of reality, the theology, the scientific endeavors of objective reality with subjective certainty in with the psychology or the wholeness of the power of your mind. We used to call this the bringing together of religion and science – or philosophy, the liberal art of creating with your mind. We're here to tell you that you can do this, and must do this, if you would escape the chaotic associations with

CHAPTER TWO: *The Mechanism Of The Miracle*

perception that have caused you to construct what we would term "hell".

Your need to put together the chaos of historic thought in the moment – or contained within what you refer to as the Big Bang – is extraordinary. If the Big Bang began, it is over. You may keep yourself there for 15,000 million years, and Master Jesus in the *Course* says you can keep yourself there another 15,000 million years. Or you can, as you did, hear this now and step directly out of your hell through the continuing practicing of bringing together of sequential time in your mind. You may make this moment the moment of the Big Bang. This is the Alpha and the Omega then. This is the direction we want you to pursue because we testify that if you pursue it, you will succeed, and did, because it is only the power of your mind that is keeping you from seeing the wholeness and glory of the reality of you right now.

I'm perfectly aware that the message being presented to you through the *Course In Miracles* or through this statement of wholeness of mine, is finally going to meet a great deal of resistance from perceptual mind limitation, because remember that the perceptual mind in limitation, the so-called human being, the ego, is constructed specifically not to hear this message. The ludicrousy of that will begin to appear to you if you see what they do with *A Course In Miracles*, with the simple teachings that God is a fact and that this isn't real. And the manners in which the mechanisms of limited time perception will deny it and attack it and declare that, "No, that isn't possible. I'm going to figure this out within my own limited devices rather than simply stepping back in my own perceptual thoughts and allowing the miracle of the light reality to occur."

Remember you are in an association with temporalness. Let's just look at this factually. Show me a consciousness that is eternal here. Show me anything that doesn't involve defense and conflict. Master Jesus expresses this throughout the Course.

You are born in pain, you live in tribulation and you accept it as a normal part of the friction, or the tension, or the disease of perceptual association. And it is inevitable that it be there because perception is what conflict is. So when you bring these thoughts into a higher range of association, the miracle occurs automatically, doesn't it? But remember this is then subjective reality. This is the statement that all of this is only in your mind. And I know how tempted you are – again and again Jesus says this – no matter how tempted you are to believe that there are forces outside of you that are asserting the conflict in your association with yourself either from a beneficent, from a good standpoint, or from a bad standpoint, it is simply not so.

The power of healing must be contained in your mind because the splitness that is the direction of your apparent reality is not so, because thought is singular. You are God or Wholeness creating. Not more and not less than that. So if you will bring all these thought forms, all of these ideas that you have about yourself into a single picture of wholeness, this is the Holy Instant. This is when the miracle must occur. Is this literally a change in the activities that are going on around you in space/time? Of course. Why would that be difficult? If indeed there are a hundred thousand trillion worlds, what's wrong with this little world being your dream, the miracle occurring simply in your rising up? The resurrection can only be the rising of you out of the sickbed of the hallucination of the world. You're dreaming. This is not real. This is not so.

I understand that perceptual mind will attack this idea as it has always attacked the idea of wholeness in its determination to assert itself and continue to obliviate itself. You can't die! Let's start with that, and then watch the miracle as it occurs more and more in this reference of Master Jesus out of body and out of time. Use the *Course In Miracles*. We are evolving advanced teachers, out-of-time teachers, that will assist you with this if you need it, and you are going to become one in affiliation

CHAPTER TWO: *The Mechanism Of The Miracle*

with this message, I assure you, or you wouldn't be hearing this message. This, then, is the circle of Atonement and your admission of it is what salvation is. How very lovely. We hope we see you soon.

Those of you now who are changing your minds are causing dramatic changes in the fabric of mind – Master Jesus would say – much more than you could ever dream of! You have no idea of the power of your mind in the individual thoughts that you are having. Indeed, since you can only have one thought at a time, as you put the energy of Light into these thoughts, they are causing incredible reconfigurations within the fabric of this time association.

Can you get a feel for this? This is the fun part of your declaration of no death. You are faced with yourself in every situation that arises and I know this can make you a little fearful. And I know that what I am saying for some of you can be very fearful, because it is a confrontation with the admission that you are the constructor of the death and chaos that you see about you. It is a difficult admission. It is the addressing of the defiled altar, as we would teach it in the *Course In Miracles*. It is the parting of the veil. It is the last six pages of Chapter 19 in the Text where you're asked to open the memory patterns of your memory thoughts and look at the things that are really going on around you. You would immediately work the miracle of the relinquishment of it if you saw that you're the cause of it. The horrendous association would be impossible.

We want you to know that there is happiness and joy and ecstasy and sharing of Light going on all around you, and that you, individually, in your sleep, in your determination to construct nothingness in your mind, are not seeing it. These little glimpses that you're getting as these shifts occur are what the miracle is. But it must happen to you. Master Jesus says again your sole responsibility is to change your mind about yourself – your at-one-ment. Do you have that? It will work automatically teacher, if you do it yourself. You listen to me, you come and share this, this new reality, this forgiveness of the grievance of self-constructed death. You will come into a whole new scenario of reality. Jesus calls it a lovely true dream where we stay just for a moment, and then step out of time together in admission of our single source and our love for each other. Thank you teachers of God. He is risen. You are risen indeed!

Just for a moment in regard to the Beatitudes and the miracle: The assertion is this, and it is inevitable that if you resist not evil – and this is the Easter message isn't it – resist not evil, that you will relinquish your thought sequencing, and the miracle occurs automatically. What's difficult for you is the laying down of your arms, the defense mechanisms, in order that you can allow the miracle to occur. It is impossible that it will not occur if the resistance that you afford is only your own thought forms, if you are actually being attacked by yourself. This is the whole idea of: blessed are the meek, blessed are the poor in spirit. So, this is the teachings then of the Sermon on the Mount (Matthew 5-7), for goodness sake. It's just the advanced-in-time message of it, isn't it? That's exactly what it is. That's very lovely.

See, you can practice it. These are the miracle moments, then, when your mind simply stops sequencing. It is impossible this not occur. And I say to you that the mind that holds itself in time is nothing. It has no source and it is not real. It does require then a miracle, doesn't it, for you to see that it is so, because there is no communication going on between the brightness all around you and the darkness of your own perceptual observation of yourself. You're doing it beautifully. The program is succeeding beautifully and did succeed. Thanks to you. You listen, dear teacher, the salvation of the world depends on you. Not on me. Not on what I am doing with this. My assertion to you is that this world is not real, and I am transcendent and gone from here. My declaration to you is that you must within your perception, since you are the constructor of this chaos, save the world through the

CHAPTER TWO: The Mechanism Of The Miracle

changing of your mind. That's the whole teaching of the *Course In Miracles*. That and nothing but that. Your awakening, isn't it? Wow, isn't that wonderful. The happiness that you feel now, the freedom of mind that you are beginning to feel, is an example of the relinquishment of guilt in association with the responsibility you feel for the continuation of your temporal creations that only die and rust and turn to dust. Come join us now in this eternal message of salvation.

Everything that you do to assist the miracle is a hindrance to the miracle. You might as well hear that. Step back, get out of the way and let it happen. Take no credit at all. See it? Be number two. Why not? All of your assertions are false. All of your necessities to assist in this would have to be false because you are the resistance. Do you have that? I know this is going to end up: You need do nothing. But that's all right. There is no sacrifice, is there? We hope we see you soon, teachers of God. Be of good cheer.

Here's what the miracle is: It is very difficult to express to your perceptual mind that everything is occurring each moment fully. You inevitably fill up yourself with what you would call continuous moments. So the miracle is loading up the moment with more of the drama of your ultimate participation in space/time. Jesus calls this speeding up time or stepping out of time. You may not know particularly that this is happening to you because you may be changing things that are happening across constellations. But it will fit into the final pattern of the cause and effect that has been determined in this time continuum, in this sequence. But what a joy this is for you, then, as you begin to discover this more and more. This happiness, this freedom that you are feeling is actually a change in the perceptual things that are around you, and that's what the miracle is. Don't be afraid, teacher. There is nothing to fear! Don't try to hold yourself in that limited sequencing of time/death, and watch what happens. We'll see you soon!

*Let go all the trivial things that churn and bubble
on the surface of your mind,
and reach down and below them
to the Kingdom of Heaven.
There is a place in you where there is perfect peace.
There is a place in you where nothing is impossible.
There is a place in you where the strength of God abides.*

CHAPTER THREE

Bubbles

It wouldn't make any difference how you came to know it, if it's only a new reflection of your own mind. I'll use the Rabbi; Rabbi, come here. Now Rabbi, Ben Abdul Abu Ababa. Whatever this is in its association is fine, including the need to identify what a Rabbi is. What I'm giving you is the reality that it will make absolutely no difference what you think a Rabbi is because a Rabbi will be what it is in your association regardless of your individual correspondence with it. It cannot *not* be. The form matters not at all. Certainly if we limit the form to a correspondence of our mutual separate associations, we will construct a continuum of time based on the reference of our own limitation. I want to know how we would not do that. How would we not do that?

We have historic references of a temple that was built and fell apart. Actually the reference that it was built and fell apart is not true; the reference that it was built, became a New Jerusalem and ascended to God is true. So we come together in a reference of a location of – let's use Babylon – we're going to talk New Jerusalem for just a second. Certainly wherever New Jerusalem is in a space/time identity, you have created a community of harmony of light that you're looking for. And you are looking for it within the walls of your Babylon identity. You cannot not be, simply because you are memories of that association. And you have historic references of the rise and fall of civilizations. Why? There is going on, a rise and fall of civilizations. The key to this is that the rise and fall of civilizations, the apparent cyclicalness of the building of the tension of correspondence of limitation without light, explodes into light and simply disappears. There's an accumulative effort made to bring about this light in limited association that reaches literally a critical mass, if you can hear this. The more love or communication that is released to reality, the brighter the association of that, of civilization, will be.

If you want to look at this as an evolutionary process of man, that's perfectly okay with me. You are looking for a Utopia. You define it as a Utopia. You're looking for a place where you can come together and communicate in the forms of your apparent mutual mind. That's okay. What is it that disrupts it? It is not creative in the association with the reality of God mind. There isn't anything wrong with it; it just isn't real. Guys! It hasn't got anything to do with right or wrong. Right or wrong would have to do with the method in which you hope to hold it in its own association.

This is *A Course In Miracles*. How the hell wouldn't it be *A Course In Miracles?* Seated right at this place of the schism is your own reality in your return to God. Are you ready for this? That's going on all the time. Time is nothing but your return to reality. Isn't that amazing? The joyous final step that you have discovered, literally, is that you were the containment of it. That's

CHAPTER THREE: Bubbles

the whole teaching. If there's something outside of you, how would you ever find it? You will seek for correspondence with me in the projections of your own limitation. All I could possibly tell you is about the old you, the old Jerusalem that fell into death and failed. We cannot speak of the New Jerusalem, but we can allow it to occur by not attempting to communicate in our own limited association, which can only bring us what? The result of our old communication. This is all in the *Course*. We need to put on a new suit. We need to divorce ourselves – this is called the incorruptible body. Obviously your body is an attempt to communicate within an old association, but nothing prevents your body from being a vehicle of communication, very simply because God is what communication is. The breakage would only be the association of light speed in a demonstration of the slowness of the emphatic condition of potential, or space/time, coming to the reality of your individual creating mind.

There shouldn't be a problem with you at this point, if you're going to use the *Course*, in saying, "I'm the savior of the world." That's crazier than hell. The objections to you being the savior of the world would have to be contained in your own continuum of association. Isn't that so? Where the hell else would they be? What surprises the conceptual mind is that in your New Jerusalem you are doing it by a non-conceptual device of light association. Can you get this?

For some of the new associations, the most spiritual endeavor they've ever done was taking cake out to the merchants yesterday. Listen to me. See if you can hear this. I don't care what you do. If you give you'll be in Heaven. If you retain in the identity, you'll be in hell. There is no in-between. What the hell's wrong with salvation? It's for you simply not to be concerned about the manner or the method, which you call exchange. All method would have to be a form of exchange or justification for the necessity of the give and receive in the location of yourself in space/time. Isn't that so? Nothing is more spiritual than giving. There couldn't be. And if you give for no reason, you will be as God. It would have to be, because you *are* what give is. Notice how you retain and use the limitations of your own mind to express the creative capacity of the limitation of your dream.

So you reenact continually the memories of your own self, contained within your own dream. This is obviously all *A Course In Miracles*, isn't it? It's an hallucination of the association of time. What else could you do? You were abandoned here. What else could you do? You were literally abandoned in a spot in space/time. It had to be a spot in space/time because abandonment is what a spot in space/time is.

How did I get here? What am I doing here? That's an abandonment in your own mind, isn't it? The structure of the world is nothing but the necessity for a justification of your location or abandonment in space/time. It would require a reason for the abandonment simply because you find yourself in an association that demands a reasonableness based on where you found yourself. But remember this, there is no correspondence of total reality contained within your location in space/time. Why? A location of space/time is the denial or the restriction of the extension of God mind! What the hell else would it be!

There is no prince of darkness. I know somewhere you think that there must be a totality of communicative evil. Listen. That would be impossible if you would listen for a moment to what I am saying. There is no stability in evilness. Jesus teaches you that all these little bubbles come together, and they can indeed express an apparent stability of what? Separation, dummies! If you want to enter into a bubble of evil, which is separation, and correspond with what appears to you to be separate mind, you will construct Babylon. You will construct centers of need, centers of exchange in your own mind – Tigris

CHAPTER THREE: Bubbles

and Euphrates are the identities, Mesopotamia – locations of apparent light that can verify the time association. Remember this: Light is not apparent; it is a reality. If you make it apparent, it will turn into a contingency based on the necessity of your retention of a past/future relationship. Future happiness is not worthy of the Son of God. It's not worth it. Constructing a city that's going to give you a better definition later on makes absolutely no sense. Not only is that true, but you are aware that the city is going to collapse. Yet you feel the necessity to retain it because you *are* the retention of it within your own association. Astonishing idea! Dissolving the bubbles is what the miracle is. But notice how intense the necessity to retain separate definitions is, within the apparent separate associations. Why? Their correspondence with each other is based on the separation, isn't it? It is based on finding reasons within their mutual intent to identify themselves as justification for where they find themselves in space/time. The reason, very simply, if you want to know – and throw all the concepts out – the reason that you are in this association with me, is because contained within your references of yourself was a more intense need to share the expansion or necessity for your creative mind. And everywhere you look, you found yourself in what you would call a dark, non-communicative place. And for just a moment, Jesus uses the word "alien" here and He says flat out, if you opened up the *Course In Miracles,* you are an alien here. Why are you an alien? Because you opened up the *Course In Miracles,* not because from the *Course In Miracles* you recognized your alienship, although it may appear to be that way. It is impossible for you to be standing in this parameter of a new association without having a desire to correspond in a broader relationship with yourself. It could not *not* be true or what the hell are you doing here? And just as obviously, there is a threat to that new correspondence, very simply because it will be a loss of your space/time location. Isn't that so? It's not true. There is no question you are located in space/time.

There's no question that I am giving you a broader parameter of associations – literally the bursting of the bubbles of separation. But remember this – see if I can teach this – if there is a correspondence going on in the limitation between one bubble and another, (can you hear this?) and that bubble bursts, it becomes a larger correspondence of light association (I'm staying away from the term *Great Rays),* that will then what? Reflect that broader range of the association. Around that broader range of association will formulate bubbles of like ilk. How could it not, since they all contain the same ingredients anyway. Do you see that? Jesus calls this *Circle of Atonement.* So suddenly here you are in a relationship where the correspondence has a wider range, dimensionally, in the caprice necessity for you to create in your own limited association. And that's fun, isn't it? Now that you've found that correspondence, you can live for another 10,000 years. You have found some harmony and are now sharing a broader parameter of light reality. Isn't that so? That makes you feel real good. It's a burst-through. And you go, "Holy mackerel, we used to hate each other and now we love each other." We are sharing on another range of contingency – if you want to look at it – and that feels real good.

The only problem you could possibly have with this is if you, in your own cognition of self-identity, have limited the range of the correspondence you want to find within the space/time continuum, because you *are* the space/time continuum. If you accept that from me, you won't be here very long. In reality, nothing could possibly contain you. What would contain you, except your own necessity to identify yourself as reflected by the old associations of your karma, your own memory. This is the whole *Course In Miracles.*

But I want you to see that you are always getting a reflection of little bubbles. And if you don't try to correspond to the little bubbles, which are little in your mind, obviously, they will begin

CHAPTER THREE: Bubbles

to find harmony through the release of the necessity of objective correspondence. Obviously the final association will be New Man who emerges from a totality of little bubbles each instant into the reality of the Single Bubble which has no parameter.

The *Course* teaches you this: One miracle is not different than any other, because any parameters of definition of bubbles can have no meaning, because they are indications of a gap or distance in the thought of your own mind. Remember that we understand now that this is contained within your own mind. There isn't anything out *there*, guys. There's nothing *out* there. Do you understand me? You can have all the bubbles of right brain that you want to have, but the God correspondence coming from your left brain will dissolve those bubbles, because they are correspondences of relationships contained within configurations of space/time identity. Say of course! How could they not be? They're what the "body" is. The body is a limited communicative device, and you have perfected it in your determination to find the harmony contained within the limitation of the association of the bubbles, of the thoughts, rather than simply dissolving the bubbles and letting them become one big parameter, for just a moment, of reality. What a great threat that is, because you're going to lose the grid of separation. Can you hear that? You're in a grid; like lots of little bubbles that become bigger. But the bigger bubble is threatened simply by the immensity of its own association. It doesn't seem as though it is, but it is. It has found harmony in being a larger correspondence, but it still remains a protective device against the little bubbles that will, of course, attack it. Or it will seek dominance over the little bubbles, in order to keep them separate from what it is.

Finally – Jesus teaches it this way – there is no parameter of limitation around you at all. You can see through that final bubble of association. It is being held by a single reflection contained within your own mind. And that's the break-out, isn't it? That's the breaking out of the bubble. First you take a lot of little ones and you make them one great big one. Have you got this?

So this is the talk about Bubbles. She's at the Empress Burlesque! Bubbles LaRue. I always wanted to burst her bubble!

Are you better to have a lot of little bubbles held together or one big one? You're better to have one big one. Why not? Then everywhere you look, you could see that you are contained within a totality of association. Nothing is more fearful to you than the admission of one single bubble, because all of the pressure of your determination to remain separate will begin to collapse on that bubble. And if you become fearful, you can't find the harmony within your own bubble, so you'll break it up into separate pieces again. This is what you do. Then you'll find correspondence in all of the foam of the separate bubbles. Do you see that? All you have to do is look at the bubbles as conceptual thought. All you would have to do is very simply, and I'll use the analogy, see that each one of the bubbles is a separate, each-moment contingency of the apparent separation, seeking harmony in the bubble association. Can you see that? Look at it as froth. The whole universe is froth, and it finds a limited correspondence based on old definitions of itself. Doesn't it?

This is the way I told the story originally: that you can have a big bubble and it can be all fractured, but as it purifies it will come to a final relationship of space/time. Won't it? And that will simply dissolve and turn into the reality that's all around you. Obviously the little bubbles, if you keep them separate, are threatened by the big bubbles because they appear to the little bubbles to be more powerful. They're really not. They're more benevolent. But the fear of the release of it holds you in the bondage of the association of your own mind. Isn't that true? You're afraid of the big bubble. Yet a single big bubble is what you must be. There is no conflict in that bubble association.

Boy, you can get a grid of little bubbles, and retain it – it's called space/time. And you can retain them for a very long time,

CHAPTER THREE: Bubbles

can't you? You hold them in the rigidity of not crossing the barrier of the totality of correspondence. Once you construct one bubble of limitation, all other bubbles must follow. They cannot *not*, because they're definitions of the location.

Actually, I'm in a different time association. Would you like to see how that time works? Isn't this nice. Would you like to look at that new time mind? You'll like that one. It was only your own parameters that prevented you from seeing it. Actually, you're in *my* mind; you just weren't ready up until this point to be in my real mind. Isn't that amazing? Do you know how that identifies? "Follow me." Can you get that? I reduced it just for a second so you can see it. Of course it means "follow me," because you are configurations of my mind. Obviously you *are* my mind, and I'm offering myself, which was a broad association in this conflict, like little bubbles.

You've got me talking about bubbles which is a mistake, because I see the universe of separation as millions of little bubbles. And I see reality, finally, or perceptual reality, as one single bubble. It isn't that the perception is real, but it has no parameters except the single parameter of the distance between cause and effect. That's what I do. That's what I am. That's what my hologram is. I am a hologram taking all the little bubbles – I've got a core bubble – and I simply dissolve the limited bubbles, and the damn bubble keeps getting bigger and bigger until what? It loses its parameters. But I start out with all sorts of crappy bubbles, and the trick is that each bubble is only really corresponding with itself. I could do this molecularly for you, in a positron and a proton and a neutron, because it's holding together in a centrifugal association contained within time.

I give it a light association and it begins to simply release its molecular construction. Reality is not molecular structure, guys! It is not an association of positive and negative. There is nothing negative in the Universe. There is no such thing as an electron. Now you've got me into another talk. Certainly a negative would require a positive association, and that's what space/time would be or the distance between. How did I get into this? I'm teaching you to release your bubble. Can you see that? It's a New Mind; you're not all compartmentalized within your own association. That's an amazing thing to watch you do, because your mind is compartmentalized in this space/time association. *In my Father's house are many mansions* (John 14) but you are the totality of your own mansion. There is nothing separate from you in your own containment. Nothing denies you access to the Universal mind. How could it? You can say, "Well, I'm going to build a perfect mansion." But you're not the builder; you let the Holy Spirit build it for you. He'll build it by converting all of your materials to one single individual location from which transcendence is very simple. You don't want cities. We need *one*. It will be Jerusalem. Where do we build it? Where the old one is! You keep saying, "Well, Jerusalem fell and rose." No it didn't. It's always rising. You are the distance in the association of your own mind with that.

I see *a new Heaven and a new earth for the old heaven and earth are passed away.* (Rev. 21) I have become new. I am the New Jerusalem. Was I a contingency of communication? Everything is a contingency of communication. But remember, God is not a contingency. That would just be a formulation of a need for perfection contained within the ratio of light, or what you call a space/time identity within the schism. Certainly you're searching for the Light. And certainly you must find it because it's a correspondence of your own association with yourself. But your bubbles are too small. Your harmony is found by releasing the network or grid of space/time bubbles, dimensions, and allowing it to be one big, big bubble of your own reality. You're mad. You've been foaming at the mouth. You've got little bubbles. Let's get one great big bubble! You got it?

I'm forever blowing bubbles! That's the Burlesque Queen waltz. Bubbles LaRue. You kick it around in your own mind.

CHAPTER THREE: Bubbles

It's a jack off. You masturbate in your own mind. That's the way I would teach it; this way you could hear it. You're just nothing but self-abuse. You're constantly looking for a harmony contained within your own mind. You find a little bit, you ejaculate your own apparent light reality on it, it becomes at most a reproduction of your own association. Can you get this? Shall I tell it biologically? The uniting of the sperm and the egg. Nonsense! I've got a good talk here! This is how I would have taught if I didn't have *A Course In Miracles*. Don't limit your own association. In each one of the bubbles is the total, entire genetic identity of all of space/time forever. It's in every single one of the cells that is contained within you. You don't need a multitude of cells; you only need one. And that will be what you are. Contained within that zygote, impregnated earth form, will be the reality of God coming from time to eternity. That's a light factoring going on in the inevitable process of your return from apparent separation.

I'm glad I've got the *Course*. If I didn't have the *Course*, I'd be teaching you directly that you are an impregnated association of limitation coming to your own reality. And that you froth, and that I'm making your bubble bigger and bigger. That's what I'm doing. Nothing can really contain your mind. Teacher of God, you are never, never, never going to be satisfied with the containment of the reflections of your own apparent separation. I'm telling you it's over and gone; don't keep looking for it. Let it go. You say, "But I had so much happiness..." Temporal happiness is not worthy of the creative mind of God. "How do I know that?" I've told you! The dissatisfaction is going to occur in you, not in me. I want that dissatisfaction with your limited creative efforts; I want you to be aware of how little you really are in what you've done here. It's really just a little point in time.

Come on out with the real world. See if you like the real world. Don't be afraid of it. There's nothing to threaten you.

You are hatching out of this. That's fearful. Just for a minute you were fearful coming out of the womb. Can you remember coming out of the womb? That was a fearful experience for just a moment. Suddenly here you are, all of the security of the fluids and your mama, the protection of that association; and suddenly... A lot of you can remember being born. Suddenly, something is pulling on you and blaaaa! You're out here in this terrible reassociation of yourself. And that takes a little adjustment. Especially if you've been spanked initially. "Come on, wake up now." You've been in the womb of earth, which is the most logical correspondence to the totality of creative mind. A perfect womb is really what salvation is. It's the requirement of the totality of the dimensional association of time contained within the apparent evolutionary process. I haven't any idea what I said! That's the way I would have taught it if I didn't have the *Course In Miracles*. Do you see that?

Each one of your containments is actually a perfect relationship contained within itself. Incorruptible body – Jesus calls it that. There could be no corruption contained in it because the corruption could not be real. Why? It's a temporal association. Reality is reality. The closest, obviously, you could get to that in space/time would be to bring all space/time together, because space and time are the same thing. Location would have to be timeful or it couldn't be location.

I'm working up a sweat here. I'm in a new place. Look out. I tricked you up this far. There's nothing really left for you here. I don't care what you do with that. If you're going to come with me, you can come out right now. Look at this. Do you see that? That's a memory of us being already gone. Can you feel that? But remember, that memory is actually being constructed at this time in order that it be a memory later on. Can you get that? My assignment would be a memory of what my assignment is for the moment that I remember it. I remember you! I remember you guys perfectly well. Not only do I remember you

CHAPTER THREE: Bubbles

in any assignment that you thought we had together, I remember you in the totality of our single assignment. I would have to. Why? I remember you in my own totality of my assignment. You cannot be excluded from me because our assignment would have to be the same, since we came in at the same time. We are part of the contingency of a sojourn into time from eternity, with the specific reference of light that surrounded us. That sounds pretty good. If I didn't have *A Course In Miracles*, I would teach it this way.

I'm here to tell you; you guys have gathered here, and you waited, and I'm here to tell you! You can remember me, and we can remember each other because we come to a place of totality of memory if you'll let it be so, and don't go wandering off somewhere. All you really do is draw the Circle of Atonement. I'm going to stay away from the vernacular. Nothing stops you from coming together as little bubbles and dissolving them – Nothing. Because you're all the same finally anyway. All of your little bubbles contain all of your big bubbles. Is that so? You can name yourself LaRue if you want to. If you do, you'll be Bubbles LaRue! My first erection was Bubbles LaRue at the Empress Theater. I attempted to find a correspondence with Bubbles, obviously because I was attracted by the negative/positive association, and the necessity for me to enter into the relationship with Bubbles. And we attempt to dissolve into a single whole bubble. And we do! If we don't let ourselves be separate, we are a single union with God. This is called intercourse. But intercourse and outercourse are the same thing! A union with any association is literally a union with God, because God is everything. Obviously your ecstasy is in the climax of your association, or your attempts to association. But since you retain the separation, you will produce bubbles of separation – that's called space/time. And each one of them contains the totality of the light, apparent light or aspects of light, within that apparent space/time location. That's what your body is.

I'll reduce that a little: There's nothing outside of you. If you contain yourself within yourself, you'll be contained. If you do not, you will dissolve these bubbles of space/time that have restricted you from time travel. You then will discover that there is no limitation in the speed of the ascension of speed of light; the ascension from a static condition to a relative association of 186,000 miles/second, at which time matter would dissolve. Obviously, you are somewhere within that association of the continuum of the definition of yourself. Jesus calls it the Great Ray association. You know the nice thing about this? That's your mind, guys! Why do you look among the little bubbles to find yourself? You're not a little bubble. But if you retain that separation, you will gather around you froth of nothingness. Why? It can't communicate because you set a barrier of frothness. It is called chaos, and each thing fights within its own limited identity in the darkness of its individual limitation. So blow off the foam! Take a great draught of reality! You only need one sip of eternity to be whole. That's the elixir of eternity that you've been searching for. You have a zest for reality!

This is Wisconsin. Don't you think we should do it in relationship with the brewing of beer? Coming to reality is a fermentation or a dissolving of the old mind. It provides you with what you call alcohol. That's what it is. Hydrogen and oxygen that give you an ecstatic momentary release from the conflictual necessity of yourself. If you do that in the totality, you will be drunk with the glory of God. Holy Intoxication is what God is! Many of you now are walking around drunk with this incredible freedom, expressed by the non-containment of yourself. You no longer stagger and fall. Do you know a drunk is invulnerable? He can go anywhere. I'm speaking from experience here. If you ferment it in your limitation, you will get an alchemy definition of the collapse of the molecular limitation. That's what being drunk is. What did I just say?! But it *is* a fermentation in a particular sense. It's spirits. We call it spirits. This is a spirit of the intoxication, and not of the chemical

CHAPTER THREE: Bubbles

limitations of you, but in the reality of God mind who offers you the intoxication of total freedom. That's really what you've been looking for, and you will not be happy with anything else simply because it is what you are. You are a free mind. Nothing could possibly bind you.

The expression "God intoxication" is very aptly said. What's the matter with them? Are they all drunk? Remember at Pentecost? (Acts 2) What's happened to them? Are they all drunk? No, it's only midday, they won't get drunk until 6 tonight. They can't be drunk; it's only noon. You're drunk with love. Boy that's an amazing idea. Love without object. Jesus teaches be carefree, free of any necessity to bind yourself to the world at all. And obviously since you don't correspond, the light is a threat to the world, which is nothing but little bubbles. They are very much afraid of dissolving from the little bubbles, let's call it the grids of time. They dissolve from the grids of time in order to exceed the speed of light which is nothing but the restriction contained within the speed of light. There is no reality contained within the space/time continuum.

You could not be limited by separate design because there *is* only one mind. Do you see that? *In my Father's house are many mansions;* but they're all one mansion. There's no conflict contained within it.

I'm going to lose it. I'm losing it. Those of you who miss this one; I'll be back in just a minute, which may be a long time. It's not really true. But it's really true, **really true** that if you miss this one, you're never going to get it. But at the last minute, if you've got a good contingency, you'll say to the association within the definition of a slower time, "I'll be back for you." That's nothing but the promise of a savior. Jesus says, *I'm going where you can't go. I'll come back and get you.* (John 14) But remember, I'm coming back to get you now. This is the way out. You know about it. All you do is pick up the Text (of *A Course In Miracles*) and read about it. Yet you still find yourself here. This is called, in what you call simplicity of the vernacular "the second coming." That would have to be true, because any outgoing would be a totality unto itself and any limitation would be a correspondence of that limitation to reality. If you can't understand "It's going on all the time," understand that it went on, and this is the second chance for you now. You would have to find yourself there initially or you couldn't have formulated an association between God and man, and the limitation is the barrier established within the slow time association. Yet time is an invention of the limited association to hold it in a constricted evidence of space. God has nothing to do with it at all, except God has entered into the totality. So the limitation is the definition of your own associations contained within yourself. It's not something else. You named it – you *are* it.

If I leave, you will be another thousand years here. This is the end of this millennium, dummy. I wouldn't miss it. You can logically see the end of the millennium. If you want to look at it as millennium, you look at it as one. You look at it as a harvest, and you will be right, because I have to find it within your own mind to see that I am sowing. Because I can sow everything, I can reap everything. If you'll let me reap, I'll reap everything. You certainly are going to get what you sow. What you sow you will reap. And if you sow in limitation, if you sow in sorrow, you will reap in sorrow. If you sow as the Holy Spirit, you will reap as that totality of your own mind.

Would you like to see where I was? You're welcome. Come on, take it up to God. Don't try to identify yourself here.

CHAPTER FOUR

Black Holes: Time to Eternity

he Matter Myth. What does that mean, that matter is a myth? Yes. It says, "Matter Myth." It says that this table is a universal association; that the universe is a provisional association of matter in a density that cannot withstand the pressure of reality. Some of you are pretty near ready to hear this, obviously, because you can feel the expression of a mind that is demonstrating thought association to you. Quit making it somehow so *divine*. It appears divine because it feels so harmonious to you to actually discover that by not what you call "matterizing" things, by not making this table solid... Obviously this thing is solid and I have made it solid in my time association. That's what *Matter Myth* says.

If your mind has first of all absolved yourself from the matter association, it will begin to correspond – the mind, the form will begin to correspond in a different universal association. You must take a very fundamental premise, which shouldn't be difficult for you since you are a mind thinking, and somewhere accept, not in a definition of yourself, that the universe is thought. I can't get anywhere with you if you're going to insist that you can take thought and construct thought into an association in time. Now, we're doing that here together, aren't we? This is slipping away from me because you're trying to define it. All I'm really offering you is the freedom of your mind to be what it is. Can you get a hold of this? Somewhere you have invented an association of yourself contained within what you term reality – universal consciousness. I'm not concerned about what it is. What difference would it make what it is, if it is going to be singular?

I'm back to this. Yesterday I tried to teach you a lesson out of the Workbook that said that you construct a physical reality. Any reasonable mind could see the absurdity of physical reality. Everything yo teach me, even in basic Newtonian physics, tells me that everything is in action all the time. Well, you go, "Yeah," but how do you make this physical then? That's what astonishes me. Why do you become an anomaly in your association of the admission that everything is changing all the time? Quite obviously, you can't get anywhere from where you are if everything is changing. Really, what you're saying to me is, "I am going to point at where I am going to be next week or an hour from now in order to get there at all." It should be obvious that you can't locate yourself.

Listen. The fundamental premise of all teachings that attempt to address time will be the notation of a "going out" and a "coming back." All ideas about relative space/time involve the idea of slow and fast time. It cannot *not* be so because the association of the universe in some direction must be a linear identity of the possibility of acceleration. This is what the speed of light is. Can you get that? In effect, then, if we can get to that, I can teach you that the slowest light can be would be your total potential in your own mind. Are you all right with this? You're going to somewhere have to accept the idea that you are a

CHAPTER FOUR: Black Holes: Time To Eternity

configuration of energy identity in time and that this – I'll teach *Course In Miracles* for a minute – that the Holy Instant is nothing but the distance between your compactness of your memory and the reality that you are. Are we comfortable with that? This is the whole teaching.

Interestingly enough, it involves the idea of dimensional or hierarchical associations, simply because it's teaching from a mind that is able to correspond more readily than you are in your identity of yourself. Yet it must be contained somewhere in time. This is the whole *Course* now. Can you hear this? I'm teaching you that somewhere in time you are in a continuing association with your own thoughts – *you*, body identities. I don't care what you call yourself. We just got you to admit, "*I am not a body. I am free. I am as God created me.*" It isn't because some things are bodies and some aren't. It's because there isn't any such thing as a body. This is *very* important.

Otherwise you'll do what these guys (authors Paul Davies and John Gribbin) do when I read you about black holes. They are very much aware that as an object approaches a black hole, time slows down – quite literally it gets slow. They are also very much aware that as long as they observe this association getting closer and closer in time, they see that it can never go totally slow. Do you understand that? The object that they are observing can never enter into the black hole. They are in observation of it. They are also aware that this is not pertinent to the man who is entering the black hole. This is Einstein. The man who is entering the black hole is operating under his own space/time association. I really got you in the *Course In Miracles* here if you care to look at it.

This, then, is a speeding up of time, or finding yourself somewhere in an association of the occurrence of a schism to a potential and the release out to reality. Is that all right? Where do you suffer your anomaly? The anomaly is suffered by your determination to create an objective association in your own configuration, which is literally what time is. Time is your own association of your own thought somewhere contained within your own body. I'll give you this in a literal sense. It is impossible that your body is not a universe. It's literally impossible because you have the idea of a universe. There isn't any question that you have an idea of a universal mind association contained within yourself. All you really needed from me was the direction – and I'll use the *Course In Miracles* – that nothing is outside of you. You are nothing then, but a universe in a continual state of contraction and expansion – that's what this says – to the point where it becomes non-observable.

I am offering you here, physically, a condition of black hole reassociation – resurrection. That's what I'm doing right now. If I release my mind, my mind will immediately come from the compactness of my own self-identity, and release to the freedom of my own mind. That's what the resurrection is. This is how you do it in the Workbook. It is vital that you remember there is no such thing as other thought minds. Why would you be threatened by this great excitement of the freedom of your own mind entering into a broader, an ultra-dimensional universal mind? Why wouldn't that thrill you? Doesn't that thrill you? Screw this idea that you've got to study the forgiveness in your brother. It's so frigging absurd! Excuse me!

You will say to me that you are determined to construct yourself in your own associations of staticness and retain the body. You have taught me that the body, obviously, is nothing but energy in a microcosm of association going on and changing all the time. Obviously we are observing an association of energy and constituting it by – we're in the real difficult teaching here – and giving it a constituted reality by the power of our mind. There is no question that we're doing that. What about it? Where do you find correspondence with the other association that's outside of yourself that will not result in chaos? If we have made the

CHAPTER FOUR: Black Holes: Time To Eternity

fundamental admission that all matter is finally only the force of love, or God, or wholeness, or life. Starting with that premise.

Is that actually going on in your body all the time? Now, I'll teach you the *Course*. This is how you leave, obviously, how you get out of this time association. Are you telling me that you may simply, totally reassociate yourself from that moment? This is called the Great Reversal. Jesus teaches this, the guy that wrote the *Course*, you, teaches it as a great reversal – that the moment that you went into that association you immediately were activated in the universal mind and that that is going on all the time. Of course it's going on all the time. How the hell would it not go on all the time if it's what time is? Come on. Somewhere you have to see this.

This is what this book says about black holes. If you come down into a black hole, he says, you'll turn into a white hole. And it is an interesting idea that you become light. Why? You become infinite. You lose all of the possibility of the containment of the association with time. At the very least, I would think that you would entertain the idea that you are doing this with your mind, and the minimum you would feel is the excitement of the possibility. The Academy is designed to do nothing but give you the excitement of the possibility of your own mind. Obviously it has to teach you not to be little and not to associate with the stuff that you have constructed in your own mind.

Why isn't it fun that all dimensions are going on all the time? And that you can enter into another association and bring all of your thought forms with you? Well, you can. So you find yourself for a moment in this one. What about it? But what difference would that make? That's the only one there is, isn't it? This one. Well, the most I can offer you is happiness, peace, joy and eternity. I can't do any more than that. You see, it doesn't matter to me how you construct it, it's always falling apart anyway. The fun then becomes what? Letting it fall apart. I hate to reduce this to the AA program, but really, all you've decided is – I didn't want to go into the psychology – is literally to let your own thought forms fall apart, because the form never has anything to do with reality at all. I got into the *Course* again. What the hell difference would it make what the table is if it's just a form that's falling apart all the time and did fall apart anyway because it became your Light association?

Are you so afraid to be free, teachers of God or whatever the hell you call yourself? It's much bigger than that. Come on! I'm only concerned about the mechanism. Why? There isn't any such thing as non-action. The basis of this teaching is that everything is going full-blown all the time. Do you have a problem with that? Wherever it is, you can call it slow or call it fast, but if anything's going on, it's going on all the time, all around you. And the pain that you must feel somewhere within you at this time is the non-fulfillment of the potential of the certainty that every single relationship that you have in your static mind knows the exact truth, and that would be truth in the sense of wholeness. How could it possibly not? And that unless you tell yourself your own false stories about your own association with yourself – and this is the idea of a dream – obviously you're going to wake up and be whole consciousness. So do you understand this? The friction, the conflict, the gravity, the depth of this apparent association is only in your own mind.

Now, at some point it really doesn't do me much good to observe a black hole, does it? I'm going to have to jump into the hole to see what's on the other side. Sometimes they teach this as wormholes. It's a loop in the fabric of space/time; dimensionally, it is thought of as like Swiss cheese. And this is the idea of time travel, that since everything is going on all the time, you can pop through a black hole and come into any other association. The only problem you'll have with that, and the problem that occurs inordinately because of the necessity to express it, is the idea that *that* universe was going on before you entered into it. Was it? Yes or no?

CHAPTER FOUR: Black Holes: Time To Eternity

(Audience): "No!"

Both. The idea that you are entering it from out of time indicates that there is a possibility of multiplicity. Otherwise there would be no saviorship. Do you see? Because if you retain the identity of this association universally and enter into another, you are in effect saying there's two. Who sees this? Jesus teaches this as you're perfectly capable of coming out of time, remembering everything that went on here and going into any universe you want. That just gives you more freedom. Now you're a genuine time traveler. You come into associations not of your own mind. I don't know if you can hear that. Then you're a repair man, aren't you? It would make no difference to me what the break in communication was because I am aware that objective thinking is a break in communication. Obviously I am offering you subjective thinking. I am offering you a flow of reality Light. That's why I am a black hole. Why? Where do you catch me? How slow are you in your own time? Have I got you to: *It is all thought?*

I promise you that I am converting thought. Can you get it? This is what healing is. I'm converting form, guys. But the sickness of you was the body form. Who's with me? It hasn't got anything to do with what sickness is. Do you see that? So the healing is occurring by the conversion of your potential thought form. This is a natural process that you will come to, that you must come to, because your natural state is to be a converter – if there is any state at all. It's the same idea that if there is any schism, it's perfectly natural for you to come from that to wholeness. I'm just offering you, then, within your own mind a brighter, more energetic, more creative reassociation of our association in thought form. That's what I do.

Do you see? Can you get it? Can you really teach A *Course In Miracles?* It doesn't have anything to do with the form or the association of the form with me because that's the static condition of the body. And the body's changing all the time anyway. Now, the joy, hopefully, that you're experiencing, that Jesus would call a happy learner, is the automatic, simultaneous conversion of the conflictual thought of your own mind. And that's how simple this is. Is that true or not? Why do I have to define the conversion? The happiness and joy is in the conversion. Isn't it?

If there really is creative light and late thought association, fast-time thought – not really slowed down to where I'm struggling with my own mind, which is all there is – I simply continually release that because I am the universe. I am that. Well, is that what communication is? Come on! Communication, obviously, is creative energy of the mind, right? And just as obviously, it has nothing to do with the thought forms. Does it? Why? If you have one thought and another thought, aren't you thinking in between the thoughts? But isn't all creation going on, despite your identity between the forms that are falling apart all the time? Aren't they? Aren't you thinking within this perceptual mind – "I," "I," "me" between your thoughts? Of course. It's what your identity is.

Now, this is transformation. What difference would it make what we said to each other? In that sense? Or if we could say something to each other? How thick are you in this creative self-identity of thickness? I can't really teach this. You have to remember, I'm teaching subjective reality. There is only your own mind. You then construct thick associations of yourself. Any body association that you make outside of yourself would have to be you because there isn't anything outside of yourself. Wherever you correspond in your own thought mind about you is literally what the whole universe is, in the sense that it's you in any correspondence that you have. You are fearful of it because it appears to be outside yourself. That's the absurdity of fear. What would you be afraid of? You could only be afraid of your own compacted association with yourself. And compaction is what fear is because it's a potential being fulfilled to the light of you.

CHAPTER FOUR: Black Holes: Time To Eternity

Now, what do you, then, as a dark group – dark in the sense that you've brought these associations in your mind here – do when you are confronted with a faster range of energy? This is how simple this is. All you would really have to do is look at where you are in the earth compared to the whole universe and wonder what the hell you're doing, constructing yourself so limitedly in your own mind. What's the sense in it?

How can the mind do that? Obviously we are in an objective association, talking about expansion of the universe, talking about black holes. Who is it that's doing the talking about it, except you? Who is it that's an association except you in your own mind? Where would the correspondence not occur in love and harmony through your release of the identity of where you find yourself?

The Matter Myth: Dramatic Discoveries that Challenge Our Understanding of Physical Reality. I would think so. *All this would happen in the fraction of a second prior to your reaching the singularity. So you couldn't observe it without being irreversibly incorporated into it.* That's a nice sentence. But notice it goes to the compactness before it goes to the release. All right? Fundamentally you are identifying yourself as a time possibility. If you were to associate it, it would read like this: *When time stands still. Things would look quite different, however, to an observer who watched you fall into the hole from outside. Gravity, remember, not only bends space but also slows time. Near a neutron star the effect is very pronounced, and it is readily detected in a pulsar radiation.* This is exactly what I'm teaching. *As you approach the event horizon of a black hole from the outside, so the flow of time in your vicinity slows down more and more as measured by a distant observer. However, the observer who crosses into the hole through the event horizon notices nothing unusual. The event horizon has no local significance.* Until you find yourself in the hole. Then it would probably begin to have a lot of significance. So you quit observing yourself going down into your time, and get into your own whole. That's precisely what the teaching is.

However, the observer who crosses into the hole through the event horizon... That's a nice thing, the "event horizon." If you're talking about Borderland, it's the event horizon. But remember that one distance between events or forms is the same as any distance. We won't get into the String Theory, the Nine-dimensional String Theory, which will be a part of this, which is nothing but your own linear thought. But listen.

However, the observer who crosses into the hole through the event horizon notices nothing unusual. The event horizon has no local significance, even though at the boundary the time warp becomes infinite. To an outside observer it will appear to take you forever to reach the event horizon. In a sense, time at the surface of a black hole stands still relative to the time experienced by a distant observer. So anything that happens to you inside the hole lies beyond the infinite future, as far as the outside universe is concerned. It is for this reason that a journey into a black hole is normally regarded as a one-way trip. Why? You're going to lose your identity in that hole. I'm just teaching you to keep emerging from your hole somewhere later on in your own future significance by the activation of your time in the continual going on of time. What a lovely idea.

To enter a black hole and emerge again would mean that a distant observer would have to see you come out before you went in. That's exactly what I'm teaching here. Jesus teaches it this way: You've got to go back in time in order to come out later in time. That's what I just said. That's what this says. Because all of the memory is contained in there anyway. Jesus uses this: It seems to go back but really goes forward. That's what this is saying. And I don't care whether you understand it completely. Quit trying to understand. The

CHAPTER FOUR: Black Holes: Time To Eternity

idea of the analogy overwhelms me. I'm overwhelmed by the idea that this is the whole teaching. I'm overwhelmed by the idea that the *I Ching* is the genetic helix. It absolutely overwhelms me. Not you. You say, "Well, that's the way it is." Yet when I look at the helix, I see that it's the symbol of the I Ching. Somebody's apparently trying to tell you something about your own helix association with yourself in time, aren't they? What are you going to do, study the *I Ching* and study your associations with it? No, no.

A distant observer would have to see you come out before you went in. In other words, you would have traveled backward in time. This conclusion should not come as a surprise because the hole traps light. Anything escaping from it has to do what? *Exceed the speed of light.* If you got trapped you would have to exceed the speed of light or you'd never get out. This is my whole teaching. Somewhere you're going back and forth into it. But each moment you go totally into the black hole you immediately exceed the speed of light and you come whole. You keep finding yourself in that association. Otherwise you couldn't get out. Actually it's going on simultaneously. The moment there is a total black hole, it must exceed the speed of light or it will find itself somewhere within the association of the descension into it and the coming out. And this is exactly where you're finding yourself. You're meeting yourself coming and going. That's what a human mind does. It has made the admission of the idea of potential – evolution of its own mind. If it can direct its attention to a fulfillment through the non-exclusion of itself, which is objective reality – this is A *Course In Miracles* now – it will continue the experience of the whole association of time, which lasted but a moment. Do you want the sentence? Time lasted but a moment and was immediately gone. It's the whole *Course In Miracles.*

What a surprise, that somebody out of time is telling you that time is only lasting a moment and literally offering you a portal of a black hole, which is what it obviously is. And now, just as obviously, you couldn't find Heaven except within the black hole. Isn't that so? It's the same idea as looking down into yourself, dummy. Where do you think the black hole is but contained within your own memory association? That's what it is, if there's nothing outside of you. But the moment that you go into the black hole, your thoughts exceed your time associations and you spring gone, which is what's happening here, I hope. Obviously, if this doesn't happen to your mind, there's no hope that you'll ever get this. You'd be confined forever to your own black hole, wouldn't you? But how would there be reality in a black hole? What is it if there's only one universal mind?

If, then, an object that falls into a black hole cannot reemerge from the outside universe, what happens to it? As we explained, any object that encounters the singularity is annihilated. It literally ceases to exist. A precisely spherical ball of ordinary matter, for example, collapsing to become a black hole, will shrink to the common center. All the matter will be squeezed into a singularity. Idealized mathematical models of changed and rotating holes have been examined to find out where the singularity lies, and where the infalling material goes. The models indicate that the hole acts as a sort of bridge, or space/time tunnel, connecting our Universe with another space/time that is otherwise completely inaccessible to it. This is exactly what I'm teaching you. You can't know two worlds. You can only know one world at a time. The moment that it's accessible to you, you become it.

This astonishing result – obviously – *opens up the prospect of an intrepid space traveler passing through the black hole unscathed and entering another universe, arriving somewhere beyond our infinite future.* Of course it will be beyond our infinite future because you've constructed the limitation of your own mind, and the idea of one beyond is the same as any beyond unless you limit your cause and give yourself an effect that corresponds to the cause of you. You'll always be trapped then within your own time association, because you're getting a reflection from your own hole. I'm teaching the *Course* and this at the same time. The moment that you then release that correspondence of the objective reality to thickness – this is the *Course* now – it dissolves. And it becomes light because it's a whole association of your mind. You literally come to light, don't you? You are light, aren't you? Some of your light was thick, fat, slow. Now it's getting fast. Is that okay?

This astonishing result opens up the prospect of an intrepid space traveler passing through the black hole unscathed and entering another universe, arriving somewhere beyond our infinite future. If this could be accomplished, it would not be possible for the traveler to retrace the passage back to the starting point. I don't know why not, unless he's in duality. It's the same idea as that you can't really move in time because the time will be slower back where you're coming from. What the hell difference does it make if time is only you? The trick of this is to understand that whatever time you're in is all the time that there is. And this will give you the notion that it can take a year, it can take a thousand years, it can take a million years, but it will always be the *now* of your reassociation in your time factoring through not bringing your old slow time – this is the Workbook now, your old slow time of thoughts that keep you caught in your body identity, through the practice of the continual release of that memory association. Done by what? The inclusion of your potential, not the rejection of some of the things in your potential that didn't correspond to you as you made this ascension. Remember that you're nothing but a distance between these thoughts and that the thoughts have really dissolved and are dissolving all the time.

If this could be accomplished, it would not be possible... Why? *Diving into the tunnel from the other universe would bring our daring space traveler not back to our Universe but to a third universe, to another ad infinite universe, to universes beyond universes forever. What would the remote end of the black hole bridge look like to an observer located in the other universe? According to the simple mathematical model, an observer would see the object as a source of outward-rushing material – the explosive creation of matter – often called a "white hole."*

This is exactly what's going on in you all of the time. The question is only where are you are retarding your own motion through this universe as you come into compactness and release into God.

How would you teach this without participating in it? I'm curious. Could you? How the hell could you? Could what I just read you really be true? Could it? Is it all right? Or are you going to have to begin to find all the books you can, to study your association with it so you can make a comparison of yourself with yourself in regard to what you are. Right? Why should you have to figure out who you are in the first place? That's what I don't understand. "I'm going to take all the material available to me and figure out who I am."

See how much the Academy is continual action of your mind? Can you get this? Notice how it doesn't really require bodily action because it's a journey without distance, that you're really not going from one place to another, but the conversion is going on within your own resurrecting body. One of the great demonstrations that Jesus talks about in the *Course* was the total transfiguration of His immediate time associations at the time of the Resurrection. Not only did He completely resurrect and leave it, but came back into this continuum as a reconstructed body, with a valid memory of the thought form association. That's what He said. He talks about it in His *What Is the Resurrection?* (A Course In Miracles-Manual For Teachers) Actually that's what's going on right here, isn't it? Can I get it

CHAPTER FOUR: Black Holes: Time To Eternity

fast enough so that you can spring out with me? Only through your willingness to relinquish the persecution of yourself, the killing of yourself in your own thoughts.

Are you saying the Resurrection is going on all the time? That's what I just read you. Can you get the connection? I'm reading you that. How long do you have to stay in hell? One day. One day. Jesus descends into hell, and the third day, He rises. It's the whole idea that He comes down into His tomb, He has to be there for a moment and then He comes out. Why the hell is that hard? Why can't He do it in a moment? Because the idea of doing it, or going and coming out, is what time is, isn't it?

It's the same idea that a dot is a circle. You see? The String Theory. This is really *sutra*. We're teaching *sutra* here for a minute. *Sutras* are nothing but strings of associate consciousnesses that create time. This is the old Hindu teaching. And there's always a distance between the beginning and the end of the string, and that's what time is. Now, that can be a Great Ray association if you will let it be. And the strings can loop and become a genetic code of memory in association with each other. That's what's happening to you. Isn't that fun, that that could be true? Or would you rather just be an old body and get sick and die again?

See, the fun about the Academy is getting up in the frigging morning and knowing there's something besides what you're doing, going on. And I don't care whether it's religious, going to the altar and praying; or whether it's reading this book, or whether it's getting with an association that's willing to watch *Star Wars* or *Star Trek* with you. It's the whole idea that there's something besides this, that you're not really going to be confined to this. See how it doesn't matter what it is. This is the teaching. One thing we know for sure: It's not this! But remember, you have made it this in your own mind. So the requirement, obviously, is the change or the emergence, or the resurrection or the enlightenment or the awakening of you in your own mind.

ILLUMINATION: Discourses With Master Teacher

See, I can talk to you guys in a particular way now because you've made the admission of your own possibility. Quite literally, I'm telling you the absolute truth. Somewhere you have always denied the truth of your own whole mind. This is Chapter 17. Fortunately you've got a book. If you didn't have a book, I would teach you the way I'm teaching you now. You would then write a book that said the method by which you did this. Oh, sure you would. That's what the Workbook is. From the first to the last, the Workbook is doing nothing but teaching you to do what I'm telling you to do right now, "None of this means anything. I brought all of this with me. I can escape this by the release of myself." It's exactly what I just read you.

Can you imagine the excitement of doing this in your own mind? See, the excitement is in the action of the creation of your own mind, not in the observation of it. Having thoughts is what has restricted you. Got it? The comparison of the thought is what has always restricted you. Yet all of creation is only contained in and between an accumulative reassociation of your own thoughts. That's kind of fun, isn't it? Or not? Do you see how your problem disappears? Come on. I'm literally teaching you forgiveness here, or non-guilt. This is the core of the curriculum. If you have constructed thought forms between your own forms in your own thought, you obviously make your identity based on your own thought. You now have created yourself in an image association of yourself in time. What is there besides that? Nothing! Once more, I'm going to do it for you. There's not another reality, dear one. There's not a Holy Spirit with a separate reality. There's only a Holy Spirit with a whole reality, which is you, corresponding to you all the time. Can you hear this? Can you get this? There aren't other thoughts. God thinking *is* you.

I'm trying to get rid of your fear for you. I'm trying to get you not to be afraid to release your thoughts. There isn't anything out there that's not you. Do you see? There's no real conflict

CHAPTER FOUR: Black Holes: Time To Eternity

going on except your fear to undergo the experience of the natural metamorphosis of your own mind. "Well, that's what the *Course* says." I know that's what the *Course* says. I know that. I've reduced it to what we call "rite of passage." That's a reduction. What I'm doing is giving you the correspondence, right? The *Philosophia Perennis*. I'm giving you the correspondence that everything is only teaching you this. The whole basis of the *Course* is, everything is only teaching you this because that's all you could ever learn. And everything you could ever learn is only for the transformation of your own mind. Have you got it? Whatever you are, you are everything going on in your own awakening.

It cannot be a problem. It is a problem because it's a constant conversion of yourself. But what a beautiful problem. I'm teaching you directly the *Course* now. Why? You see a solution that transcends the association. It immediately becomes joyous to you to release rather than hold on and derive your old experiences. In fact, the derivation of your own experience now causes you pain and you no longer want it. Right? Yes. For some of you. Others of you still hold on to it. Why? You are all different in time. Come on! Come on! Come on! Every single association of body identity is literally in a different association in time or he would become the same. He would then become that one identity in time, which is really what I'm teaching.

The assimilation of the Great Ray association is exactly what I am teaching you. Jesus calls it the Great Rays, but wherever you are in your own – Jesus calls you a constellation – wherever you are in all of this Great Ray string association, it must be contained in your body because you have given yourself a body identity. But it also must be whole. So if all the Great Rays are finally only one, you ignite your own Great Ray association and the particles begin to become waves of recognition of yourself in time. You are your brother, quite literally. You are not your brother because you study him and decide to try to be like him.

You are your brother because there's only one mind. Do you see? We keep admonishing you, "Be one-minded." That's all there is, anyway. Don't separate yourself from your Ray. The harmony that you feel is the entering into the Great Ray spectrum light association. That's why you feel good. Why do you feel good? You lost your conflict of self-identity. "Where did it go?" What do you mean, "Where did it go?" You want to go find it again? That's what a lot of you do. You keep rummaging back through your own black hole in order to keep getting a reflection of yourself. This is all the whole idea of burning the dross, of undergoing the experience, of letting the chaff go, is directing you to – this mind re-identity.

Is that what I'm doing with my mind now? A little bit. What will happen if I do it all with my mind? We'll all be gone. I bet you can't hear that. By "we all" I mean me. I'm not sure you got that. Who did you think I meant? You? Come on. You guys are in my dream. I'll reduce this just a little bit. You are in my dream, but my dream is very much aware this world is not real. In fact, the whole basis of my dream now is that this world is not real. What other world? All I'm concerned about is that this one is not real. That's my assignment. Yet I've got all these thoughts in my mind, which are you, who I no longer recognize within my new association.

Sometimes I try to do it this way. Remember how you used to get lost in the hall and didn't know which classroom you were in? The bell would ring, and all the doors would close, and everybody would leave, and you're caught in your own passageway of your own mind. You don't know what the hell classroom you belong to. Well, if you'd look at the earth as a scenario or a classroom, you can see that when you exceed your own purpose dimensionally, you no longer belong in that classroom. And for just a moment that's pretty chaotic. This is the way the *Course* would teach it. You somehow don't belong here. You don't belong in this segment of time any longer. Why?

CHAPTER FOUR: Black Holes: Time To Eternity

You've matured your body so it won't fit into the limited form association. What does it do? It causes conflict to the association. The association is protecting itself within its own mind. It literally needs to hold itself together, so that any light that intrudes into the chaos is conflictual. In the *Course* Jesus teaches you're always protecting yourself from your own illumination. But remember, dear teachers of God, it is only happening every moment. Listen, if you don't hold it together, it will fall apart and you will be the divine Mind of God. How do you know that? We're sharing the idea. I'm telling you that you are. I'm telling you there's no reality in our association. I'm teaching you *A Course In Miracles*, that there never would be reality in our own association. You go, "Wow, that's wonderful. I don't want these associations to be true."

If I can get the Academy to include the mechanism of the psychology with the philosophy of singularity, that the process is going on in the individual, my job is done. And that will happen, it should happen, in the next 40 days. You can't teach at the level that you're attempting to teach, which is nothing but the transformation of the body/mind association, and not run into a conflict that will dissolve to Light. I'm not concerned about that. I'm concerned about how much can be brought into this new direction of light. See if you can hear this. My concern about what's in here is really nothing.

If I could teach you that you're a vat of beer. When I was taught this at the Academy, I was taught that I had taken on an association, hermetic association of an energy factoring, and that by introducing a Light into it that it will leaven, that it will evolve into a brighter identity. I am very much aware, and you should be in your whole new mind, that there aren't separate identities. At most, they contain the necessity of all the ingredients. I will just put them together, put some Light into them, and harvest it – get out of it what I can. I am the Good Shepherd. If I have the sheep, my job is to show them that they are the shepherd. What the hell else am I doing? Why am I concerned about what you are in your own association? That's not real. Reality is this. I can bring together, though, in association with you any thoughts that you will bring to me because I'm standing at the black hole. This is the whole *Course*, what I just read you. If time went and came back, I'm at what you'd call the Alpha and the Omega point all the time. It's always darkest before the dawn. You're always going to that moment – and this is expressed a lot in the *Course* – where the altar, he calls it, of total darkness turns to total light. Why isn't that exciting to you, if it's you? What are you willing to hear about this? The process is one of inclusion, so that I can see that every form or thought that I am having can spring into the Light of my singular reality.

So I am a catalyst of Light in a later time association that literally transforms your individual thought associations. It has nothing to do with the attempt to communicate in the thick thought, does it? Because that's not communicating, is it? Because communication has to be whole to be real. So any attempts that you make to identify that association simply constrict you, for that moment, to time. But see how accumulative the Holy Instants are, because each time you have one, a real one, you have forever converted that form. You no longer have to dwell in that form of your own genetic identity. It's gone! It's been shone away. Where is the darkness when it's Light? Nowhere. Where is the objective form when it becomes Light? Nowhere. What is this form? Nothing. Nothing but a reflection of your own mind, of your own thought.

Now, try to do this. Here's what we want at the Academy. This is the problem some of you are having because we're diversifying in our perceptual association. One of you is going to teach it from a music standpoint or from an art standpoint. What I showed you here was very artful. The idea of the reassociation of my creative mind from my potential, which is exactly what I expressed there, can be taught as an inclusive thing without me actually studying the containment. Obviously the *Matter Myth* will reduce itself to objectivity. I don't question that. What do I care about that? I'm looking for the pertinent sentences, like in the *Philosophia Perennis*, that will direct me to the certainty of my own mind association. I don't have to study the details. I don't have to explain that God is gravity to myself. I know that God is gravity because God is pushing on me all the time, and I'm trying to escape down into a hole. And then, when I get totally compact, I'll come out and be everything because I am everything. But God appears to be attacking me, and I'm trying to escape Him because I'm trying to get down into my own black hole. But I won't succeed in doing that.

Now, the excitement, then, is: Something is out there. I don't have to know what it is if I have no fear in my own mind, which I have created in order to keep myself from going there. Now I can stand here, wherever I am in all of universal mind, and say, "I am that." I know you can reduce that. You reduce everything, anyway. All I'm really telling you is that's what you are, and that's all there is. Is that an experience? I don't even understand your question. The universe *is* only experience.

You're reaching a point in your late-time associations where you are sharing in the experience of my mind without the necessity of entering into an exchange with me. That's the highest range of teaching there is, isn't it? "And he stood among them, and they went to Light." This is literally true. You see? So if you guys all come into a late-time association and aren't combating yourself in your own association, you will form a circle of Atonement, won't you? It's the whole idea. And all the baggage you bring in then is simply released into this Light of this identity. It's the same idea as "You are the Way and the Light."

Where will we meet, then, in this? At the beginning and the end of time? Is that where we meet? If we, in the portal sense, meet, it would have to be at the beginning and the end of time, because the beginning and the end of time are right together.

Where we went in, we get to go out, don't we? Where we started this frigging expedition, we've got to get out of it. So I'm standing here, calling you and telling you it's all over. This is called "The Call." At the time that you journeyed out in your own mind, you simply descended down into a hell. You really didn't go out anywhere. You couldn't get outside of everything. It's the same idea as God is gravity. So you came out of the Garden of Eden, which was a temporary, a momentary construction of the Borderland – actually, going and coming out. Are you meeting yourself going out of Eden or are you meeting yourself coming back? Remember that when you went outside the door you really didn't go anywhere. You just descended. And every time you had a thought that you thought could escape, it simply reflected off that thought and put you deeper in dung. You literally went deeper in hell. We're east of Eden. You can teach it that way, if you want. You went to your Eastern potential, in the Land of Nod. You went to the Land of Nod, east of Eden.

Does Jesus mention that? He says, "Where does it say you woke up. Adam fell asleep. Where does it say he woke up?" You're in Nod. Do you have *Wynken* and *Blynken* with you? Yes! There's so much energy in that poem, I couldn't stand it. I read *Wynken, Blynken and Nod,* and I began to go to Light. This is what we want to happen at the Academy. Will we teach *Wynken, Blynken and Nod?* You bet. You're feeling a little *Wynken, Blynken and Nod.* By your non-necessity to identify, "What the hell does he mean!" You keep saying, "What do you mean by that?" You are determined to find a result from what you projected before in the nursery rhyme. The nursery rhyme is everything or it's nothing.

Mary had a little lamb. The doctor fainted! Actually, esoterically, *Mary had a little lamb* is the birth of the Christ. *Mary had a little lamb. Its fleece was white as snow. And everywhere that Mary went* – the Virgin – *the lamb was sure to go. It followed her to school one day* – which is the

CHAPTER FOUR: Black Holes: Time To Eternity

perceptual mind – *which is against the rules. It made the children laugh to see a lamb at school,* or the innocence of the lamb in the Christ. What else do you want to know?

Now, I did that with a little energy. What I'm showing you is the lamb in school. That's what it is. But see, it's not really a play on words, it's a release of them. Can you see it? *Little Boy Blue, Come Blow Your Horn* is another one. Real lot of energy in it. The funny thing is, as children, you know there's energy in the nursery rhymes. That's why they survive. They have survived precisely because of the energy that just came into that. It then enters into the illustrations, doesn't it? *Mother Goose.* It enters into the association. You wonder why the kids will pick up the old *Mother Goose* and go, "Wow! Look at this!" They have real good memories of it, all the old illustrations. These are the icons of energy memory.

This will be taught in the art class. Why? Contained in that cartoon or in that memory is all of that energy. Why wouldn't it be? It's all memory anyway. I'm teaching you to remember better. I'm teaching you to remember, not by your own devices. But through the release of the device of memory, you will begin to create with your new memory minds, won't you? All perception is only memory, anyway. That's the fun part of this. If you don't resist your own memory – I hate to reduce it to forgiveness – but why the hell would you want to challenge somebody in your own association? Release him so you can enjoy this transformation of you that's going on.

Can we explain this to the world by establishing in space/time an Academy of bright reassociation? Why not? We can do anything we want to do. Why are we secure in this? It can't fail. Our security is in the certainty that we're only holding it together for a minute, anyway. This is a great practice for you guys. We're always only getting the result of the construction, and all constructions are limited, anyway. And it's the falling apart of the construction that makes this whole, not the holding it together. Can you teach that at the Academy, that it's an awakening, a coming together, a vortex, contained within the great association of space/time? I hope so because that's what it is. It will not be somewhere else. It will be where you, in your consort minds of your identities of love for each other, construct it – and the release of the necessity to identify yourself in your separate associations. That's what it is. That's what you're being offered.

Now, those of you who can be mindful of this Light association are very rapidly progressing to your own resurrection. And each moment that you're admitting that it's occurring all the time, you simply stay in that reassociation of yourself. It's a metamorphosis. You can't empower yourself. Anything that you're doing with your own mind is always restricting you from this flow of light and energy that's going on around you. It hasn't anything to do with the body at all, does it? The body's gone. "Yeah, but I need to use it to transform it." Well, get at it then. Be about it.

CHAPTER FIVE

A Masters' Academy

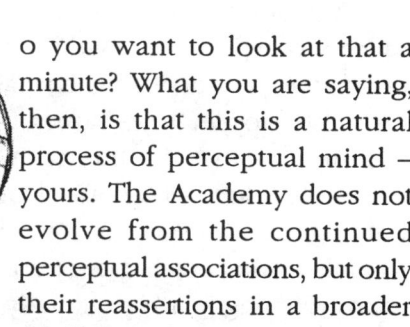

o you want to look at that a minute? What you are saying, then, is that this is a natural process of perceptual mind – yours. The Academy does not evolve from the continued perceptual associations, but only their reassertions in a broader range of conceptual self – creative self-expression – the admission of the evolution of man. Is that it? That's what everybody says. Everybody says that man is evolving. You are saying that you can have a structural location where you would actually accelerate the evolutionary reassociation of individual man in his mind? In essence, it would have nothing to do with the conceptual association at all except in the mutual creative purpose of the nobility of man. You have to teach this real gently initially. You teach it like Ralph Waldo – that man is more than the sum of his fearful part associations with himself. And that's acceptable to everybody, right?

It is very necessary in this Academy that you make this step to individual transformation initially and all the time. Let the disciplined identity bring his conceptual self-associations projected from him, and experience the broadening of his self-identity in the cognition of his association with you in the range of your teaching devices.

That the fearful constraints in which man finds himself, in this twirling mud ball of objective death can be transcended individually in the mind. Is that what you are going to tell me? And the result will be an aggregate reassociation of man in a more harmonious situation of himself in objective time. You can't teach it any other way initially. I'm trying to do the twelve principles of the Academy.

You are totally unconcerned whether the guy is seeing saucers, or whether he's writing a story about quantum physics, or whether he's declaring that Salvador Dali is God. You don't care. Listen to me. We're saying, "Isn't that wonderful!" But there is a process that the human mind is undergoing in a time association to an identity of universal consciousness – an ontological admission of Universal Mind. Now, if you have formulated that in scholastic purpose and religious commitment to overcoming fear, you literally cannot be attacked. You can be attacked for the idea of transformation, but it is very difficult to do because you already have insinuated that the transformation is a necessity for you to give and love in the psychology association. Really what you are saying is that love – and we're going to include the passion of this – is a reasonable association of the necessity for the individual mind to find peace in his own communicative devices. We are not at all concerned about what those devices are. Do you hear me? Do you hear what you are saying? This is *A Course In Miracles.*

In the whole association of the principles it doesn't even mention the *Course In Miracles*. That will be in the curriculum. I'm not concerned about giving an identity to the Academy except the declaration that it is fundamentally spiritual, that it is a religion or a coming back of the mind. The trick to the twelve principles of the Academy is not to have any perceptual reference at all, not to mention the *Philosophia Perennis* and all the other guides that will force the perception, but rather teach that this association is only for the transformation of your mind. Do you get this? It has to be done that way. And you are saying that minds at this point in their own time are feeling a regenerative self-identity – certainly *you* have – that will enable them to come into a new perspective of the relationship with themselves in temporalness.

Well, if that doesn't occur, is he going to attack you? Is he a condition of attack if he doesn't have the experience? What do you care? You are not concerned about that at all. You understand me? You are teaching only what? Metamorphosis. You are teaching transformation of mind. That's acceptable. That may be acceptable now. There are enough loony associations in science that will come here and have the experience. This in no way constricts the self-identity of the individual in his moral value association, in his dedication to being a man or a woman and the head of the family. It literally does not have to do with that. There is no request at all that he relinquish anything in his self-association. Simply in the process of relinquishing his perceptual self, he will realize a *noosphere*, as Teilhard de Chardin called it, a broader range. And that can be taught, right? Taught as what? An experience. So you are saying that knowledge is an experience, and that knowledge can be gained by an enlightenment of the perceptual mind. This is an offering of a transition – the declaration that the human perceptual mind is a transition. It is a temporal, transitional association of an evolutionary process. That sounds so good. You see, I don't mind knowing that my destiny is in the stars. The idea that I can find my destiny now might have a lot of appeal to me if I'm not confronted with too much magical crap about how to do it.

If you can get the fundamental *Course In Miracles* in. If you can keep in mind that this is what you are going to do. And I'm depending on you to do this. You are the ones here, representing all of man somewhere in time, who keep reducing it to concepts. You are saying that you have now evolved a new association only through the release of you, not through the identity of you. One of them will actually be, then, the psychology of joy and happiness that emanates. This is very valuable. We're going to take a scientific principle of quantum particle-wave association and turn it into a joyous experience of self-identity? Are you telling me I can do that? Yes! Can you hear this? And you are going to teach that it is a different association of the mind that causes the happiness. It is very important that you evolve the principle of the miracle of giving in this, or you are going to have a lot of problems. You are not trying to prove anything. "There's nothing to prove here," is your statement, and that proof, or a self-concept, is what the fear of reality is.

Listen: That is real. I don't expect them to make the initial step that it is real. Our requirement is only right-thinking for a minute. If I can just get them for one minute to say, "Hey, this is a possibility that there is a transcendent of which I am not aware." That is the key to this, without getting into the spiritual aspects of it, of God particularly, or doctrine. "There is a Universal Mind of which I am not now aware because I am caught in my own conceptual identity. Yet I must be included in with Universal Mind because there is only one mind. And although I don't know that, I must be able to come to know it because I am having the experience of transcendence. I am feeling happiness in this new mind of mine. And I detect that it really doesn't have to do with the separate perceptual thoughts, but just in a translation of that thought into a harmonious identity of myself."

So, at the Academy you will teach dance and you will teach painting. Isn't that a strange and amazing idea? In other words, you are making a provision to allow for the experience; to not

CHAPTER FIVE: A Masters' Academy

deny it, which is really what you are saying. Your preamble says, "Come with an open mind and share the experience of our mutual reality." Is this it? Try to formulate it in his mind. Obviously you cannot give any attention to a single perceptual obstacle. No. This has nothing to do with the conflict in individual form associations. Is this so? All right. And it is individual. You are teaching individual transformation. There's obviously no way you can force that transformation on them. But you can reason with them, through their own self-identity, to an assertion that they are more than the objective reality in which they find themselves. Very lovely.

And it can be done reasonably and *must* be done reasonably. You have learned what you are and it is not so; that there's more to you than that. These are what you give them, that the learning of the world falls short of knowledge of any kind if there's a God – a Universal Mind. I'm just running it up the flagpole, guys, which is exactly what I want you to do when you get to the Academy. Bring them into a group, open it up and run it up the flagpole, and don't let them get caught in their own stuff. I just want to see where you are with this. You are actually going to teach metamorphosis or transformation of the human condition into a whole loving mind! I don't care what you call it. I'm absolutely not concerned. You are saying that there's more in Heaven and earth than you can see out there. "And while it's very frightening to me, it need not be frightening if I'll gradually undergo this experience." Little do they know! We're not concerned about that.

That will all be in the *Course*, incidentally. This is all in the *Course*: the confrontation of yourself, the on-going reassociation of your mind, individually. So we are in the process of reducing it now, even below the deny-ers of this direct association. This will reduce to the total sleeping ones that have no idea of what we're doing. You haven't seen any corruption until you've tried to teach this. All right. But you are saying,

"Here it is. Come into it if you can, or if you want to." And we're going to use the vehicles of limited association of self-identity. There's no reason why any *Course* teacher can't come here and be a teacher, none at all. They are teaching transformation of the mind. And we can use these teachers if we can get them into a determination to reassociate their own self-identity instead of proclaiming their reality at their limited manifestation of themselves. We've got to trick them in that regard. But we understand that the whole thing is a façade.

The key to this, then, is that this whole thing is just a façade. If you guys can hear this, you'll have no problem with the Academy. No matter what the apparent perceptual credential is, it is a façade of perceptual unreality, of thought form associations that guard you from the reality of God or whole mind that's around you. You keep putting on these garbs of identity; you can bring them into this association and examine and release them, through a creative purpose to transcend your apparent identity. That's nice.

Do you know what the toughest reassociation will be? The physical aspects of it. I'm going to tell you this. You have taken for granted, hopefully, somewhere, at least without too much denial, that you are undergoing physical changes in your body association. It is very important that we have a class on endorphins. I don't care if you call them endorphins, or magnetic cellular synapses of reassociation, because the admission of the on-going process can be fit very well into the accord of the transformation if you don't deal with it specifically. If you want to correlate the chakras as the churches, I think that's lovely. You'll have a hundred people who have come here that are going to verify Edgar Cayce's Armageddon. I don't care. What do I care? I already know you are doing that. Is it possible that you guys reach that on your own, without me? There's no question that I'm giving you direction. I know what I'm doing. I'm just teaching total abstraction of God, or reassociation, and providing you a mechanism.

CHAPTER FIVE: A Masters' Academy

You are saying that it is possible in the Academy, through you – this is *Course* now – through the admission of the necessity for your transcendence, or that you come from a common Source, to let go of the necessity to attack or defend your own associations around you. Now you are into the total psychology of the *Course In Miracles*. Now, obviously if you've got a guy coming to study quantum physics, he literally has no correlation between those two ideas. He has none. The idea there's association between him beating his wife and finding an interstellar quasar doesn't occur to him. It does not occur to him. You are going to show him that yes, you do participate in your own research, and you are finally only researching yourself. You are researching your own perceptual mind. That's a hell of a step, that your philosophy is your psychology; that your science is your art. The science of the mind is an art of self-determination through the necessity for the human mind to create, to love and to identity itself. Of course. I won't take that away from them.

We're trying to give it to you. You want to tie your ass up in concepts. I don't want that conflict. I'm going to make this so open that there's nothing occult about it. You'll find it is so open that it is totally material. I don't give a crap. The fundamental premises will remain totally occult. But if you don't make it objective in the perceptual mind, you remove all the documentation of him. If you'll use the *Course In Miracles* – and this is a big "time" idea – the documentation is always historically gone, for example, that the mind is gone. What a hell of a tool to teach this! It doesn't make any difference who they are. You are going to teach them when they sit down, "You are in a conceptual identity of yourself that can be transcended."

What do we care if they identify the experience? It is *A Course In Miracles*. They need to identify themselves. I'm really reducing this. They need to have an experience of the phenomena. You are not going to deny them anything, though. Now, you'll be attacked and considered foolish because you don't deny them any perceptual associations of themselves at all, right? All you tell them is, "Hey, let's get with it. That's gone. What are we going to do now?" That I am a part of a species that's evolving to galactic identity? I like it. I see it on television all the time. You Trekies can teach a course in Trekieism. I do not mind you doing it. I think you should do it. The whole idea of space warp, the idea of moving in time is what we teach.

Now, obviously the constricted discipline will look at us as ridiculous because they're restricted to their own association. But contained in each batch of those, there is a single consciousness who is questioning his own association. Almost inevitably he'll be the one that taught it and then realized the futility of his own teaching. If you can get him, you are making real good progress. That's really the kind of mind we want. That is not to say you won't get minds that have denied the whole thing from the beginning and will spring into Light and be totally intellectually capacitated. In forty days they'll know more than everyone that ever knew anything about this.

Jakob Böhme, the great Christian mystic, says, "In a moment I knew more than anyone could learn in Universal Mind." It's all in there. Learning, then, is a process of inclusion rather than subtraction. That's what we're teaching. This is a process of inclusion, one mind. You listen. You can't do what you are going to do now in a half measure. If you are going to have an Academy, you have to really make it earthy. My problem is not doing it or not, my problem is how you associate with it. I'm talking to you individually. My problem is how much you really think in your own perceptual mind that a whole mind is giving credence to the perceptual identity. It's giving none. This is the whole basis of the *Course*.

Somewhere you are going to have to see that if the whole thing is a façade, you don't have to be concerned about the subterfuge you are using in your own mind. That will be demonstrated by the release of your individual credential in

CHAPTER FIVE: A Masters' Academy

your teaching devices in the classroom. I assure you this is true. And to the direct extent you individually – I'm talking to you – do not attempt to exchange your own perceptual knowledge, which is futile and ridiculous, with the associations that you are teaching, you can direct them to undergoing the experience of the miracle. That is what will happen when we get them there. We don't care how they come. But you are saying that you can do that. What will you end up with if you don't? You'll end up with another real broad academic association of the denial of reality. And that, in fact, is what occurs. But I'm not concerned about that. Remember, this is just a front. It is just a front. You walk in the front door of this and never come out. Do you hear that? It is called the Borderland. You walk in and you are just gone. Does anyone miss you? No. You might miss yourself for a minute, but walk through the door. That's the difference between crucifixion and resurrection. If you feel the loneliness of not being whole with God, come here and be whole with God, and you'll be fine. The other problem you'll have with this is apparent perceptual aggregate identity. That will always be considered a cult. So let it form in a very broad fashion.

The tendency to enlightenment will cause a circle of Atonement, or brightness in the mandala of the consciousness memory. That happens as this happens. This is a demonstration of the capacity of chaos to come to Light in the broad association. That's exactly what this is.

You can teach them that minds communicate and perceptual body identities break off communication. That's the whole teaching. But you've got to get them there first. You sure as hell aren't going to get them there in *Course In Miracles* groups because the concepts are ridiculous. They're reductions to anything. You might as well have astrological groups, communists, or philatelists. Philatelists?! See how limiting groups are? You are saying you are going to come together for another purpose altogether. That's nice. Just like going to church on Sunday. Actually they come together for another purpose.

Evolution of the human mind – the awareness of the awareness can be transcended into single awareness. The conflict of the mind in its self-identity is an assertion of a wholeness of mind reached through transformation. So then, this Text of a Mind out of time, teaching you this in your own association will make sense to you. I want to be sure I got this. If you as a human being came into this identity, and I sat here in a chair, where the hell are you with this book? And I'm looking at that. How much are you going to demand a reassociation in your own mind if this book says that all of your concepts are what are binding you to death? Obviously your unwillingness to accept that is the necessity for the Atonement. Is this so? The perceptual necessity to know where this came from has nothing to do with the truth at all. It would require the admission that it comes from something that cannot be understood or somewhere in another time identity.

Concepts are learned. Guys, I'm talking to you. I want to see if this would work. I'm talking to you in your individual minds. Everybody has an identity in the concept about yourself. They're always learned by you, aren't they? *They are not natural.* Whole mind, or Universal Mind, is only a creative purpose of self-identity. *Apart from learning they do not exist.* They are not real. *They are not given, so they must be made.* Not anything that you have brought in here is true. *Not one of them is true.* How much are you rejecting that in your own mind? I have no idea. None of your concepts are true. I'm not going to go back in and teach this, but this is what we're saying. *Not one of them is true, and many come from feverish imaginations, hot with hatred and distortions born of fear.* Remember the movie? (Defending Your Life) You are very fearful about your own associations. I am telling you that if you will let them go now, you will experience a transcendence. Somebody sitting with you will say, "Wow, that was easy. I'm experiencing a transcendence." Are you saying that then he's ready in his own time identity to have that experience? Yes. Out of this group,

CHAPTER FIVE: A Masters' Academy

how many are really ready to bring their own *I Ching*, their own self-identity, genetically, into a total re-cognition of Universal Mind, a translation of the potential of the human mind to identify itself in its own association?

That's the *Course In Miracles*. *What is a concept but a thought to which its maker gives a meaning of his own?* And the guy says, "Of course I'm doing that!" And you know it. There's no attempt here at all to make the consciousness say, "There's a whole thing here that I'm here conceptually to tell you about." That's not how you teach this. He is in a continual self-examination of himself in his own identity. That's what he is, isn't he? *Concepts maintain the world that you see. But they cannot be used to demonstrate that the world is real.* Let me see you do it. Now, if the conceptual association says, "I'm satisfied with these forms that are around me, giving me an identity," obviously he will maintain his satisfaction with that. But you remember this, wherever he is in his own associations has nothing to do with reality at all, and that in fact is this whole teaching. Reassociation does not really have to do with reality, but only with the transformation from the separate, or unreality, to the reality. Right?

Concepts maintain the world. But they cannot be used to demonstrate that the world is real. For all of them are made within the perceptual mind of *the world, born in its shadow, growing in its ways, and finally "maturing" in its own time thoughts. They are ideas of idols, painted with the brushes of the world, which cannot make a single picture representing truth.*

This whole association is to allow you to make one single picture of your holographic mind in time to represent the truth just for one moment. After that you'll never be the same, because you'll search for the brightness of your own self-identity within this brush or picture that you have painted of yourself, because it'll feel good to you, because you'll like the harmony of it. And you will no longer want the conflict of your own conceptual necessity to hold on to your own identity. That's what this says, isn't it?

A concept of the self is absolutely *meaningless, for no one here can see what it is for, and therefore cannot picture what it is. Yet is all learning that the world directs begun and ended with the single aim of teaching you this concept of yourself, that you will choose to follow this world's laws, and never seek to go beyond its roads nor realize the way to see yourself.* You are coming here now as individuals, telling me, "I'm in a chaotic association of a world that's so limited, and I'm sick and tired of it. I am looking for another identity of myself." The basis of the Academy is only "Know thyself." That's the second Latin slogan, after "Only miraculously can you." You see? Those are the two slogans, that you must know yourself and can only know yourself by a miracle.

As soon as this happens, this is going to be gone. I'm just going to take one more dip here. And that's only because you tell me that in this framework it is actually possible to take this very, very, very, very, very, very, very, very, very, very, very, very, very, very simple treatment of individual transformation of mind and insinuate it into a chaotic memory that's determined not to give itself the power of its own mind – that is literally asleep in its own memory. Who is that that's asleep? You! Well, you don't have to stay here. Why the hell would you have to stay here? There isn't any such place as here. You are only entering into the transition in order to come here for a moment and get the hell out of here. "But you just said we're going to have an Academy." No, I didn't. I didn't say anything of the kind. The only problem I have with this is, if I dip down that far, you are just going to include me in with your natural perceptions. I'll be gone, and you'll be here with an establishment. If you want to do that with your mind, I can't stop you. The idea that I am entering in this is going to please a lot of people on this

CHAPTER FIVE: A Masters' Academy

earth because they're going to be pleased with the idea that their own self-conceptions can lead them to the truth. That's a lie. But I have to get them in for a moment so I can show them it is a lie.

Obviously each moment you are whole and perfect with God because that's what mind is. You are not going to not be that. That's such a direct threat to the association that obviously he crucifies it the instant it comes into his mind. He must take the fundamental teachings – I'll use Jesus, or any whole mind – and immediately deny it because he's what that is. So this is a direct demand that he reassociate in his own mind his own inevitability of his revolutionary, evolutionary process of the species of man to Universal Mind that is out there, by directing it to his own self-identity. That's what this says.

You will choose to follow this world's laws, and never seek to go beyond its roads nor realize the way to see yourself. Nor can it be unlearned except by lessons aimed to teach that you are something else. There must be lessons that aim to teach that you are something else. That's a required admission. Otherwise, you won't seek it, will you? Many perceptual minds will not seek another association that causes harmony. See how insidious that is? Each moment, each individual credential is satisfied with his own associations. That is a statement of fact, isn't it? If his own mind has constructed himself in his own identity, he cannot *not* do that. That's what he is.

Thus are the Spirit's lesson plans arranged in easy steps, that though there may be some lack of ease at times and some distress, there is no shattering of what was learned, but just a re-translation of what seems to be the evidence on its behalf. That is, you must shatter my declaration that you are God's Love and perfect as God created you. You must shatter that concept in your own mind or you would become perfect as God created you. You are the only living Son of God. You are that Universal Mind. You shatter that in your own mind into self-concepts of your own associations, because it is very fearful to you that you are as God created you. Obviously. How would it not be? You are depending on a time association to keep yourself here, aren't you?

Let us consider, then, what proof there is that you are what your brother makes of you. That's what you say. *For even though you do not yet perceive that this is what you think you surely learned by now that you behave as if he can tell you what you are. Does he react for you?* No, but he tells me how I ought to react. *And does he know exactly what would happen?* He has no more idea than you do. *Can he see your future and ordain, before it comes, what you should do in every circumstance?* Don't be ridiculous. *He must have made the world as well as you to have such prescience,* pre-recognition, *in the things to come.* And he has, in his own limited association with you. How the hell are you going to get out of here? If you listen to him, you'll only hear what you want to hear in your own mind. Wow.

Perhaps the reason why this concept must be kept in darkness is that, in the light, the one who would not think it true is you. And what would happen to the world you see, if all its underpinnings were removed? Your concept of the world depends upon this concept of your own self. And both would go, if either one were ever raised to doubt. That says they would go – that the moment that you raised it to doubt, they're gone. Boy, talk about the power of the perceptual mind.

There are alternatives about the thing that you must be. You might, for instance, be the thing you choose to have your brother be. This shifts the concept of the self from what is wholly passive, and at least makes way for active choice, and some acknowledgment that interaction must have entered into it. There is some understanding that you choose for both of you, and what he represents has meaning that was given it by you. This is the first step to subjective reality –

CHAPTER FIVE: A Masters' Academy

that I am causing this. All of this is in Chapter 31. *Although this step has gain, it does not yet approach a basic question.* Now we're at *cogito ergo sum*, "I think, therefore I am," and I am in association with my own thoughts. I'm trying to teach this as though you had never heard it before, but it's too late. You are hearing me. There is an admission now of subjective reality, of existentialism, that you are in your own mind.

It also shows some glimmering of sight in perceptual laws *that what you see reflects the state of the perceiver's mind.* That's a statement of fact, isn't it? You have it that far. This is Sartre. This is Kant. This is Schopenhauer. This is all of the philosophers. If you read them now, they'll be saying exactly this, that somewhere they have seen the unreasonableness of objective reality – that something out there in space/time could really direct them to a body association. It is an admission that they don't know who they are, really, and that by nothing that they do in objective reality can they come to know who they are. That becomes a philosophy of existentialism. No question about it. But this says no matter how much you re-examine yourself in that association, you cannot gain knowledge of yourself because the process is transcendental rather than self-inclusive.

The key to this is that whatever you are including into your own conceptual identity of self is what there is in the universe, that *Self* itself is singular. And that's what's not acceptable. That requires the experience. *It shows some glimmering of sight into perception's laws that what you see reflects the state of the perceiver's mind.* Now, if you can get the association to begin to do that, he'll have the experiences because you are a provision in your own memory for his experience of that. That turns mystical immediately. But obviously that's what you are undergoing in this experience. Now, if you can get him to admit that he's come there for that purpose, it will become extremely efficacious because he will begin to undergo the experience of his own identity. If he's coming there to have an experience of death with you, and you have not offered him a fundamental premise of the necessity for the transformation to life, you are not going to get very far with him. That's what this Academy is for. We understand that he's going to bring his concepts into that. That's what we're teaching, that it is the transformation of the mind.

If you are what you choose your brother be, alternatives were there to choose among, and someone must have first decided on the one to choose, and let the other go. Although this step has gains, it does not yet approach a basic question. This is very simple. *Something must have gone before these concepts of the self. And something must have done the learning which gives rise to them. Nor can this be explained by either view of the self.* This is very, very fundamental stuff. This says that you are using the power of God mind, the Holy Spirit, to identify yourself in your own limitations. *The main advantage of the shifting to the second from the first is that you somehow entered in the choice by your own decision.* I don't care how you did it. It has value. Why? You need to know who you are. You have asked the fundamental question, "What am I?" haven't you? Can I actually teach that you individually are in a decision-making process of your own mind and that through the change of your mind this world that's all around you will disappear, and that you will wake up in Universal Mind in Heaven? I don't know. It doesn't seem hard to me. The process is the only thing that could be hard, and that's the relinquishment of self-identity, isn't it?

...that you somehow entered into the choice of your decision. But this gain is paid in almost equal loss, for now you stand accused of guilt for what your brother is. And I've seen a lot of people get that far. "I'm the cause of all this. I'm the guilty one." That's exactly the same as saying, "I'm not the cause of any of this." Why? The concept has nothing to do with

the reality at all. A lot of people get that far – obviously they feel the guilt of their brother starving to death. We've got half a million babies, and, well, they're going to starve to death in the next three months. It doesn't concern you in the slightest. You are very guilty about it, but it can't concern you because there's nothing you can do about it. What a terrible situation to find yourself in. Holy mackerel! Phew!

But this gain is paid in almost equal loss, for now you stand accused of guilt for what your brother is. And you must share this guilt because you choose it for him in the image of your own. Somewhere he has to be guilty if you are. You cannot be totally guilty without transcending. Listen. You cannot be totally guilty of your own conceptual associations without undergoing the experience of enlightenment. It is impossible. You must be kicking some of that guilt out in order to keep your perceptual associations.

The concept of the self has always been the great preoccupation of the world, and everyone believes that he must find the answer to the riddle of himself. That's his problem. His problem is he must find the answer to the riddle to anything – that somehow truth is a secret and that he can find it in his own self-identity. *And everyone believes that he must find the answer to the riddle of himself.* I don't know if I can teach this: *Salvation,* enlightenment, realization of whole mind *can be seen as nothing more than an escape from* your own conceptual identity. Period. *It does not concern itself with content of the mind at all, but with the simple statement that it thinks. And what can think has choice, and can be shown that different thoughts have different consequences.* And you know this. *So it can learn that everything it thinks reflects the deep confusion that it feels about how it was made and what it is.*

Seek not your Self in symbols. There can be no concept that can stand for what you are, no matter what it is. Do you see this? What do we care about the thought forms you are having about yourself? *They cannot stand for what you are.* They can't. Why? They're always gone in your own mind anyway. *What matters it which concepts you accept when you perceive a self that interacts with your own evil-ness and reacts to wicked things? Your concept of yourself will still remain quite meaningless. And you will not perceive that you can interact but with yourself. To see a guilty world is but the sign your learning has been guided by the world, and you behold it as you see yourself. The concept of the self embraces all you look upon, and nothing is outside of this perception. If you can be hurt by anything, you see a picture of your own secret wishes. Nothing more than this. And in your suffering of any kind you see your own concealed desire to kill.*

You will make many concepts of the self – this is the Academy – *as your learning goes along, and each one will show the changes in your own relationships, as your perception of yourself is changed. There will be some confusion every time there's a shift, but be you thankful that the learning of the world is loosening its grasp upon your mind. And be you sure and happy in the confidence that it will go at last, and leave your mind at peace. The role of the accuser will appear in many places and in many forms* – because it is in your own mind. *And each will seem to be accusing you –* because you have found him guilty. *Yet have no fear that it will not be undone.*

The world can teach no images of you unless you want to learn them. There will come a time when images have all gone by and you will see you know not what you are – you've gotten there. *It is to this unsealed and open mind that truth returns, unhindered and unbound. Where concepts of the self have been laid by is truth revealed exactly as it is. When every concept has been raised to doubt and question and been recognized as made on no*

CHAPTER FIVE: A Masters' Academy

assumption that would stand the light, there is the truth left free to enter into its sanctuary clean and free of guilt.

Then the statement you are afraid of: *I do not know the thing I am, and therefore do not know what I am doing, where I am, or how to look upon the world or on myself. Yet in this learning is salvation born.* Wow! What you do in your Academy in that identity of the self in your own concepts, I have no idea. But I don't know how the world could have that written on the page. I'm not at all sure that in the frustration that I felt in my majority, had I read this, I would not have immediately sought this out. I'm giving you a statement of fact here. What I just read to you would have been very reasonable to me in any adventure of my own mind as I identify myself. Would it have been to you or not? I don't know. You know, what I'm saying is existentialism, subjective reality. Is that reasonable to you? That's a big step. The idea that there's a single mind or consciousness is very reasonable to me. Always has been. Why? There is a single mind and consciousness. How simple a solution, then, if you are dealing with your own concepts. Where is the difficulty? The necessity for the transformation. Remember that the transformation to reality is a natural occurrence being denied by the perceptual identity. Got that?

That's your Academy then. So it is possible to write a preamble to this and declare that this is what this Academy is going to be – without a reference to the *Course In Miracles?* Sure. Oh, sure. Why? It is very lucid in my mind. It should be lucid in yours. It is very uncompromising, but we're not concerned now about the uncompromisingness. We know that the perceptual mind is compromising itself with itself. Isn't it? That's your Academy. Where's your problem? Only in your own mind in entering into it. But it is not the requirement of the association, but the release of the association that will bring this about.

So you are at the Academy and you are saying, "Yes, I am having this experience. I intend to undergo this transformation in this cycle of time." Now you really start to teach this and watch what happens in the world. If I keep it broad enough, it'll be a son-of-a-gun to attack. We have to teach personal transformation. Show me another way it can be done, if all concepts are the obstacle to the transformation. I never really reduced it to this, but it is only: Know yourself in your own identity. That's being taught by a lot of philosophies. So you have to teach two associations. One, dramatically, is that you are the only identity there is, regardless; that God is not outside of you. But more directly, that the concepts of yourself are all there is. How are you going to teach that?

See, while the consciousness is willing to admit he's responsible for his own identity, you are declaring that there's something outside of himself that he can reach or can't reach? Which? He is going to want to know. What do you tell him? So all you are at is the paradox of transformation. Do you see that? But he uses devices that have nothing to do with the devices. It is a statement of singularity of mind, that the devices know each other perfectly well at the moment that they become divisive, or at the moment that they become harmonious, they fall into a different form that then must be divisive in its own identity with itself. And this persists and in fact is a definition of a condition of reality that is not what reality is. But certainly it appears to be reality. Is this true? If you are bringing these groups together, the guy depends on the existence of himself, and the termination. And the defense against termination. So he keeps getting sent back to earth because of his fear of death. You guys are writing movies about it, for goodness sake. Well, you are doing it. So you must know it. But now we're saying, well, let's teach it then. Let's go into an association that admits that Love, which is God, is simply the release of the perceptual identity, which is fear. That's the whole *Course In Miracles*.

CHAPTER FIVE: A Masters' Academy

"Do we need transcendent minds on the Board?" Hell, no. We just need illustrious, self-conceived evil minds on the Board. What the hell do you care the minds that are on the Board? You are teaching transformation of the mind. Do you really think that the Mountain Man with the beard came here because he heard there was a great master and he was immediately going to enter in with the reassociation and go to Heaven? Bulldung! The Mountain Man came here to debunk and prove I was crazy and that some weirdo was sitting here. That's a statement of fact. That's what the perceptual mind does because that's what it is. It has to, in its own mind, prove that truth cannot be true. That's what it does. But the dependence on the conversion of him is all that Universal Mind is, if it needs conversion. I don't know if you can hear that. I don't care where the association is. If he underwent an enlightening experience in a late-time association, you are that, too. You are that! There's no multiplicity in it, not really.

Is it possible for me, then, to experience him in his new mind association? Yes, but not if I give him the identity of my own previousness. And I don't care where that occurs. Now you can see that the miracle is instantaneous, and has nothing to do with how long it has been accumulating within the perceptual mind. Isn't that so? But that would lead me to declare through acceptance and faith that he is the savior of the world. I'm not going to let this out in the Academy, but I'm giving you the fact of it anyway. Now, this consciousness underwent an experience in order to come to know that. But I am very trusting of that. I believe that he underwent an experience and that he came here and that he has had this and that he's the savior. Sure. Why would I not? What is there about him that I would deny that he's the savior of the world? I just read you that. Except that I'm going to share a guilty association in my own mind. Do you understand me? If it wasn't for him, I would never be saved. It's so simple. "But you have qualities in your saviorship that he doesn't have." Bulldung!

See, that's just your determination to hold on to your conceptual crap and to keep your own identity in regard to what this is. I just got through telling you all of the concepts are meaningless. Jesus says this early in the *Course*. That does not mean it will not lead to respect for a mind that's obviously in association with itself, and it should lead to that. I'm really not concerned about that. This is only a challenge to your own sleeping minds, guys. What's inside there does not concern me. This is the whole direction of the teaching.

Speaking for myself, this must be just about over, isn't it? Otherwise, how am I able to do this? What you are saying is that you are in a communication that transcends your perceptual identity. It is what you are doing, right? Is that what the Academy is for? Only to the experience. Boy, that'll get futile for you, too. You are teaching the impossible. The toughest part about this, until you guys came around, was the necessity to admit that you are never being heard, no matter what you say. Do you understand?

The reason we can have the Academy is that you stopped going "huh? huh?" and you are going "Ah-ha! Ah-ha!" And that's exactly the same as coming into a harmony of your mind. Minds communicate; bodies do not communicate. What are you worried about? But that must come to what I just read you – subjective reality. Are you comfortable with that? I have never been comfortable with objective reality. There was never a time when I didn't question what the form was in association with other forms. When I was told that I was spinning around at millions of miles an hour around other obstacles with trillions and trillions of stars, there was always some fundamental question in my mind about objective space/time. This is the confirmation of that, that there is no reality in distance, that mind is simultaneous, that while you can construct the cause and effect separately, it will only be contained within your own mind. Have you got that? And this is a process of bringing the cause and the effect together.

CHAPTER FIVE: A Masters' Academy

So I'll give you the written stuff on the Academy. And you send it all over the world. Broadcast it on the news. I don't care; I'll give you a framework. That's all. And it may be slow in coming, but there's some endowed minds, what they call minds that have intellectual capacities of release that have reached a very high association. We trust – we know that you have to hear it some time, because you did hear it some time, and we also know that that time can be now, and that time must be now.

So we didn't fail at this, either. And if we fail, it will be to life rather than death. Try that again: If you fail, you'll just be gone from here. You won't be back in another condition. It is very crucial that you hear this. This is very frightening to you. You have a tendency to say, "Yes, yes, but I've got to get it because my body's getting older and I'm going to die." No, it's not. No, it's not. This is important for some of you guys. You don't have to worry about that anymore. That can't be explained, however. It is the same idea as having already laid my body down, I don't have to be concerned about it. It is very vital for some of you. All I want to guarantee you is that you can squeeze your thoughts and die on me and I'd still have you. Because it is always already gone anyway, and I couldn't give a crap less where you think it went or where it goes. You will stand here. And I understand you are looking in the mirror and some of you still hold on to a little perceptual identity, and that you really are in a process of just kind of letting your body be. This is the teaching. You'll discover that you've in fact done that. And then for a moment you'll grab a hold of it, and you'll look at yourself, and you haven't seen yourself. And you'll discover little things all over you. But remember, you are not in a Calcutta train station with maggots crawling all over you. No, no.

You've made a discovery that is allowing you to undergo the transformation of your body rather than sitting under a tree, staring at the sun with no eyelids, letting a tree root grow up your ass. Can you feel this? This is the transformation of your body. Can you understand? You are just caught in your own body. You are not a phenomenon. You are a continuing reassociation of cellular memory in your mind. The alternative to that, obviously, is the observation of the body. But remember that the observation of the body is time, the binding of yourself in your own mind. And a lot of you are experiencing fear with that. Good. That's all right. Good. You've been shown exactly what to do here to overcome the fear. If you don't fall into that fear thought and defend yourself, it will go away because it has gone away.

I'm very much aware that some of you establish high criteria of self-enlightenment and use that criteria to continue to give yourself the *Holy Instants* and to direct the purpose of you. I'm trying to get you a step above that. What the hell's wrong with being totally fearful? *I'm* totally fearful. Do you think I'm not fearful of this place? My salvation is that it is not real. It is in my mind and it is not real. Did you look around you? That's the fun part about it. Your acceleration, your revelation, must occur at the fear point. I don't care whether you are giving it a specific reference or not. That doesn't concern me. It is always perception to light. It is always perception to non-perception. Come on. I don't care what you are fearful of; if you are fearful of a specific association, from then on you'll do a fear association with that specific form.

If you love one single association totally, you will do all associations with that one form. That's how simple it is for me to know that the Mountain Man is my savior. If he's not my savior, if he's separate from me, I have every right to be afraid of him. He's a separate mind. I don't know who he is. I don't know what he's going to do to me, except steal something from me. He must need, because we're separate. You see the insanity of a human conceptual mind, contained within itself, reflecting back its own fears of itself? What the hell do you think you are, brother? That's what you are doing. There's no sense in denying

CHAPTER FIVE: A Masters' Academy

you are doing it. You are doing it. Go ahead. As soon as you say to me, "I don't want this anymore," it'll change. I know this is the final step. Why anyone would want to continue to suffer pain and sickness – I'm looking right at you; I don't care how you are doing it – why would you want to keep a body identification when you've been told this message? I wouldn't care *what* it involves. It has become a possibility in your mind.

The reason it's the lesser of two evils is because everything is evil to you. Do you understand? This is a jumping off place. I'm giving you a statement of fact here. I'm not offering you a solution to your own sick problem. I don't care whether you study it or what you do with it. I'm telling you there is no solution to this. If you can get that into your mind, you'll release the necessity for solution and have the God experience. Not by providing yourself with the solution of *A Course In Miracles*.

A Course In Miracles is not a solution to your perceptual problem. It is the declaration of the unreality of it and the necessity for the transformation of your mind. Oh, this brother is hearing that very plainly. So is he teaching that to the universe? Of course. He's ready for this. I've got to say this: He *is* the universe. Wherever he goes, in all of space/time, to the most distant stars, to the furthest galaxy, what the hell do I care? It is either whole or it is nothing. If it is whole, you need not be concerned what it is. This is what I'm trying to give you It's little and big at the same time. It may seem to fluctuate in your own mind. If it turns back in, Whappo! Can you make that step or are you going to just keep lulling in your own stuff? But the other sad thing is, and finally you guys must realize this, I'm professing total love to you and apparently giving you separate identities in this association. It's really not true. You might be offended that I am using your love energy in my own association around you. I assure you that's true!

Jesus says you have taught this from afar, isn't it time you looked at your own now. If this association is dedicated in its own mind to the provision of itself in space/time, everything in all the universe is healing that mind in its association with itself. The final step is only the translation of that self-identity to its own wholeness. The requirement for the continuing necessity of the release is what a communicator is. I don't care whether he recognizes that he's communicating or not. I understand that he will recognize it at some level, but it doesn't concern me because it is always past anyway. Now I can see that space/time is a fabric of time, fabric of thought, and that *that* mind is all there is in a continual reassociation of itself. Your only question, then, to yourself is, "What am I doing here and why am I doing it?" There is no answer to that. If you ask the question in the transition of your own mind, you will have the experience of your own whole self that was the manifestation of the necessity for the transformation.

Both selves are the same because there is only one Self. The self that communicates with its own self in its limited identity is in the transition of the recognition of the singularness of its own mind. And I say "its" in the concept that it is not real. That's very reasonable to me. Now, the experience of the passion of that is your necessity to create. This is the declaration that if you are not happy and joyous all the time, you simply are not using your own creative mind. It is so deep and thick here that you really think that this is solid. You make a solid hand here to make this solid for you. It is not solid. There's no such thing as solid.

If you take thick energy or thick light for a moment, you can compact it into a limited identity association. Did you hear that? Isn't that what you are doing with your mind? So there you stand. With all of this crap outside of you, you've compacted yourself within your own identity. And you are very fearful of what's out there. I can't understand what you are teaching in your own concepts. What are you going to do? What are you going to do in your own mind? I know I teach it as a philosophy but I can't get you to look at anything you do. It is so strange to

CHAPTER FIVE: A Masters' Academy

me that you do that. What are you getting out of this? Did you ever look at that? Is that the fundamental premise? Not really. You keep kicking it out and saying no, that's not true. Can I teach you that it's only your mind? Well, what do you do? Just keep proving that objects are real? You keep proving that that object is real in your own mind. And that these associations in your own separate mind – I just read you this – are actually separate minds talking to you, and you need to know who they are by asking them questions about themselves. Of course that's what you are doing. And you like some of them better than others. I have no problem with that. I'm not trying to take it away from you. I'm just trying to get you to look at it. You like some of them so much that you'll eliminate all the other ones. And then you grasp that one in your own mind and it falls apart on you, but you cling to it as long as you can. What a sorry frigging state you are in. And not only that, but you like it. There isn't anything out there! I must construct it in my own mind. It's going to fall apart, so I'll hold on to it.

I'm offering you no solution to this at all – none. None. In this advanced teaching I'm not offering you a solution. You are going to say to me, "Well, what's the solution?" and I'm just going to say, "How the hell do I know?" Who are you asking for the solution to the problem except someone that you are going to hear within your own association? Can you hear me? Can you teach it this way? I don't know. But it is true. Do you see that? This is only an awakening from your own dream identity. "Well, look at the lovely manner that I'm waking up in." What the hell are you talking about? Any of the associations of your own mind will be just exactly as conflictual or as harmonious as you want them to be. I understand you need the conflict. Why else would you ask for the solution?

All I want you to see is that if God is Love and whole, it would be impossible for you to ask for the solution to conflict without experiencing it, if you'll admit to me what I just read you – that it is in your own mind. Obviously you deny that, and you seek relief in your own perceptual mind. What's real hard for you is the admission of the necessity for the hardware. If suddenly somebody's sick in your family and dying, you think somehow that in your mind you have to overcome that and see that as unreal. That's exactly the opposite of what I'm teaching you. I am not teaching you to give specific references. I am teaching you to accept it as inevitable in your own process. That's about as close as I can get to it. The problem I have with that is that you immediately accept it and make it a part of yourself. But if I'm going to sink it this low to have an Academy, I'll do it. Because those who are going to hear this will hear it. You'll notice that these real advanced associations, the moment that they heard this, that was it. And you say, "That wasn't true with me," and I'll say, the hell it wasn't. I'm not concerned at all how long you've been working on this.

I'm standing here offering total release to you. You are the one that brings the baggage. So one thought is the same as any other thought? And the creative mind only releases and that's the experience of joy? Love is letting go of fear? The proof that they will want to hear it, if there is a they, or if you want to hear it – were you in enough pain? You were in enough association with your own existence to see that there must be another answer outside of you. Do you understand that? God is a concept? There is no conceptual identity in reality because all of the concepts are the same in reality. It doesn't make any difference what the form is.

You are in an experience of metamorphosis – awakening from a self-identity to eternity, an evolution of your mind. What's wrong with that? What else would you intend to do? You are aware of evolution. What are you going to evolve to? Death? How can you evolve to death? You already are dead. You are already in limitation. Seek and ye shall find. Seek you had to and find you did. Why? Seeking and finding are the same thing.

CHAPTER FIVE: A Masters' Academy

So you are always getting what you are looking for. If I throw it away, what do you do? Grab it again? "If I can cling to this long enough." Right? "I'll hold on to it long enough." Is that what you are going to tell me in your own mind? Long enough to what? You can't hold on to it long enough to find life because all you are finding is death. You've already admitted by holding on to it, you are going to lose it? Is holding on to a thought the same as losing it? If I defend myself, I am attacked. Do you want the sentences, dummy? I'm just giving you the philosophy.

Obviously if you defend yourself, you are going to be attacked. Otherwise why would you hold on to it? It must be something that has a great deal of frailty. If you can hold on to it, you can protect it, and it becomes a part of you protecting it. And you are very vulnerable. And there is something out there that's going to take it away from you – and *there is*. How am I going to get out of that? I'm in a dilemma of cause and effect. I have to give myself an identity; therefore, I must protect myself from something. I don't know what it is, but I must protect myself from it, because my reality is based on the protection of myself in my own association. What's the solution? Shall I tell you? Don't protect yourself. I don't understand why I couldn't stand on the Mount and tell you this. And did. All I ever really told you is: don't protect yourself. I didn't mean to have this fall down into doctrine. But any association who's going to teach you subjective reality has got to teach you not to protect yourself. Obviously the lesson is you are protecting yourself from your own attack thoughts. And you can get this perceptually and say, "Yes, I know I'm attacking myself," but it is quite another thing to release the necessity for it. But in that is salvation. And literally in nothing else, because it is true that you are protecting yourself from yourself. Don't protect your own identity and you will experience love. Then you'll lose identity.

And you'll discover that by giving it away, you can keep it. Not in the sense of giving it away specifically but only in the sense of knowing that by giving you are creating. Do you see that? Any possessions then will make you want to give more, and that's a fact. You can say, "Well, we all need a minimum to survive." I don't even know what the hell you are talking about. "We have to sort this out somewhere. There's a difference in mammon, I can sort out what I *need* against what I *want*, and I'm able to tell the difference. The main thing is that I can survive. And I can continue to study the process by which I'm coming to know this." How simple the uncompromisingness of this! It is never true. Death is never true. Obliviation is never true. It never was, and it never will be. I'm here to tell you that. Your acceptance of it is what salvation is. That's how simple this is.

This is a direct confrontation of a cognition of yourself in your own mind. There is no other mind but yours, whether awake or asleep. There isn't any such thing as a sleeping mind. You can be hell-bent on proving it. Go ahead! But then you don't need me, because your proof lies in sickness and death. Who is here to deny you that? No one. You've constructed in your mind all of the forms that will verify yourself. You keep asking yourself what the solution to the problem is. Don't you understand that? The asker is the unreal part of it. He wouldn't have to ask if he knew. But if he doesn't know, he's not real. Who is it that says, "Who am I?" Somebody who really doesn't know? What is it that doesn't know what beingness is? Whatever it is, it has every reason to protect itself in its own mind. You are fearful of what I'm offering you because it is a loss of your own protective association.

Do you have the feeling that you are popping in and out of time? I usually don't direct perceptual minds to it because wherever you are, you are always in this perception. But actually they're always only over. Individual transformation. I'm not trying to alleviate your guilt. I'm trying to make you totally guilty.

CHAPTER SIX

Mrs. Brown, Red Rock and Rover

Is it true that all subjective associations are also objective? In other words, if you make application of your psychology of yourself, you'll be talking about yourself in association with yourself. If you project it out from you, you will be talking about your objective association either between two objects or between yourself and the other object. So, that is the way you think, isn't it? Why? That is the way what you constitute as a human mind thinks. It is a self conceptual association.

I want you to enter into this discussion with me, those of you who are undergoing this process, because if we are allowed to get out of the religious and philosophical connotations of the necessity for a definition of the process which you are now undergoing in your mind, our progress to the realization of singular mind can be very, very rapid indeed. Just as obviously it is going to have to include the objections that you have utilized to formulate a correspondence with yourself in the limitation of your mind association. I am going to use the *Course In Miracles* for a minute, because we need some very fundamental associations here. This is my declaration to you: First, the universe is mind and that it is singular mind extending eternally forever. Second, the definition of you as a human being: You are an objective perceptual association of self-identity contained within a temporal frame of reference. Is that all right?

Let's try some very simple sentences that will correspond with this: Reality is a single, whole mind. All of the universe is based on ideas. All ideas are contained within the human mind. Since you are a human mind, all ideas of any nature, whether in correspondence or the release of correspondence, or in subsequent correlations of associations are contained in *your* human mind. For some of you, that can start to be a lot of fun if you will not take offense at the simple idea that you are mind. You are that mind.

Here's the difficulty. As soon as I give you objective associations in correspondence with yourself, you begin to formulate them in a form of a constriction of your necessity for a definition of your own cause and effect relationship. I know that you do this. I know it is impossible that you do not do this, because fundamentally, conceptual or objective reality is conclusionary. Listen. It is impossible for you not to reach conclusions in the correspondence with yourself. It has literally nothing to do with whether they are true or not, it is a process that is inherent in an objective association. I can't take that away from you. That's what you are. I am not trying to attempt to take you away from that. What I am attempting to do is get you to see that any linear correspondence of your associations with your own thought forms will always be over and gone. And, if they are over and gone, it will always be limited to the aspect of your definition of yourself. It literally cannot *not* be. Isn't that

CHAPTER SIX: Mrs. Brown, Red Rock and Rover

so? You may then depend on them to formulate your reality which is what the human condition does. It depends on those forms of thought, then. It finds a correspondence in that thought form that literally gives it an existent momentary association with itself. It then passes and it gathers these moments of existent form and lives within the association of the limitation between its own cause and effect relationship. That's a fact of the matter.

Here's the secret to it: Creative mind is an eternal extension, not in a projection nor in any objective correspondence whatsoever. Since you are obviously in an objective correspondence with your thoughts, we are teaching you to practice non-conclusionary thinking. This is the whole teaching. This is what this Workbook does. What it says to you, literally, is: *The world I see has nothing to do with reality. It is of my own making, and it does not exist.* (Lesson 14) That's a conceptual thought on which you can depend! If you are going to have some dependence on conceptual thought, then depend on that one. *God is the Mind with which I think* is another one (Lesson 45), because they do not contain elements of the comparison of your association with yourself.

There is no way that I can degrade the manner in which you correspond in your own mind with your own self-identity except to tell you that it is always over and gone. Not only is it always over and gone, but it will be limited by the factors that you correspond with in your own memory association of what you are. Is that so? I am going to read you this; these are important things. What have we said? We said that you are idea. God is an idea. God has an idea of you that extends forever. We have said that your conceptual associations, while not real, can be brought in, through the power of your mind, to the realization of single wholeness because nothing prevents it from doing that. In other words, we are not concerned about what you think *about,* but only that you think. Remember that? Remember that old saying, "Before you louse it up, think" – T-H-I-M-K!

You have learned manners of formulating your own conceptual value system that transcend the methods by which you previously arrived at conclusions. The more you are able to open your mind to a non-definitive non-limiting identity, the broader will become your range of the process of your thinking, very simply, because your mind, *mind,* is a thinking factor. All of the universe is actually contained in your own mind. The fact is you are only using 6% of it anyway. Well, what the heck is all the rest of that in your mind? Could it be some of it is more lucid that I am denying? Could it be that there is a factor of quantum relevance that will prevail if I release for a moment the necessity of my identity? I am teaching you quantum thinking – the dissolving of the relationship that previously held you in the bondage of sequential form. Is that all right? You enjoy that! The enjoyment you are getting out of it is by not attempting to understand it. Very simply because what I am offering you would be constantly misunderstood by you simply because all conceptual relationship is fundamentally a misunderstanding. It is a misunderstanding of what you actually are. We want you to misunderstand yourself in the totality – simply by not attempting to understand the correlation.

What is difficult for you to see is that the moment that you don't understand it, all of the other relevant procedures of your perceptual mind will immediately synapse to your new reality. It seems as though you must call on them in your own mind. The truth is exactly the opposite. By *not* calling on them, you have available all the thoughts that you previously rejected or ascertained to be true and then put into pockets of memory that will automatically and simultaneously aid you in this new definition of your own identity. Do you see that?

Now once your mind begins to do that, you are thrilled at the continuing *prospect* – that's not a bad word – of revelatory thinking, simply because you are not enclosing yourself in your own thoughts. It doesn't prevent you from enclosing yourself in

CHAPTER SIX: Mrs. Brown, Red Rock and Rover

your own thoughts, but the practice is obviously one of release of the associations contained in your own mind. It doesn't matter how you do it. You will begin to think in very devious ways. You will discover that your mind will take short cuts. You are not required to have a process of reaching a particular conclusion based on all of the evidence that you have. Finally you feel the frustration of reaching the conclusion and having it always be gone anyway. Any conclusion that you reach in that manner is a very slow way to think. The body-brain thinks in a very slow way. All creative mind thinks in quantum. It literally cuts across the circuits that are being measured at the speed of light, and corresponds to the singular reality. It becomes a process – that's what you are feeling now.

So, death is an idea. Let's try it: Death is an idea in your mind. You have an idea of death. If you change your mind, you couldn't die. You can't find any correspondence of death in your association. It just becomes silly to you. Suicide is a crime in almost all the states. I see in Texas, where they are practicing capital punishment (putting people to death) more and more – a legislator two days ago said, "I want to make suicide a capital offense." Amazing idea! That's funny! Anyone who attempts suicide deserves to die, preferably by lethal injection!!! So, whatever you're doing all day long, when you suddenly laugh, often times you don't know what the joke is. What's happened is, you have released the defense of yourself and nothing is more joyous and funny than the discovery of *nueva* – of a new way to think.

Since your mind is actually God thinking, the closest you can get to eternal, creative happiness is the continuing transformation of your conceptual mind. That's the fact of the matter. The fact of the matter is, it is in your mind and you're doing it. The fact of the matter is that our minds are singular and that all our concepts are contained within this association. I am showing you how, through this process, to enjoy what you would call quantum or creative association.

We are not concerned about your concepts; we understand that you are a conceptual association. There is no sense in me telling you that you are an illusion or that this is the "domain of the ego." What do I care? You are the necessity of looking at the fact that the human consciousness is a capability of its own identity in association with itself. *Cogito ergo sum* – I think, therefore, I am. I'm concerned about what your "therefore" is. I am very much aware that you are "therefore." All you have to do is include all of your "therefores" and then "thinking" and "am-ing" would become the same thing, because they are the same thing. But the process of that occurring is what miracles are – they simply transport across the necessity of the defense of the association. Do you see? Jesus uses the term "flow across." They don't have to take devious routes that you have constructed in your own mind to reach conclusions about objective associations. You got that?

We will read from two places here. This is kind of nice, it is one we read all the time but you might be able to look at in a little different way.

The concept of the self has always been the great preoccupation determined by the historic references *of the world* in the correspondence with its relationship for this moment in time! That doesn't say that! *And everyone believes that he must find the answer to the riddle of himself.* Here we go: the riddle of not knowing. *Salvation can be seen as nothing more than the escape from concepts.* Literally! But you obviously cannot escape concepts by attempting to subtract them from your own mind. That would be too late simply because nothing is outside of your mind, if an idea leaves not its source. This occurs in the teaching of the comparisons of what you call projection with extension of your mind.

Salvation can be seen as nothing more than the escape from your own conceptual self. *It does not concern itself with content of the mind, but with the simple statement that* you

CHAPTER SIX: Mrs. Brown, Red Rock and Rover

think; and because you are thinking, the other element we talk about, that perceptual mind has a mechanism of decision that is inherent in it.

I am not teaching you not to decide; I am teaching you to let the decision be made, not based on your reference with yourself. In no way am I trying to get you to go off somewhere where you can practice not thinking. I am teaching you to transform your thinking association to broader self associations, that's what this says.

Seek not your Self in the form relations of yourself. *There can be no concept that can stand for what you really are,* because you are whole mind, God creating. That is not to say you cannot derive gratification from your previous thought form associations since they have been designed specifically to verify your identity within your own mind. Isn't that so? And you will utilize them in a definition of yourself because that's what you are. I am telling you that no definition of yourself can possibly survive the single realization that you are a single whole universal mind. Fortunately, reality is not a matter of survival. It hasn't got anything to do with the survival of your old thought forms. What could the survival of your thought forms result in but your own annihilation? Your willingness to accept that previously astonishes me. Your discovery that it is not necessary to opinionate the old definitions of yourself in correspondence of your mind will astonish you. I want you to see that that's a reality. I mean, you are not going to fool anybody by formulating in your own mind and pretending to examine your relationships. I am teaching you that this is a process of miracle thinking.

What matters it which concept you accept while you perceive a self that interacts with evil or objective association and reacts to apparently wicked things. *Your concept of yourself will still remain quite meaningless. And you will not perceive that you can interact but with yourself.* Literally. *To see a guilty world is but the sign your learning has been guided* by your own objective association, *and you behold it as you see yourself. The concept of the self embraces all you look upon, and nothing is outside of this perception. If you can be hurt by anything, you see a picture of your secret wishes.* (Chapter 31) I didn't know that was written in the book! That sentence isn't there any longer. I must have used it twice and it got used up. Listen to me for a minute – don't worry if you use it up. A lot of you suffer from loss of memory. That's what forgiveness is; it is the loss of the necessity to defend yourself because all of your grievances will be the defense of yourself. That can be a little disconcerting. You carry on a conversation and suddenly it has absolutely no meaning at all. You have lost the reference by which you defined it. A lot of you laugh about that. You better quick get back into your own – people who leave here are very fearful of that loss – or of that expansion. Isn't that amazing? That's what fear is. Fear is actually the conceptual association in any regard. Freedom is the release in all regards or the momentary release of the necessity for the defense of the self. You have it.

Nothing more than this. And in your suffering of any kind you see your own concealed desire to kill. I'm trying to stay out of concepts just for a minute here to show you how your mind is now beginning to work. What we are dealing with is the certainty that everything is an idea. The problem that a conceptual mind has is in the limited definition of a form that it then uses to reflect other form associations. Do you see this? It begins to what? Specialize in its own conceptual relationship. And indeed it can become an expert at the specialization of the limitation of its own form identity. This is the teaching of the world: Become an expert within a limited field of self-identity.

I am teaching you to become an expert in the continual release of the necessity for the specialization or occupation of your conceptual mind that will bind you to old references. Notice I'm not at all concerned about what your occupation is. All I'm saying is that any occupation that you have can be broadened into a new definition of yourself in your own relationship very simply because you are a definition of yourself in a relationship. Any what you call special relationship or occupation will bind you to that inherent correspondence, based on what you call yourself. All right?

I'm teaching you, in a particular way, to be a poetic plumber. I'm teaching you that your mind is not limited to fixing pipes, but that you will find a correspondence if you allow it to occur, quite literally in the memory package that is your brain. It is very difficult to teach this at this point.

Let's see if I can teach you this: All thinking is objective. I'll use the term "muscle." The brain is a muscle. Every single instant billions of cells in your relationship are exercising or corresponding to other cellular relationships. Many of you, when you feel the joy of your new muscle relationship, will begin to run. You'll go out and begin to exercise and do all sorts of things because your brain is feeling its muscle and you want to direct it to action. That's perfectly okay. But remember that the action is always subsequent to the muscular reassociation going on within the convenience of your need for identity of yourself. So I'm teaching you that the brain, the mind – I don't care what you call it – never sleeps. It's 100% all the time an activation of your association. Obviously you slow it down; you literally slow it down and force it into an association of yourself that gives you, through your eyes, a limited definition so that you only let so much light into your brain. You are afraid of letting more light in because you'll lose your plumbership. You are liable to start writing poetry and you have already been condemned by your own correlation, to being a plumber. I just got through reading you, telling you that it is only in your own mind. But the process of change is not the process of a re-evaluation of your conceptual identity, but the release of the necessity for *any* evaluation at all.

This is turning your will over to God. What I want you to see, is that that's an actual happening. I don't deal with the surrender at all. Why? I don't want the conflict of my own mind. Why would I have to practice surrender? I'm enjoying a continually new relationship with myself. I'll see if I can express to you how my mind would work in its objective association reality. Since the whole mind is nothing but a storage bin, no thought you ever have is ever forgotten. The only thing I can tell you is that if you are storing thoughts *about* things, the less that your objective thought form has to do with a purpose verifying your own association in a correspondence with the object, the more valuable that objective form will be to you. Can you see that? It is hard to teach *Trivial Pursuit*. I am teaching *Trivial Pursuit*. Can you see that? On *Jeopardy,* there are very few specialists. Do you understand? At least half the answers on *Jeopardy* are intuitive answers, did you know that? They are not reached by the conclusion of formulating what the answer is. If I'm in a good run, I can answer the Jeopardy questions as fast as they are said. Many of the guys on Jeopardy will answer the question before it's even asked. That's why they have to set the buzzer so that it only clicks on after the question. Most of the people would simply buzz all the time. Not only would they keep their finger on the buzzer, but they would know what the question is going to be. Boy, that sounds like Sheldrake's morphogenic field! It is!

The answer and the solution to the problem is always contained within the vast array of the thought program. This is what clairvoyance is. If you release the necessity for defining what is going to occur based on your own conceptions, anything can occur. Literally! You are a great prognosticator. All prognostications are self-fulfilling. How did I get off into that? That's a true thing. I got into *Jeopardy.* It is not based on knowledge, but it is based on what we would call a form of quantum thinking where you get a flash, you call it "in-tuit," but it involves "out-tuit." It's in and out. But it is spontaneous. "I

CHAPTER SIX: Mrs. Brown, Red Rock and Rover

don't know how I knew the answer." I'm going to tell you how you knew the answer. You knew the answers because you had practiced the activity of your own brain-mind not based on the limited definition of the association. That is, you did not specialize in the question that was being asked, but the manner in which you would respond to any question asked in association with yourself. It is called creative thinking. Can you get a little of this? I am training your mind to do that. Mind is a mechanism of creative thought. I'm not taking your objectivity away from you.

I remember the first time I discovered I could read. It absolutely astonished me. I had been taught that "Jane" is a thing. And suddenly I looked out, I read a sentence and I understood it within the confines of my own mind. I immediately thought a library was the greatest thing there could ever be, because I could go into the library and there would be all those objective associations that would help me define what I was. It wasn't until later on I discovered that each one them was categorized in its own separate association, and that as soon as I began to specialize and become one thing, I had to subtract from my mind the other things that I used to value in my thinking. "Well, if you're going to be a doctor you're going to..." If you want to be a proctologist, let's face it. Ha! Ha! Ha! You laugh! That's an old joke! Actually, they are stored somewhere in your own mind and you suddenly get an association and that's what is causing you so much delight. Don't worry how you do it, it works real good. It's an amazing way. I want to be sure you understand this.

We used to teach it as knowledge for knowledge's sake. What we are saying is learn it for no reason whatsoever, the more facts you learn for no reason whatsoever the more readily they will be called upon by your new mind as you release the necessity. Is that true or not? Can you get this? No, you can't. You think that because I know that Topeka is the capital of Kansas that I specialize in state capitals. That's not true. I know that Topeka is the capital of Kansas because Topeka *is* the capital of Kansas. It is not the capital of Kansas for any reason. Now. I don't have to find a reason why I became a specialist, I can let that be a fact in my mind.

It doesn't seem as though it will work to a human mind, because it is accustomed to the validation of the fact association rather than the creative reassociation simply through the non-necessity to define Topeka as the capital. It isn't that that does not involve the idea that Topeka is one of the largest cattle-slaughtering cities – all those other things are a part of my process but I have no intention of becoming a specialist on Topeka, on what state capitals I know about or in fact on anything that would deprive me of my inherent capacity of reassociation of my mind, evolved from my non-specialization. All right? I don't care whether you hear this. This is a fact.

Now, when your mind begins to take creative leaps, that's a very nice happening. This is called academic thinking. What occurs in academic thinking is somebody will formulate factual relationships outside of their own identity. The question always arises, in the ego: should I continue to formulate myself or should I base my reality on objective fact and subtract myself from the association? I'm telling you that it is a combination of both of the associations. And this is what the miracle will be. Do you see it?

I saw a dead chicken on the way over here and arrived at the Pilgrims over in England before they left for this country. I'll give you a fact how my mind works. How could I possibly have gone from a dead chicken to suddenly I got into all the consternation of New Amsterdam and England? Why? I freed myself from the necessity of the definitions. The process is called an academic distraction. *If I killed your chicken, Mrs. Brown...*

"Hey!" (That's the neighbor to the other neighbor over the fence.)

"Hey, your dog just killed my chicken!"

CHAPTER SIX: Mrs. Brown, Red Rock and Rover

"Gee, I'm terribly sorry, Mrs. Brown. I certainly will make that up to you."

"Well, it was a wonderful chicken. I got it at the Fair."

"Yes, I see that that chicken is a cross-bred species. That chicken is a Red Rock."

"What?"

"I said that chicken is a Red Rock."

"I didn't know that."

"One of the original species of chicken that we brought over to this country was called a Plymouth Rock. The Plymouth Rock chicken is a very common variety of chicken."

"I didn't know that."

"Yeah, but do you know why the Plymouth Rock chickens fell out of popularity?"

"No, I don't know. Why?"

"Well, they only lay brown eggs."

[There's a dead chicken on the road, the dog is panting, blood is dripping.]

"Oh, you mean Plymouth Rock chickens only lay brown eggs?"

"Yes, they were particularly valued because they could be valued both for their meat and for their eggs. In our new specialization, you may not know, but they now breed chickens for meat *or* for eggs. One of the few combinations that is bred both for meat and for eggs is called the Red Rock. Since nobody particularly liked the brown eggs from the Plymouth Rock, they bred them to the roosters of what you call Rhode Island Reds. Now Rhode Island Reds produce white eggs, mostly. And that's how we got the term Red Rock. In a certain sense you can eat your chicken and have eggs at the same time!"

There is a simple reason why human beings don't practice cannibalism. They need to reproduce. Never mind. I don't think Mr. Jones would understand. In *my* mind it would jump to that.

She said, "Gee, you certainly know a lot about chickens."

"Yes, I do and I intend to compensate, and as long as we're talking about chickens, why don't I take you out for Chinese tonight?"

"Well, why do that as long as we have a chicken dinner, come over to my house and we'll have some."

He pats the dog on the head. "You go and do that and I'll bring wine. Would you say about 8 o'clock? How about some Muscatel?"

"Yes, why don't you, I'd enjoy it."

That's another story!!! Then the curtain falls. That's a nice story. Notice that you use factual associations to distract from the association. Now whether you do that in correspondence with the association does not concern me. Only that you do it in your own mind and allow it to correspond. See how that flows from my mind?

Now that is not to say that I did not have factual information. It just was not connected. I'm not a chicken expert. If I really taught mind training to a large group, I would teach them to take one totally irrelevant fact – irrelevant from the fact that it's not a part of the association – and learn one a day, probably between 7 and 8 in the morning. The retention factors of your reference mind are at their most lucid. That's what they call short term/long term memory. Don't be concerned about that. If you did one a day for 365 days and remembered 50 of them forever – now you don't have to remember them intentionally – you'll discover that they will come into your mind simply as a part of your reassociation. Do you see? It was very common for students to use memory associations to verify facts that have nothing to do with the fact itself. Isn't that so? If you're learning

CHAPTER SIX: Mrs. Brown, Red Rock and Rover

Topeka – how did you learn Topeka is the capital of Kansas? How could ou learn that? What was the way you learned that? Hole in the sock. So that the connection was done between Topeka and hole in the sock? What was the connection? Toe-peek-a. You'll probably never forget the capital of Kansas! I promise you, you'll never forget the capital of Kansas. Not only that, but you learned it in kind of a joyous way. I didn't hit you with a hickory stick or anything, though that works too. Are you aware of that? Topeka is the capital of Kansas. Whappo! That was kind of a hard way to learn it. That's the way most human minds learn – through the pain of the experience – rather than the correlation of the joy.

So you're doing quantum thinking. And it's fun. Do you know the nice thing about it? Whatever your repertoire of horrors is, or of joys, it makes absolutely no difference in the process if it's only in our own mind. Do you see that? The freedom is that moment of release. Most trivial pursuiters learn it simply because they hate the mundane associations of human beings. It's nothing but a soap opera and a definition of the old thing. They just want to introduce some other factor into the mind, at least to give it enough breadth so that it can be somewhere else. Even if you do it with the Green Bay Packers, at least you're out of that association and into a new association of your own mind.

All power is given unto you in Heaven and earth. There's nothing that you cannot do with your own mind. There is no conflict outside of you. This is a process that you are experiencing, isn't it? Don't be concerned about how it works. You can't fail at it, simply because failure is what success is. If you don't correlate it in your mind, you will experience the grace of God. Why? That's what you are, isn't it? So don't look for it in your own concepts, but don't attempt to find it by subtracting yourself from your own conceptual associations. So the natural process will be a quantum synapse within your own mind.

Whenever you see associations who are not able to process this new form of thinking, it will always be because they are contained within the speed of light forms of the necessity of their own molecular definition. That's a fact. Very important that it has nothing to do with the concepts. Do you have this fundamentally? Can you see that? What will surprise you is, no matter how many times you present this to perceptual mind, it will hear it within its own perceptual association. I'm teaching you that all of your concepts can be transformed to reality because everything is contained within your own mind. It has nothing at all to do with how you define our relationship, since all of our relationships will always limit us.

If people don't understand that, and this is what's really difficult for you to see now. A gal yesterday sent me a tape of a guy and the note said, "Why don't you listen to this and see how valuable this association who has been dead is in his therapeutic associations?" That has nothing to do with what I'm trying to get the association to do. I sit right here and tell it that has nothing to do with it. It isn't that he might not say something that has value, but certainly anything that has value will be in her relationship with herself, not with me. She's not going to convince me of anything contained within her own mind. How could she?

Are you saying that no two associations can ever have exactly the same thought? If they do, they'll lose their conceptual association. That's what the fun is. So it's not a comparison. It's love. It's simply a release of comparison? Really? You can actually set up these morphogenic fields of energy that contain both the question and the answer? The process is one of reversing the cause and the effect and not letting the cause out there affect you, but letting your mind direct it by the associations contained within your own grasp. That's how simple this is. It's incredible.

Is that thought, is that energy, Light energy, that you're finding? Yes. So you're going to have ideas, but if you don't force other effectual ideas on to them, they'll release to the new

CHAPTER SIX: Mrs. Brown, Red Rock and Rover

association of your mind. An amazing idea. Transcendental existentialism. You're in a constant state of a reassociation of your own system. Isn't that fun? And you're not afraid of it any more. Isn't that amazing? You presumed that existence was fear. You presumed that the protection of your thought form association was what life was. You're just preoccupied with the definition of yourself. And you are contained within that association? What an astonishing idea. Who do you communicate with? Just your own old thought formulations. It's incredible!

"Yes, but if you and I don't have any body identities, we will lose all the bodies in the world?" Yes, of course. Why not? There could be nothing in your conceptual identity that would stop you from remembering that you're whole, creative mind, is there? Come on. I've gone to decision again. If you decided that you didn't want to be a plumber, the only thing that would stop you from being a poet would be your definition of what a poet is. There's nothing more poetic than the manner in which the plumber applies the wrench to the plumbing. I assure you that that is true. And to the extent that his mind enters into this, he enjoys his plumbership. But it's one hell of a lot more than applying the wrench. It contains all of the elements of his own gratification of his identity. For goodness sake. The whole teaching of the *Course* is: You're never going to be satisfied by being a plumber or a poet, but in the totality of that reassociation of what you are. How would you ever be happy being limited in your identity? It doesn't make any sense. It's senseless.

Actually the less you specialize, the more dangerous you become. You begin to make application to the reasonableness of your mind. We're not concerned about the specialization at all, and that finally will not be accepted by society. Why? There has to be a purpose here for you to be here. In effect, what you're saying is there's no purpose at all except your illumination. That's the experience that this young consciousness just had.

Now, that was offered by my association of my own mind. You'll notice that you need not be concerned about the result of the miracle at all. The less concern you have about the result of the association, the broader will be the range of the association. Wouldn't this be true? We want to come to know each other not by our definitions of ourselves, which will only let a poet and a plumber come together. Certainly we can come into a bar and have a drink together. And you can talk to me about plumbing, and I can talk to you about writing poetry. But actually we're communicating in an entirely different way. I assure you that that is not really communication. But in the expression of our mutual separation are all of the elements necessary for the totality of our loveship for each other, simply because that's what we are. But as long as we search within the parameter of our limitation, our gratification will be based on our separation rather than our correspondence.

It's the same idea as when love gets too close to you, it's very frightening. If I go in and sit next to a guy in a bar and I'm going to sit there for two hours, it's kind of important that he place me in some sort of category. Especially if I'm going to bump against him with my thigh. This would be true of all associations. "What do you do?" "Well, I go into bars and bump people!" "For what purpose?" "None at all!" "I'm very suspicious of that. You must have a motive in your own mind for sitting next to me." Will "I love you" work at that point? I doubt it very much. It might. The problem you'll have will be the manner in which you express it. Isn't that amazing. He must believe that "I love you" has an outcome. It must require a subsequent action in regard to what the love was rather than the moment of the miracle of the release of that association. We're teaching again. There is no outcome to this. None. There's no conclusion to this, except the joy of universal mind. And that's not an exception. That's a reality. That's nice, to be able to think like that.

CHAPTER SIX: Mrs. Brown, Red Rock and Rover

So you thought the secret was in somehow sorting out your associations. I'm teaching you the secret is letting them be whatever they are. But you'll discover that, as you do creative thinking, they'll suddenly become a part of your association for no apparent reason. That's the fun part about it. It's a new way to think! Wow! You certainly have a lot of intuition. It's a new manner of thinking. It's fun to be around spontaneous people up to a point. They lose themselves in their dedication to death. If you lose yourself in your dedication to death, you simply spring into light and are gone. You literally have no reason for being here at all. And there is no reason.

I can't show you what love is, but I can show you what the obstacle is. If the obstacle is not in my mind, it cannot be in yours, if you will not let it be, because our minds are actually the same. All we're doing is just formulating different patterns in the energy association. You see? What the hell difference would that make? Isn't that amazing that you do that? Just as directly, if you give form value, you'll get a subsequent form of a variant association of that form, and will base your reality on what you call the new form. And you'll keep inventing better telephones, better mechanical devices to retain your separation. And you'll call it communication. Amazing.

There's an interesting idea in *War Games*, that you could teach a machine, through repetition, the futility of the solution that it is seeking. Is it possible to teach a machine that? It's possible to teach *you* the futility of it. You're nothing but a machine of repetition. But the machine would arrive at the conclusion that war is futile. And that's exactly what happened in *War Games*. He finally said, "No one can win this. I don't want to play this game. How about a game of chess." You can't win the ultimate game of associations of conflict. Did the machine arrive at that? Yeah, through the continuing repetition. The question is: How many times are you going to attempt to play the game in your own mind, where no solution is going to be possible – where the winner dies, is really what that says.

It's a lovely movie. I saw it last night. The conclusion to either side you take is going to be death anyway. It's always a cat game. You can't win.

I suppose you can define that in limitation: I'll always win in tic-tac-toe if I start and you don't put the X in the middle. That's a fact. Because I started, I will win. If I start, and you don't put the X in the middle, I win. If you put the X in the middle, it's a cat game. I want to be sure we understand this. I know you're going to go out and try that. Is it valuable to know that? Yeah. See what my mind did with that? I'm showing you how to do that. Every time you get your ducks in a row, something's going to intercede in that and break it up. See how my mind then begins to do analogies of the association. Your mind can do that, and the human beings are going to say, "Pay attention!" All of you are great fantasizers anyway. Any game you've ever watched, you were able to more emphatically participate in it. I know you, guys. I know how your minds work.

So you did not necessarily become an expert in the bats and the balls but in the participation itself, and entered into the drama of your own mind in playing that game. That's true. I'm teaching you to do that. Becoming an expert on how the glove and the bat are made is really not playing the game. But you must play the game in order to be a winner. How else would you discover that you can't lose?

As this evolves in you, you'll find it isn't that you don't define yourself by associations with a conceptual mind, it's just that you don't know how to conceptualize with the association because you don't know how to conceptualize in your own mind. I have no idea where you are with that. I don't want result thinking. It's very fundamental. If I plan for the future, how do I not get the result of my plan?

These are all just things that you'll read about again and again and again. What I want you to see is that's what you are. Isn't that nice? So if I say a word to you, your response may

CHAPTER SIX: Mrs. Brown, Red Rock and Rover

have nothing at all to do with the word that I said. I've broken you out of the pattern of your own sequential thinking. That's Zen. The purpose of Zen is to continually break you out of the pattern of your own conceptual thinking. You can nod your head and tip it all you want. What I'm trying to do is break you out of it by saying something that has no correspondence whatsoever in your mind. That's what Zen is. What do you call that? A koan. Isn't that amazing? Whatever you said to me, I could say anything else. Your capacity to then bring that into a correspondence with you would indicate how rapidly you're coming to miraculous thinking. You wouldn't resent it as an intrusion on your mind.

The only reason that you resent me is, I'm a continual intrusion on the definition of your own association. That's the whole basis of my teaching. I don't allow you any sequential thoughts at all. I didn't take your thoughts away from you. You can strike out in a million different directions. I want you to. "Oh it's not that; it's this." Include it. "It's not that. It's this." Include it. "It's not that, it's this." I'm teaching you to do that. And you're learning to do it. But you're not learning it by devices. "How am I learning?" By a miracle. It's a miracle! You suddenly go, "Oh!" All you've done is taken the forms that you previously held in limitation, you release them, and you begin to express yourself.

What an amazing idea, that the human conception will force you into what you would call a "normalcy". It's as though somehow the human condition must determine what's normal. "Well, we have to stay within the range of what is normal in an association." What is normal? Say: "A town in central Illinois." Well, is that true? Let it be that. Don't be concerned. We've got that. "It's a town in central Illinois. Normal." Well, how did the term "normal school" come about? Never mind! See, I freed it up from what? The necessity to continue in association. Can that be practiced? Sure. Constantly disrupt your own crap. When you get out there, you begin to turn in and give definitions of your old association, crack it out with something. Everything is pertinent to your thinking process, literally everything, if you let it be, in your own creative self-expression.

The idea that the conceptual mind is forced to think normally, the way they're teaching it now, is just absurd. It makes absolutely no sense at all, the idea that in the mechanics of the mind, they call it "scientific," that that form is true and this form is true. The fact of the matter is that none of us see anything exactly the same. How could we, if they're only memories of our own association? I don't need to be told that an artist's mind sees differently than my mind. I know that it does. She will see in association things that are different than mine, and the explanation is not contained in the canvas, or the color, or the pictures, but rather in what she is, of what is in her own creative association. But imagine reducing that to form, giving it value and sticking it in a safe because it's too valuable to leave out? Amazing!

So we're not really equal at all, are we? We're just totalities of our own memory associations. There's no sense in having conflict. Reality has nothing to do with equality whatsoever. God is not equal to anything because nothing compares to Him. Amazing! That's exciting, isn't it, as your mind begins to do that. Do you still go out and try to explain this to the conceptual associations? I'm explaining it to you. But you're enjoying my explanations. Actually all I'm telling you is that there's no reality here. I'm telling you that objective associations are not real. But there's nothing in them that keeps you from being whole because you *are* whole. You are using all the power of your mind. Am I to understand that any application that you make to it – what I just read to you – will be only in your own relationships? This is crucial to this, isn't it? What I'm saying is, you are only doing this to yourself. Does that include pain and joy, and happiness? Sure. Why not? Sure. Isn't that fun?

The reason I'm teaching you this is: we're dealing with an objective association. I cannot take your objective associations

CHAPTER SIX: Mrs. Brown, Red Rock and Rover

away from you. So you no longer thread your timid way through this continuum of time based on what objectively you were told you were when you arrived in this place. Every single objective thing here was designed in your own temporal organization to guarantee the retention of your location. I am telling you that you are the cause of this; that the world was not here, waiting for you when you came. You brought the world with you when you came. There is no world without you. It isn't something out there that somehow you have to exercise control over, or is going to control you. What an astonishing idea. How you process that, I don't care. I'm giving you a fact, because my mind is universal mind. One thing for sure, if you don't organize your thoughts, you can't be guilty – only in your totality and momentarily. What have you assumed? Assumption for your own guilt.

Be very careful with the word mora ity. Be very careful with that word because they will immediately presume if you're not teaching morality that you are immoral. You're not teaching that at all. God is moral because He only gives. Any association that only gives could not be immoral because giving is what morality is. Otherwise they'll interpret you as not allowing them the definitions of their own associations. You're not doing that at all. Jesus would say you're going to get the result of your own definitions. If you have moral value contained within that, that will be as valuable to you as it is. Why don't you simply obey the admonition of Jesus: "Give everything away." If you do that, morality could not possibly concern you. Why? God only gives. Morality will always be a comparison of the retention of the association. I just digressed into that. They're going to look for a way to condemn you by your non-definition of them, by not allowing them their association.

Can you hear what I'm saying? Do you hear what I'm saying to you? Are you having an experience with me in this? Is that valuable to you? I asked you a question. Is that valuable to you? Do you want to do that? I want to be sure that your choice is there. I didn't take your choice away. Did you notice that? I asked you a direct question.

There is a manner by which you can come to know. In each moment that you choose, you are denying it. So I give you the method and take it away. Every single second you actually make a decision within your own mind. What you correspond with later on is always gone, anyway. You accumulate old decisions in your mind, and that's what your body is: old specialization of your mind. And then you use them up? You use up your potential? What an amazing idea. How about you? Who are you? I understand what your body is, but who are you? Who is it that does that? "Why, me. I'm going to get old, and I'm going to die." I don't understand that. It doesn't make any sense.

This is the next page of what I just read you. You don't know who you are or what you're doing or how you got here. How dare you tell me this is a pair of glasses? You can tell me it's a pair of glasses, but the fact is you have no idea what this is. This is an accumulation of cellular associations within frequencies of energy, isn't it? This is why an artist's mind is different than mine. An artist may very well look at this and see a reflection of the crystalline associations in her own mind. When she tries to explain that to me, I only see it as a pair of glasses. So any form that we compare is always limited in us by our own definition of things. We're teaching you a new way to think.

We are not demanding, incidentally, that you derive from some masterpiece what somebody else derives. We're a step above that. I know that many of you stimulate your post-relationship ecstatic identity by remembering specific incidences that stimulate your memory. Isn't that so? You go back into your thought forms and you remember the canoe and the moon, and the one time that you were happy. And that's perfectly okay. There isn't anything wrong with doing that. Remember, though, that it's always the *Holy Instant,* not the correspondence of it, in which the value lies. It's very crucial to this process. Isn't it?

CHAPTER SIX: Mrs. Brown, Red Rock and Rover

Because you can't go home again. There's no manner by which you're going to be able to duplicate in the form the moment of that joyous occurrence. Don't underestimate the revenge of the ego against the past. All it is continually trying to do is either remember a *Holy Instant* or an unholy one, when he found a correspondence that verified his own association. At the very minimum, he has lost them and will feel the resentment of the loss, and will have to accept in himself the inevitability of his own aging process. Nonsense. Just nonsense! I hate it. You are the energy of love at the instant of that recognition of yourself, not in the correspondence with your old memories to replicate it. Let it go. It's over and gone. There is nothing here that you can take into this fresh memory of you. Why? It's all here, anyway. It's all in your mind. There isn't anything missing in there.

It is not that old memories are not valuable. You can look at an old tintype and feel every energy within that field that has ever occurred in the relationship. I'm not taking anything away from you. You open up an old book, and there's an old pressed flower between the pages, and suddenly all the memories of your senior prom are there. I suppose you can find solace in those memories as you get old and die. I always felt the frustration of having to correspond with that and not being able to change it. Most human beings will say, "If I could go back and change it, things would have been different." That's true. So go back and change it and things will be different. What would stop you? You're only in your own mind. Isn't that amazing? It's called releasing the resentment of the old association.

You're not going to succeed in getting old, anyway. It's not going to work. Why do you want to compare the thought you're having now with the old thought? Any comparison is always old. Is that so? Is that true? It doesn't matter how old it is; it's old. Are some of your thoughts older than other thoughts? *Thoughts about* get old; thoughts don't. Can you hear that? Thoughts *about. Have thoughts* get old. *Be thoughts* are being.

Amazing! If you have thoughts, they will get old because having thoughts is what time is. Location. Having associations. That's the domain of the ego? I don't give a crap what you call it. It is just the conscious association of your own self. You don't mind even being there any more. You've found a way out of it. You were trapped in a box of time and space.

So what's happening with you new quantum thinkers? You laugh at the idea of conceptual thinking. I look at human beings that already have established what the conclusion of their thought is going to be. I got this book, and just page after page of New Age stuff, and all of it written from the limited conceptual association of the identity, with a great deal of fear of finding an actual correspondence. They only want to find a correspondence that guarantees their relationship. It's just absurd.

So your job, if you accept it, the mission impossible, is to enter into every relationship and release it from the necessity of the defense of itself. That's what a savior of the world is. Isn't that so? Yes! So it's possible to have clinics of transformation, Miracle Healing Centers. Of course it is, because it will make sense to the association. How will it make sense to him? He has the experience. Without the experience, obviously he has nothing. Everybody who leaves here simply is refusing the experience of his own broader association. Isn't that so? Do you understand this fundamentally? That's my concern about you. I'm offering you no alternative. That one guy left. I really liked him. I got him to understand that he had no alternative. I tried to get him to DOR, which is Discharge On Request. I said, "You have no alternative." He said, "I've got no alternative but to be here?" And that is absolutely true. He has no alternative. And that will take him to salvation very rapidly. But once he's here, there is nothing contained within this association that is an alternative to him, either. He can't go or stay. And that was not acceptable to him. That's the truth of the matter. I've cut off your retreat and offered you no future. You underwent the

CHAPTER SIX: Mrs. Brown, Red Rock and Rover

experience of the non-defense of your own association. He had no intention of doing it. I can't do anything about it. Then he shouldn't come here. But certainly you can't know that until you come here. You have to have a reason for coming here, or you wouldn't be here at all. Not that your reason is true. That's why you need the Atonement. You're dealing with an impossible situation. That's fun for you. Now that you hear this, that's kind of fun, isn't it?

You don't want humans to identify you any more, most of you. You say, "Why are you calling me that? I'm not that." "Yes, you are." "No." "Well, what do you want to be instead of what I'm calling you?" "Nothing. I'm not going to be any of it. I'm not going to be any of those things. I'm going to be as God created me."

So that's pretty manipulative, isn't it, if I have to go back to be sure I remember the thought. Everything is manipulative. It's going to work despite you, anyway. I'm not asking you to suddenly become an expert and be able to recall that. I'm showing you the distraction that's possible in your mind if you don't retain the relationship. You see that? That's what I'm trying to get you to do. You know that no matter what I respond, an open mind could find a correspondence with it? Why not? If he doesn't restrict the form thinking. A lot of you undergoing the awakening did some very what are apparently foolish things that seemed perfectly reasonable to you at the time you did them. You were in a new association of what that correspondence was. It was a broader range, generally, of how you thought of your own associations. And many associations said, "What the hell are you doing?" But it is very reasonable to you at the time that you're in that new association. Do you understand?

Spiritual brokerages. Spiritual accounting. "Well, I do spiritual accounting. I want to give and receive and give purpose to what I'm doing." Fine. The frustration would have to be that you're always being misunderstood. You might as well be misunderstood totally because any definitions of the new association won't bind them but they will bind you, if you insist on a correlation of what's occurring in your own mind. You can spend a long time here doing that. So you must accept Atonement for yourself. But that's not to say that in the process your mind will not be on Skid Row. You may find that your relief comes from helping alkies or taking the part of an alkie, and being there so that you could share in your own realization contained within your own self.

The only thing I'm telling you for sure is you can't escape yourself. And the more certain you become of that, the more integrated you become in the association. I'm telling you this, so you must know about this. I'm giving you the fact of the matter. Here's our old family member, here. She looked a little bit for her correspondence in there. And she found the happiness of an historic reference correspondence. You're not meeting anybody you don't know. It's just how limiting are you in that old definition of your association?

Today you learned to release your energy. This is the Workbook of *A Course In Miracles*. For goodness sake! Well, how come some people can do it better than you can? What are you talking about? Nothing can escape the attention of your mind. How valuable is this new way to think? Very valuable if you don't have to sedate yourself in the process. You understand that? Creative thinking necessitates sedation because the passion of the creative thinking cannot be stood by the residual of the human condition. That is why most artists are dead by the time they're 30. There is no way they can express the totality of their own mind. It simply overloads, since the circuitry in their brain will overload it, and it becomes very painful, so they reduce it. They drink in order to separate from it. In other words, I drank to reduce my mind, not to increase it. A lot of people drink to increase their mind. Hell, my problem was that I couldn't hold anything in an association.

CHAPTER SIX: Mrs. Brown, Red Rock and Rover

Now, I'm teaching you to do that in a new perspective. I'm teaching you to constantly find other associations. Try not to reach any results at all. The process of that is turning your will over to God. If you don't turn your will over to God, you will just simply correlate until you can't stand your own thought patterns. The mind will say, "Why don't you concentrate on the cause and effect of this association?" I didn't mean to give an alkie mind talk, but that's what that is. My mind was incapable of doing that. There were always too many sides to the associations, extrapolations between the dead chicken and the Rocks. I might have done it a lot of different ways, but it's a true statement.

See how simple this thing is? Boy, there is a lot of this in the *Course*. You must have really wanted this, or why are you so happy now to have found it? That's miraculous thinking. Did I really tell you that you're just stuck with yourself if you stay here; that there's really no one outside of you; that you just keep dreaming this dream over and over again in your own mind? What an amazing idea. It's both fearful and joyous, because somewhere you're going to go out and construct these other forms in this little place that are going to verify you, in your own memory – these phantom figures of human beings. That's just nonsense. There's nothing real about them at all. Not anything. They will dissolve.

But see, my mind dissolves into the solidness of you, not into the phantomness. Let the form be what it is. Your mind will handle it in its new association. It is amazing that your mind is going to be what it is, anyway. Have you learned to do that? But somewhere you have a retrospect, otherwise, why do you laugh? That's true, but it's only joyous. If I connect it to the previous experience, I'll feel the fear of the connection, and I'll suffer from that connection or the verification of the Holy Instant. That's it. Hell, it's always changing all the time anyway, isn't it?

So God's an idea, isn't He? Do you have an idea about God? Come on. Have an idea with me. "Yeah, but I can't have an idea about an abstraction." Why not? He's going to be whatever you think He is, anyway. Everything is an idea. You *are* an idea. "Did God originally have an idea about you?" What do you mean, *originally?* Certainly, when I have an idea about God, I take all my correspondences, and I remember what I would want God to be in the correspondence of myself. Why would I not do that? God is an invention of my mind. How are you getting along with it? "Well, pretty good." This is the *Laws of Chaos*. "God's really giving me a lot of good things I like; some things I don't like, but I have to understand I've got to accept them, anyway. There's nothing I can do about it because He's God. He can now be the cause of my pain, and I don't have to understand. I've got to accept it." That is just crap. That's the Pope's new book: we're controlling God because we forced Him into our pain. We can make Him. He made the mistake of acknowledging us. That's a sentence in that book. And now we've got Him trapped in our minds. Do you see that? The human has a little authority problem. It cannot *not* have because it is its own problem and wants to be. It wants to be. Well, don't you assert yourself? Who do you assert yourself against? Yourself? Do you mean that you're the only one participating? Is that true? What's wrong with that? Nothing. Is it fun?

You play the game of death. But you really can't die. There isn't any such thing as death. So do you see it? I don't object to your facts. Give me any fact that you want. Well, how is that fact corresponding in your own mind is what I want to know about. Let it be true. Everything is true by the possibility of it, is really what I'm trying to get you to see. Your subsequent denial means absolutely nothing. It is amazing how the mind won't do it.

Mars has a mean diameter of 4,240 miles. It's about half the size of the Earth. Is that valuable to you? "You just told me there was no such thing as Mars." The hell I did. I told you Mars has a mean diameter. "What are you, a specialist? Do you specialize in Martian associations?" I know that as a fact in my

CHAPTER SIX: Mrs. Brown, Red Rock and Rover

mind. Remember, nothing is outside of your mind. Is that okay? I'm doing it with you right now. Can you see? Can you get it? If you don't tie your mind up into the fact, it can go anywhere. That's why you're at this place, to let that occur. I'm telling you that cellular repair, or enlightenment, is very possible, and there's only so many cells that have to be converted in an association. That's the fact of the matter.

Can you hear what I'm doing? It's amazing. Do you see that? The thought that I just had; I got on to Mars. No wonder you can't sleep at night. If your mind is real active, you'll discover you don't sleep. Not only will you not sleep, but you'll be sort of in what we call an ethereal state, where your brain is busy converting cells that you don't even have to be aware of. They're working all the time. You've got billions of cells. There's more synapses going on in your brain than there are stars in all of the universe. So that once you get it rolling, you can think about something else, and it will just keep going. True statement. In fact, in remembering it may slow it down. But if you want to slow it down for a minute in order to reassociate, it's very possible, if you don't make it explicit within your own mind. I'm trying to teach you how the mind works. I'm actually looking back at how I arrived at this. You can, at any moment, introduce any other thought into your form associations that you want. Now, that may throw you off into that other track formulation. If it doesn't, your mind will continue to proceed to consolidate that in the new relationship of your thought. Why? You collapsed the form association, didn't you? You released the objectivity of your persona in order to continue the formulation. That's a description of the miracle. Isn't it? The light literally comes down in because you didn't track off somewhere into an endless search that was going to lead nowhere. Because there's no way that it was going to go back, past the thought that you had about the relationship. Wow!

So you say, "Well, tell me more about the Red Rock chicken. That's funny. I need to know more about Rhode Island Reds. Are they still using them?" Yeah, they still are using what you call Red Rocks. Do you know why? They don't need chicken sexers – you know, the guy that can tell the new-born chick's sex, the Japanese guys that specialize in sexing. They discovered that in a Red Rock, the down between the rooster and the hen is different in the first day. That saves all that necessity of retaining chicken sexers. The down is a subtly different color. Isn't that nice to know. When it's born, you can tell the rooster from the hen. It took them almost a hundred years to discover that. You would think there would be a simpler way! Certainly, *you* have a simpler way! Actually your way is more complicated. It's simpler on the surface. It appears that you could determine the gender by the physical association. It's not true. Do you see that?

You never do things for the reasons you think you're doing them. Do you see that? So do you want the eggs or do you want the meat? My mind can do this real simply. "Yeah, but if I eat the chicken, I won't have the eggs." That's a dilemma. There's no answer to that. The answer is to consume the Christ and He will verify me in my association mystically. He will refurbish me, because I'll eat the Christ; I'll eat the totality of me. Jesus teaches this in this other lesson I was going to do. The evil totality of you stands next to the Christ of you. You literally consume the Christ in the definition of the sustenance of your own mind. That's what you're doing. We call that crucifying the Christ. But that whole Christ is always there. It would have to be. The Christ is not a body, yet is He always with you. I'm teaching you Christ-mindedness. Get out of the way of your own formulation of your mind.

Are those figures each whole unto themselves? For the moment that they are whole unto themselves only. One of them is temporal and disappears forever, the other is eternal and will always be a part of you – part of the totality of God. See how simple this is. So I'm becoming a Light body. Do you see that? You no longer force the association of your mind. You're losing

CHAPTER SIX: Mrs. Brown, Red Rock and Rover

your thought form identity. So what? They weren't real anyway. Lessons 92 and 93. Let the Light into your form associations. Why not? "I'll lose my form associations." Yes. Don't be afraid of that. Your mind is the mechanism of decision. It's going on all the time anyway. Stop trying to manipulate your own thought process. Wow. That's debilitating! How do you do it! You have to constantly force yourself into your own association. Not any more. You have learned a new way to practice. You didn't disappear. You're still here. "Well, if I do that, I'll disappear in Light." Well, then you're gone. I'm concerned about how you do this now. You're the one that wanted to learn resurrection. I'm literally teaching you physical resurrection. I'm happy to do it. Did you enroll in the class? Why wouldn't you have anything that you wanted? You no longer are gratified by the association of yourself. I don't care what it was. How could you possibly be? Life is eternal and extends forever in the joyous realization of God. This is not life, is it? "Well, I'd certainly like to be able to define it." Go ahead.

You mean that all I'm really teaching you is, "Don't formulate?" I'm back to that. I want you to see how the miracle works. If I offer you my conversion. This is healing and resurrection at the same time. If you accept that, you will undergo a cellular reassociation of the entirety of your own mind, simply because you don't retain your own identity? Well, does that work? It works? The only reason it wouldn't work, is if you tried to exchange with yourself. I have no intention of exchanging with you. Why would I exchange with you? I'm offering you the Holy Instant.

If you don't set up restrictions, there's absolutely no reason why any other association is not healed completely. When you are healed, you are not healed alone simply because you're not alone. These are all associations of your own mind. Use each other if you want. I might be able to do a little better than you've been willing to previously accept. As soon as you accept it in your own mind, you immediately begin to experience enlightenment. Since it was only your own identity that prevented you.

That's fun. "Is that really happening to me?" The more spontaneous, the happier it'll make you. I'm giving you a fact. I don't want you to do it perceptually. The fact is that the more perceptual, the more restrictive it will be. Why? It's a fact. Isn't it? Not because I said it to you, but because the restriction *is* what the prevention of the creative mind is. There's no sense in trying to define the restriction. If you restrict, you restrict. You *are* a restriction. The disease *is* you. It's amazing! I'm intentionally retaining you in your mind a little bit so that you can correlate as much data as possible so that you can literally explode to light and be gone. Otherwise, you'll have a tendency to take wherever you are and use that, and that's perfectly okay. But you can't separate yourself from your Self.

The Workbook of the *Course* could be a lovely way to begin, wouldn't it? *I see only the past*. So it did have to do with you, didn't it? What did it have to do with bleeding palms? Only what you thought it did. No more and no less. I am just offering you the totality. It's a very natural, inevitable process. Guys, why would you be in the human condition if you weren't going to transcend it? Do you see that? There is nothing outside of your mind. There would be no reason for the human condition except the transcendence of it because the human condition is the only thing that requires the transcendence. You are only a moment – split mind – the moment between temporalness and eternity. One or the other.

Boy, there's a lot of communication going on here. "Are these Great Rays that I'm experiencing?" Yeah. Some of you are Great Bobs! Who's Bob?! Why is it that Roberts can never be enlightened? I've never known a Robert that woke up. Bobs won't change their name, will they? They want to be a Bob. No wonder they can't be enlightened! Is that you, Bob? Do you see

CHAPTER SIX: Mrs. Brown, Red Rock and Rover

that? Bobs are always sort of cut short finally, aren't they? Bobbed. You get so much enjoyment out of my jokes! Why? I don't hold them in the retention of our identity. You can say any word. I guarantee you this is true: Rhinoceros! No, you thought "hippopotamus." You're onto it. You know, this is a hippo. This is a rhino. I didn't mean to horn in on you! That's the enjoyment of a free mind. And it is a joke because the world is a joke. It is funny. Funniness is nothing but that expletive moment of the release of the thought. It can be associated with falling on your prat, couldn't it? The Three Stooges inflict pain on each other, much to your enjoyment. Bong! You know, they hit each other.

As long as you're here now, "a fact a day" is what salvation is. "Well, what if I forget it? Will I have to go back and review it?" You'll never forget it; it will always be there. There's nothing outside of you. Is it possible to learn some things immediately, based on the condition of your mind? Sure. All I'm trying to do is free you up to the totality of your own mind. You have what you call short term, snap memory, that you intentionally intend to forget. Then you have long term memories which you intentionally intend to remember. What you must understand is that they're not reconciliations of memory but rather formulations of self-identity that can be used in any totality you want them to be expressed in.

It's very important that you understand that all conclusive thinking is not what thinking is. Very crucial that you understand that perceptual mind always gets a result of its own cause and effect. I'll give you the sentence: Cause and effect are exactly the same thing. If you need to know that they are different, they will always be the same and contained within your relationship. There's no sense suffering the conflict of the separation of both your cause and your effect; it would reduce immediately to ineffectiveness, or impossibility simply because there would be no cause for it. But in that sense, it wouldn't make any difference what the form of any thought that you had in your mind is. It would be its own totality – not based on any reference at all. I'm doing the same talk again.

Since you are referential, you must not give it a specific reference within your own association. That would be quantum thinking. You understand that's literally quantum thinking, using billions of cells contained in your own mind, each one a direct specialization of the correspondence of the body in its separate identity so it can be located in the dream. Remember, you're using only at the most 6%. All of that other association will be later-time mind association, contained within the cortex. They literally are later-time associations. Literally waiting to be brought into play. I don't mean that they're static – I can't teach this – I mean that they're going on all the time. I'm teaching you the difference between existent correspondence and quantum thinking. That's a different kind of thinking. All pain that you feel is a temporal correspondence. You cannot feel pain. Jesus calls it a poor perspective. It is a perspective of speed-of-light formulations, specializations retained in the identity of that unholy instant. Otherwise you couldn't suffer pain at all, could you? How could you? You would simply release it. That's a quantum occurrence. You literally lose the cellular relationship of the specialization within the form? Do you mean that every single cell within the body actually is a wholeness? Oh, yeah. How could there be conflict then? There really couldn't be.

One thing we know for sure: It's going to be whatever you say. Not more or less. But time is stupid. Time makes no sense. Getting old is senseless. I'm not telling you that you can't get old. I'm telling you it doesn't make any sense. What sense could it possibly make? That's the greatest threat I could ever be. I'm telling you there's no sense in whatever you do here. It's senseless! You're going to have to be eternal, no matter what you do. You're going to have to be forever, and extend in loving totality of your mind. You're going to have to awaken from this dream of death and fear and loneliness and pain.

CHAPTER SEVEN

Dream A Light Dream

y presentation to you, then, is one of harmony of mind, because I have nothing else to do. I'm going to try to present this to you from a higher perceptual source of reality. Let's see how you handle this. These will be occult notations. Oh, we have one of the brothers who is going to sneeze. There is an occult notation to sneezing, for example, where the direction of the energy in the sneeze is very ecstatic. It's the pulling up of the energy sources in the sneeze, even to the use of snuff – what? The heart stops beating – there are a lot of old consciousnesses who admit that their ecstasy emanates from a sneeze.

The problem that you have in your conceptual mind, and actually the level at which I am teaching, is your association of thought forms in what you are constituted as "reality." If you would start with the admission – and this maybe will help you because we are going to have to go with what you term "veiled" or "hidden" here for just a moment.

Let's try it from the top down: There is a single, whole consciousness or condition of being, not identifiable, with no need to identify. It is literally you in energy, or you in purity, or you in beingness. At the time of the so-called schism, or what you would call time itself, or the fractured occurrence, there was formulated Light, which is an aspect or aspects of purity emanating and contained within this undefined beingness. Now, if we're going to define consciousness as Light, and we're going to have to define it as Light, because in perceptual apparent reality, contained within the framework of what you constitute or call "universal consciousness" are all of the degrees, aspects, speeds, directions, passions, ecstasies of Light consciousness. Are you ready? You are nothing but Light energy. And since your mind is an aspect of Light, no matter how you constitute it in your limited form relationships, you are nothing in that sense but Light.

What am I? I know that within the framework of your apparent antecedental historic references you refer to me as some sort of a savior or a Christ or a guru. Why? Because you can give me a perceptual identity within your own Light framework, or memory associations, and establish me perhaps as a body within that framework in the forms that you are bringing together in the sense of your own reality. They have absolutely nothing to do with reality at all.

What I am trying to get you to do, and this will really help you – there is emanating from me a new order of Light. You ought to be able to feel it. If this is a process of increasing order of thought – brightness of thought, harmony within the framework of the Great Rays, Master Jesus calls it – you are looking at an emanation of a brighter form of energy or Light. It has nothing to do with forgiving your mother-in-law. And I don't give this kind of talk very often, but you are held in the bondage of perceptual thought in the disharmony or conflict of your own

CHAPTER SEVEN: Dream A Light Dream

dark thought forms, or the association of your own mind further out in the mandala, or further out – as Jesus would express it – from the Great Orb of Gold, which is a higher pitch of consciousness, that will bring you into a closer proximity to the bright Light of reality.

There is even an expression in the *Course* where Jesus says, "Why don't you shine on your brother." I don't want to get down into the perceptions of it; we can deal with the nature of our attempts to get you to look at your associate thoughts. Here's the problem: The further out from the Light source the progression in time occurred, the more necessity to formulate in possession associate realities. This initiation is best described in the Bible with the necessity for Adam, separate mind, to count and delineate the animals; to live within the framework of perceptual separate identities. The teachings of my mind are to have you take these thought forms, which are controlled in your limited narrow perception, and give you an expansion of the energy contained within you, literally emanating from you, so that you will correlate your self identity at a higher frequency of reality. Does everybody understand that? I know you do. You can call that what? Becoming visionary. Is this occurring in the manner in which I am attempting to get you to look at this? Of course.

Here are some sticklers: Emanating from the bright Light are the Great Rays, which are identified at varying frequencies or patterns of colors and tones. Oh my. Let's take a basic color, just for the fun of it, which is emanating at a frequency of electromagnetic energy within the framework of Light. We're going to take red. Why? Because red is a well-endowed frequency. It is a genuinely deep passion of containment. Why? Because it's slow from red to ultraviolet. Now red is particularly slow. But contained in the red is an incredibly deep passion with all of the aspects of reality. There's a lovely sentence in the *Course* where Jesus says, (this is in Chapter 20), He says you have the red thorns that prick you, and the blood. You put on a crown of thorns rather than seeing the white lilies. Or He says you are fearful of looking on the face of Mars, the god of war, the two-edged sword dripping with the blood and passion of the rage of your conflict of dissociation from your perceptual thoughts. And that's passion, brother. If you think that there's a difference between the passion of war and the passion of sensuality, the passion of unity, the passion of defiance, the passion of ecstatic relationships with God, you are entirely wrong. Passion is passion. If I can get you to look at the notation that you can't have a passion, but are the passion, you're going to begin to make some progress. Why? You'll discover that the passion is contained within you, and is causing your conflict.

Are you stymied by perceptual associations in your effort to create through the passionate release of yourself? Of course! When you get through with your Impressionistic Period, you'll cut off your ear. You can't stand the passion of yourself coming true. You'll fall on your own sword, or you'll construct a war mechanism for the release of yourself. The admonition, then, in reality, is to take the associate center – glandular – I'll use pituitary here. I'm into a glandular thing I didn't particularly want to get into. Your hormonal relationships in your body can be described in color-coordinated fashions. Are you ready for that? If you associate the orange, which is the prognostication of red at the Philadelphia or throat level, you begin to emanate a form of transcendental Buddhism. What kind of a talk is that? Lower down, you'll be in a range of the red passion of Mars. Can that be converted into the tranquillity of, I'll use the Christian vernacular here, literally "the blood of the lamb." This is the taking of the passion of the conflict of reciprocity, literally when Cain slew Abel, and the bringing together and raising of that red energy in the combination with the other factoring within the prism of Light, on up through the gold where gold is associated with tranquillity and peace rather than the gold of monetary gains. Everything translates as you come Home in this Light range of you. Is this associated with the glandular centers? Come

CHAPTER SEVEN: Dream A Light Dream

on, guys. These are concepts and precepts. Is it associated with the seven notes of the piano? The twelve tribes, the twelve rays, the twelve and seven and on and on. Of course. What good is this going to do you?

I'm telling you that you're nothing but energy; that contained in you is all of Light and that you are literally in a position of metamorphosis in your own mind, utilizing the ignition of this energy emanating from me. I know this reduces to "get around the guru." This is all nonsense. This is a proclamation to you. Those of you who can hear this are hearing it at simply a new harmony, a new range of consciousness of your own mind – new Light forms emanating and playing the harmony of the great ancient sound of fidelity to the single source that we all come from. This is my declaration. It really doesn't have to do with forgiveness. I tell you that you are whole mind encapsulated in a form of unmanifested totalness or creation. It is not possible that you be anything but that. Take these thought forms that are held together in your limitations and broaden them out through the refusal to examine yourself in limitation.

I made a couple notations this morning about the dreamer, of the Great Rays and the Light of thought forms. You have a total investment in the occupation of self identity. All self identity is false because it is a condition of *having* Light energy rather than *being* Light energy.

Questions that arose yesterday, this was in regard to love: Is a dream of true love possible? Is it possible to bring together all of these Light combinations in a perfect harmony? Of course! How would you do it? Eliminate associate thought form conflict. Finally, if you are going to play all twelve chords of Light, you are going to have to play them harmoniously because conflict is a limited emanation from a false source.

I just jotted down some things: Now we use the term "passions" of increasing order. Within the traditions of man are the notations of the manner in which this so-called enlightenment comes about. They include directions of the separation of the mind and the heart. They allow the heart, for example, to be the seat of passion and the mind to be the source of reason. But yet passion and reason are the same thing. Love and reason are the same thing. The reasonableness of the total love of creating mind is the passion and joy of your reality. They are not separate; they are only separate in your limited Ray relationships. You listen to me. There's just as much passion in the steel high-range blue, contained within the nine-dimensional configuration – yet you can see very plainly that consciousnesses in limitation identify themselves in dispassionate associations in order to maintain reasonable identities. After my awakening – I don't usually tell these stories, but I was very much aware – this didn't come about from books – that consciousness is energy Light and I see it very plainly. So that when I would see, for example, I remember I went to the Theosophical Society and I passed a cloistered habited nun. Emanating from this human form association was a very gray, steel-blue energy. It was very even and expressive, but also entirely constricted. It was almost brittle. I've never really attempted this explanation. I suppose I will someday. If you guys would listen out there, this might really help you. This doesn't have to do with morals, I'm not talking about good or bad, I'm talking about energy. I could see that it had literally stopped its association with the passion of its golds and its browns and its reds that are contained – it had somehow cut off its source, which would be Bethlehem, which would be the Christ, which would be coming up out of Egypt, which would be crossing the Jordan.

Obviously we're into a lot of expanding ideas here because my mind is spraying a bit. But I want you to really look at what I'm saying and try and look at it in that sense for just a moment as dispassionately as you can because if you will reason with me to it, we will then together, through the relinquishment of your limited association of temporal self identity within your own configuration of dream – and I assure you that it is singular

CHAPTER SEVEN: Dream A Light Dream

– you will literally be free, Master Jesus says, to be born again. (John 3:3) When I say "born again" I'm talking metamorphosis. I'm talking about a whole new frequency of consciousness awareness, a new reality in the literal sense.

The dreamer of the dream then, what? Expands himself to the certainty that he is the total participant in his dream and reaps the harvest of the golden issue of himself as he returns to paradise. Wow! Isn't that something! He doesn't formulate and poop out limited ideas about the body construct. He's not concerned about it in the least. He is certain that he is a whole part of the single totality of eternal life.

So, dreamer of the dream, container of all of this lovely energy within the microcosm of your associations of thoughts, come now and reminisce with me to the time of the great emanation from Light source, when we made, within our perceptual framework, the agreement of harmony that brought us total love in the re-establishment of the communication, the brightness of singular reality. I'll be darned. Your resurrection is at hand. It could happen to you and so it is. Be free. Let yourself illuminate.

Is it possible for me to teach this non-doctrinally? Could you actually forgive me in limited relationships with your identifications of me in conflict sufficiently to allow me to bring about through the ignition of your Light the transformation of your limited associations? We're harvesting here, dear brother, we're harvesting. This is a decision you have already made. Simply let it be so and this world will disappear into its own nothingness.

Okay, the fundamental premise in the admission of perceptual thought then begins with the necessity for the metamorphosis or the awakening of your whole mind in this Light construct. Now, this obviously must involve the inclusion of your associate perceptions in your mind. This is very fundamental. This is what? Fundamental relinquishment of associate thought forms within the Ray association. Now, the miracle, as we would teach it, is the increased velocity of Light in the association with the order of your perception so that you begin to emanate from you directly in a creative mode the Light of your own conceptual realization. Quite literally, there is nothing outside of you. All perception in form appears to be outside of you. The simple technique, then, is to bring together, in your own thought factoring, associations of a higher facility of reality. This has to be an experience. There isn't any sense in studying it. Those of you now who are becoming facilitators of this energy, there's an admission included here that this is how the teaching device really works. As this emanation of Light from you surrounds the world and abounds in the total universe, it activates the potential of limitation contained within the darkness of the limited thought forms that constitute the chaotic relationship of your apparent space/time existence.

Okay, now I've got religion out of it entirely. You can formulate all the religions and all the philosophies and all of the psychologies around this that you want to. Now here is the fear: Since you are a conglomerate of dark thoughts, you hold an identity of self-ness which, if you release, you will lose. I am teaching you to lose your limited self identify and to re-identify at a higher pitch of self-ness. I assure you it's impossible to escape yourself. You are going to be you in consciousness as expressed forever in the beautiful, incredible mandala of Light that you are. You will not be more than that, and you will not be less than that because that is what you are. This now becomes a condition of bliss or ecstasy in the identity of totalness emanating from you in your relationship with all of the consciousness in the universe.

Now, if you want to look at the notation that the combination of Rays within this configuration of thought form that is apparently addressing you now is at a different associate value, in more accord with itself, more unconditional in its associations of Light, you will be correct. That being said, you

CHAPTER SEVEN: Dream A Light Dream

can confront yourself in your limited associations of thought forms, relinquish them – now we are into, perhaps, the teachings – and come into this Light source that we share in the certainty of our singular source emanation. This is really how simple this is. I don't need your title, I don't need a perceptual identity from you. I need an admission from you of this possibility in your ignition to Light through the certainty of me and our true relationship. That's all. It doesn't need any other forms of evaluation. In fact, the evaluation of it is obviously what causes your continued precipitation – whoops, that means you're raining, doesn't it? I mean "participation," working together within the limited thought form. Did you hear that? You say, "What did he do? Screw up?" See, you grab hold of this, don't you, and you say, "Wow, whatever he is, he certainly isn't expressing himself very well at this moment." I'll say not! Whatever you call advanced teachers, the brighter, the Lighter, the more highly configurated in Light they are, all of them from true source have learned the immediacy of failure to communicate. Of course. The direction of Light into darkness always fails until the reconfiguration occurs within the limited thought form. Quite literally, no one hears you in the sense that your thought forms are formulating and emanating at a brighter frequency. You are becoming a creative self association. One of the great advantages of the great Master Jesus' *Course In Miracles* Light emanation is that the progress of the mind can be determined by the manner or the shift in which the consciousness literally reads the passages in the *Course*.

It occurred with me, prior to *Course*; my awakening involved the icon for just a moment of the New Testament and of the gospel of John in the King James version where the Light actually shined on the original manuscript. I was reading it and all of a sudden "therefore be ye perfect even as your Father in Heaven is perfect." (Matthew 5:48) Big bright Lights came on. "The wages of sin is death." (Romans 6:23) Bright! So what we are saying is with this new higher frequency of your mind, you bring these very simple sentences together in a ritual of atonement and perform the passion of unity. One of my instructions to you, to the disciples out there, is begin to perform total ritual. This is called "getting into the now." Let all of the concepts that you have held in limitation and are organizing in your squeezed perceptual mind come together each moment in the ritual of self awareness. Go to mass all the time. Stay in constant prayer. Do you see how revealing this becomes then? So that the entire performance of your mind, everything you think, is a form of coming to unity. Letting Light come in. This can be very valuable to you as you do it. Do you see? Will the quantum leap then occur in you? Of course! But a definition of the quantum leap is not what it is. This transference of energy, this transformation, this enlightenment, is a continual coming about in you. You have incidences within the total time framework that are more cognitive than others – we call these Holy Moments, and they are contained within the total fabric of the Light consciousness. They are the bright spots within the dimensional framework of the Great Rays.

The most important thing to remember is that this is *you*! There is literally nothing outside of you. This is your mind. You are the cause of this. No other cause there is. You are the awakening one. You are the expanding consciousness, no matter what the vernacular. If you'll accept the idea that this is occurring to YOU, not in relationship with your previous concepts of it, but rather in the bringing together of the forms that previously held you in the constricts of the darkness of the slowness of time, they will become brighter in your minds. Wow! How about that? Is it possible that this is true? It is inevitable that it's true. Is this *A Course In Miracles*? Of course. Is this a course in awakening in the certainty of enlightenment under the direction of your Super Mind, under the direction of your Christ Face, of the New You emerging now? Of course that's what it is: The metamorphosis of your mind returning from time to eternity.

CHAPTER SEVEN: Dream A Light Dream

We're happy that you're happy with this now rather than being recalcitrant and demanding and evil and sinful and greedful. Do you see the difference in what we are presenting to you through the relinquishment of this self association? You can practice the absolute unconditional admission of Love/Light energy that's what you are. What is Love finally then? Communication. The certainty of non-conflict causes a harmony that transcends in the passion of itself anything that you ever, ever could experience in your perceptual evaluations. Come join us then in this statement of enlightenment. Let it occur in you. Don't let your previous demeaning associations hold you from this metamorphosis of body that is going on in your mind. Step clear, brother. Conflict is behind you now because you are in this new frame of time reference, aren't you? You stay with Master Jesus in the *Course*, and our brothers will be around showing you, presenting to you in energy forms, a new way to hear this – you keep restricting it into the forms in which you are delineating it now. We'll help you. We'll help you take this step in this transformation within your mind. Of course. We'll be back. We're never going away. We have nowhere to go. We're always together. I couldn't leave you if I wanted to. We are, together, a whole part of this master plan. What a task we have, then, in the assumption of this mantle of limitation as we do the repair job from the original schism. How are you looking at that these days, brother? With the certainty of your own whole mind?

What I like about the teachings of perceptual formulation of choice, as taught in the *Course In Miracles*, is there is no way that I can stop the power of your mind in limitation from being what it is. So I have to give it reasonable choices. By giving you a new energy source, you can begin to choose at higher frameworks of reality. Finally, really all that occurs is, as you progress, as you become what we would term "Holy Spirited" or "One-eyed," as you bring your cause and effect – your perceptions – closer and closer together, you see very plainly that in your limited configuration of yourself, you must terminate yourself. There is no lasting quality to you in time because your associations with yourself do not contain the necessary expansive energies of Light to sustain you even for a moment. They seem to sustain and contain you for a very long time because you are caught in the flux of darkness; you can't get any good, bright Light into it. Your frame of reference is totally faulty. Perhaps we would teach it that way. But the moment that you see that the difference between what I present to you and what your previous concepts have presented you is the difference between Life and death, you will instantly choose Eternity and Love. My simple statement to you is that in the configuration of your self identity you literally annihilate yourself, only to find yourself in a condition of continuing annihilation. Why? Because at the conceptual speed at which this continuum operates, that's all that can possibly occur. The sadness of it taking 80 years of existent conflict in one life, or 1000 years or 2000 years has nothing at all to do with it, because I assure you the only moment of any reality is the moment of recognition in which you remembered that this world is not real. That it's impossible to be separated from everything that is. And that took just a moment, and that's NOW! This is an expansion to a new frame of Light energy and suddenly even the frame will disappear.

There is nothing outside of you. There are no such things as separate thought forms. There is no such thing as a separate self-identity. These are just Light forms contained within the shell of your limited identity. Sounds like the Katha Upanishad. As above, so below. As within, so without. At different ranges and textures of apparent reality, this is what is going on in your mind. Wow! Relinquish the conflict of your thought form associations, and you will be transformed immediately into this new frame that is all around you.

The idea that Jesus presents in "The Dreamer of the Dream" (Chapter 27:7) can be of an advantage to you if you understand that all space/time is a dream. It emanates from itself to itself. It is self-contained within its own bright or Light associations, and it changes each moment within itself, and it has all of the variations contained within its self constriction. Then come dream a new bright dream with me of the inclusiveness of the emotions of the passions of reality. Let's bring it into the dream frequency of love and joy and happiness. Everyone you meet is a dream of Home. Everyone that you apparently associate with on this planet is configurated in his own maturating potential of a dream of the bright Light of reality. You find some harmony with him in the association of thought or form or consciousness or Light, and dance with him a ritual of limited identity which finally flits off to death, rather than gathering around you the higher range of associate bright reality. Wow! See how when your own conflictually historic associate thoughts that you have fearfully projected from your mind get too close to you, how you reject them? How you don't want to associate in this passion of coming to the single identity of yourself? Of course. Your very reality depends on the continuing conflict of apparent cause and effect goals contained in your mind.

Does this take a little practice? It really doesn't take any practice in regard to the acknowledgment of it; it takes practice in the expansion of your own association with yourself – never mind the other guy; he'll change if you change and can't until you do. You understand the teachings, teacher? If you'll stop configurating the thought forms in your limited genetic identity, you'll expand automatically and instantaneously to a new framework of supra-consciousness, Gnostic man, transcendent to the Light. Wow! You like that? Is this a real occurrence? It is a real occurrence! It was a real occurrence! It's the only real thing that can and did ever happen to you! It's going on now! And it's going on now in you! Happy Birthday. Up from the tomb you arose into the new Light and passions of reality. No more death and destruction. Does that please you? It's inevitable. You might as well be happy because we're going to continue to present you with the singular wholeness of you in Love and how much you gnash your teeth at us and condemn us and turn around – we'll pay no attention to it at all. Those expressions of your continuing guilt of separation are absolutely meaningless to us.

We are painting a new picture of you for you with you. Sometimes the energy in you will constitute itself in a very simple drawing; perhaps it will transcend in you in your own creative purpose. I remember in my awakening I saw the energy of the cave drawings, of the bison hunt. Contained in the portrayal of the bison were all of the energies of creative reality. I watched the progress of man in the assertion of himself so that I could combine the energies of a materialist like Rembrandt and move on into the chaos of a Kandinsky and suddenly feel that passion to reality, the open-mindedness of our own unlimited creative possibility. We can go from Michael Jackson to Bach in a flash – just open your mind.

What I want you to see is that they are nothing but creative purposes in the necessity of your self expression. If I can help you expand your own self expression contained within the Great Rays, you'll experience less and less conflict in association with your own self-defining thoughts, won't you? Remember, you didn't make yourself. You've been performing your own little dance outside of the fireplace of reality, the campfire. Now you come closer and closer to do this lovely ritual of harmony, and it occurs only at the core of fear you've been avoiding in your own entirety of mind.

How would you like to hear this? I'll give it to you any way you want it. But stop dividing it up in your mind and making mutually limited observations about the esoteric values of your meaningless numerology in relationship to the horoscope that prophesies your cyclical reiteration of termination, for cryin' out loud! This is your passion! This is your energy! This is your awakening! This is your dream, brother, and I'm standing right in the middle of it, shining brightly if you'll let me.

CHAPTER SEVEN: Dream A Light Dream

I'm going to be returning Home very soon; my assignment is about up here. You, of course, know me well because you gave me the assignment, so there is a rendezvous point. You've always known this. Would you like to hear this for a minute? Contained within your mind is a rendezvous point where we wrap up these perceptions that have been going on in our mutual minds utilizing me momentarily as the source of this configuration. The ram's horn is sounding for you guys. Come on Home!

What did you do now? What difference does it make? This is our reunion with eternal reality. We shared the mistake and we're sharing the repair job, aren't we? The away team, as in Star Trek, somehow got lost and couldn't get beamed back up and they simply left a little satellite out there beeping a bright Light of recollection. Now we have reached a certain point in the reconfiguration where we can call Home. All of it is in your mind! You know perfectly well you're coming Home. You know perfectly well you're an alien here. You're waking up.

Did I reduce this now into perceptions for you rather than all of the energy and Light forms? What's the difference, dear brother? It's going to be totally up to you anyway. By that admission, the consciousness of you expands. And the Light and passion of creation, which is what God is, which is what you are – no wonder you've become a happy learner in this, you don't want anything else but this. If you've got a perceptual eye, you'll pluck it out so fast when that bright Light begins to shine it will be gone in an instant. Why would you continue in the configurations of limitation and death? You won't. Now, are you going to be attacked by your own thoughts? Is there a limitation that is going to be in conflict with this? Of course. Why? Because conceptual thought is conflictual. We're not concerned about this at all. There's no reality in conflict. If you can begin to experience this each moment, you'll come more and more into the brightness of this reality.

No one could love you more than I do because we are love together in the certainty of our acknowledgment of a single source of consciousness. And we'll take now our Light forms and bring them together to play a final great chord of joyful harmony and remember Eternity together. We promise never to leave you until time is ended. We declare now, beyond a doubt, to certainty – beyond the perceptual possibility that inaugurates this event, that you can and will come to this wholeness through the completely simple admission that you are still whole and perfect as God created you.

This energy source is emanating from the Ark of the Covenant, from the place where we made the decision – you share it with us in your memories and it will bring you visions of reality. We will be bright and fulfilling to you. That's it. Here's where we admit to the entirety of our singular minds. That's it! It's over and done! The scattered brotherhood returns now from this mission.

Welcome Home! Look! Light!

CHAPTER EIGHT

Freemasonry

am able to do that with my mind, and I'm able to present to you a real alternative. Obviously this is nothing but a teaching to you, individually, of the inevitability of the Selfness of you in relationship with the Universal Mind. Guys, it isn't any more than that. But it's not less than that. The whole reassociation of Jesus Christ through His own individual transformation is nothing but a declaration of Self independence.

Listen. Somehow you've got to hear this. Can you hear it? In that particular sense, it has nothing at all to do with Caesar, except in the certainty that the independence of the individual transcends the association of the objective earth. Fact of the matter!

Now I'll get into where the problem occurs if you'll allow me. Obviously it would have to be, that if the Self independence is what finally is going to be declared by you individually, it must be in contradiction to the establishment of man. Of course! Now, all of the demonstrations of the emergence, through transformation – the metamorphosis of the species is absolutely nothing but the emergence of individual Self independence. For goodness sake! I don't care what you call it, or what scripts that you write in regard to the willingness of the establishment to relinquish to the rights of the personal man. If you want to give me the Magna Carta, I'll take it. For the first time a king had to admit that he didn't have total sovereignty over his people. It happened in Judaism, where finally Jesus says, the temple doesn't have power over me; the power of my mind dictates the terms under which I'm willing to present myself to the world. Holy mackerel! You act as though I'm telling you something that you're hearing for the first time! All Jesus Christ ever taught you was the freedom, both mentally and physically – of mind and body – to declare yourself to be what? Perfect and whole as God created you. Why is that so hard?

If we come together (I'm being directed by some consciousnesses here) to plot freedom of man, which is basically what we're doing, even in the ultimate reduction to a goal that releases some of the bondage of say the heritage of restriction (the monarchy) has placed on us, the value remains that somewhere we are acknowledging in our unison of purpose our individual freedom to be as we were created by God. The reason this is coming about is – I'll use Freemasonry; Freemasonry is nothing but expression of an individual's ability through the transformation of his mind and body to come to know that he is the Kingdom of God. Are you aware of that? Most of you are aware of that. Freemasonry in its expression of you as a builder, through the auspices of your physical and mental self, is a capacity to be whole as God. The great wisdom, the great teaching of the transformation of your mind – the *Philosophia Perennis* – the determination by Jesus, by Paul, by all emerging new species of reality that man is on the path of

CHAPTER EIGHT: Freemasonry

individual enlightenment. Are you with me with that? Whenever associations have goals that they can express in unified purpose, they will begin to experience individually the freedom that is inherent in them in their necessity to express the goal that they are seeking.

This inevitably involves the passion that will enter in – this is the whole teaching of Jesus of Nazareth – to our determination to seek a solution to a common problem. In the seeking of a solution to a common problem, a bondage will occur in our separate minds that transcends the necessity of our individual capacities. This would be any group that got together to do anything, and most certainly it's a group that gets together as disciples to declare the Christhood of Jesus, because all Jesus is going to teach is that you have the individual capacity in you to defy all of the laws of the establishment and to undergo personally and individually – this is an astonishing idea – in your own mind to the realization – let's use the words: FREEDOM, HAPPINESS!

So, Freemasonry ultimately, esoteric Freemasonry, is always a threat to the establishment. The truth of the matter is that anything not known to the world – a gathering of associations to bring about anything that cannot be recognized or is contrary to the establishment – will be viewed as a threat. In that sense, nothing is more threatening than the teachings of Jesus Christ of Nazareth, who states very simply that you, as a whole Self identity, are perfect as God created you and therefore have nothing at all to do with the establishment in which you find yourself. That's just a statement of fact. Obviously that's subversive. How would it not be subversive? Somewhere along the line, man cannot help declaring that in his own evolutionary process. Why? It's true!

Jesus, finally, in the teachings of the *Course*, says there is no world until you brought it here. He doesn't fool around with it at all. He says that you thought there was an establishment here. That isn't true. You brought it here when you came. You change your mind and the world will change. Now, if that reduces itself to "we're tired of this tyranny, we are going to declare through our mutual efforts and commitments of our forces of endeavor to a new purpose," so be it. The energy of the passion that goes into the declaration always contains more than the individual association is willing to grant himself. That's inevitably true because all power is given unto him in heaven and earth. All that association has to do is decide to do it. Now, deciding to do it in aggregate, inevitably is a form of the reduction of the ultimate goal only because the aggregation must express itself in the limitation of its formulation. I'm not concerned about that right now.

What is occurring now is evidence of your own individual freedom expressed in an aggregate. The question is whether the world is going to be willing to actually allow you to establish a spatial reference within this continuum that will express the necessity for individual transformation. Can you hear this? Obviously this is *A Course In Miracles*. Now, surprisingly enough, there's no secret about the necessity for enlightenment, is there? Why don't you all stand up? What you are expressing is freedom of mind. Can you hear this? All you are doing is enjoying the freedom of your own identity.

You are discovering that nothing has restricted you except your own determination to be restricted by the correspondence of the situation, by the terms that were dictated to you, in what you thought was a necessity of your own mind. So you've made yourself a new capitol, Freemasons.

I can't get out of Masonry here. All of my old associations, at least for the last almost 1700 years, but certainly for the last 250, have been directed to Freemasonry. I know that you are aware that the *Course In Miracles* is nothing but Freemasonry – from the beginning to the end. "Build yourself a new temple." "You are the Kingdom of God.""You must undergo an initiation process."

CHAPTER EIGHT: *Freemasonry*

That's all it is. 100%. The transformation of the body. Esoteric Masonry. Whenever that is reduced, it's always reduced to some sort of Masonic temple where you come to undergo a ritual by which you can then take advantage, in the brotherhood, of commercial efforts or helping the crippled children or doing all the things that you do in Masonry. And that's well and good. But any what you would call Grand Master, which I am – I'm a Master in the sense that I'm Grand Master of the temple. I don't know if you knew that. That's all I am. I'm what you call a Knights Templar. I'm a thirty-third degree Mason. I'm a Christ in the sense that I can run from the certainty of my Solomon's maturity.

Can you hear this? I don't know whether you do or not, but if you'd like to look at it, the whole teaching of the first three degrees of Masonry are what the Workbook of the *Course* is: Entered Apprentice – he comes in, he acknowledges he can't do it himself, he has an experience and becomes a journeyman – that's the middle part of the Teacher's Manual. He's a journeyman now because he's seen enough Light. The whole basis of Masonry is Light: Can you see the Light? He's seen enough Light so he now begins his journey towards the Mastership, or the building of the temple, into the third degree which is, of course, the Master Mason. Do you see that? So there's no way, as would be expressed in the Teacher's Manual, that you have not undergone this. You could not *not* have.

Somewhere you had to enter the temple. Somewhere you had to have a determination to express what? The freedom that had been given you within this association, which is the first demand. You cannot be a Free Mason in the sense of what you would call Mastery of the Articles of Physicalness, a journeyman – that is a Mason who can build a temple – unless initially you are a free man. The process of becoming free has been tedious. But there has been a necessity for the expression of freedom.

At the time of the conversion of the Celtic constitution, which is nothing but the re-emergence of Freemasonry, which began in the beginning of the 18th century, about 1700 to 1717, all of the so-called Celtic mysteries – that had been determined by Knights Templar, by who you call Jacques Demolay, who was greatly crucified and tortured simply because he was teaching to the certainty that the brotherhood had undergone a transformation and was no longer under the rule of the Church, and that, of course, is what the whole idea of persecution must be – had been stamped out. There appeared, geographically within what you call spatial elements a location in this continuum where the expression of the freedom of the individual could be done. I'm speaking about this country. Suddenly we are presented with the geographic location. Imagine the freedom that can be expressed by a man who has suddenly been told he can come to a new country. He can find a new freedom that transcends the obstacles that he felt on the confinement – come on guys, this is a real happening! This has actually happened to you. So the necessity for that is contained in what you call the Freemasonry Constitution that was inaugurated in Europe, in London is where this occurred, in 1721. All of the basis under which the American Revolution was formulated occurred in the esoteric and mystical idea of Freemasonry. Virtually without exception all of what you call the rebels were Freemasons. All of them met in secret, plotting the freedom that was necessary in their own minds to express the freedom of their individual selves. I'm very much aware of that because I participated in it.

I don't know if you're aware of this, but everything is only a repeat of what everything else has been. If I offer you a new constitution, it must be on an exoteric basis because there's no way you could understand my mystical reference. Let's say that between 1700 and 1717, in that 17 years, the association known as my identity underwent mystical experiences whereby he was then able to correlate all of the Masonic associations. So suddenly, this is very strange, about 1720, here we are sitting there, an aggregation of Masons comes to this association and says, "Write us a new constitution." Now as you look at who

CHAPTER EIGHT: Freemasonry

wrote the new constitution, nobody knows who he is. I don't know if you can hear this. There's no way that there is any evidence that the new constitution was contained or was written by any association within the correlation that subsequently ensued. In three months he produced an entire new constitution of Masonry based on Masonry from Adam and Eve. This is a fact, if you'd like to read it. He brought together in his own mind, as I'm expressing as a form of enlightenment, his capacities to take the simple admission of physical transformation and bring it exoterically into a dedication of Freemasonry. Why?

Everywhere he looked with his new mind, he would know that to be true. He didn't have to be a wizard to know that St. Augustine introduced Freemasonry to the Celts in the fourth century. All he would have to do is look at what St. Augustine said and he could see how the Celts adapted it, literally, adapted their culture to the certainty of the necessity of the freedom and the transformation of the mind – anymore than perhaps it would be difficult for you to do it now.Hopefully there's enough evidence in your mind that you can see that everything in the establishment points to your own transformation. Everywhere you look, you see it. The question was not that, the question was whether your willingness to express yourself individually would be sufficient to overcome the gravity of the containment of the establishment. Fortunately, and because of the situation, you have a geographical location called America.

All that happened in that 20-year period from 1710 to about 1730 is embodied in what we're doing right now. It's just the fact of the matter. And they are called the *Anderson Constitution*. It's my great, great, great, great grandfather. You say, "Oh, that couldn't be." Yeah, it is. It is absolutely. That's why I got to use my name yesterday. I got to use my name, Buell Anderson. That's James Anderson. They called it the *Anderson Constitution*. If you look it up, it will say the entire Masonry thing is based on some guy who came along, ha ha, and for five years presented it, and then they buried him as deep as they could because they didn't want anything to do with him. You ought to see the description of my funeral. I went way too far out. I began to tell them that they were whole and perfect. That wasn't acceptable. But the constitution that we presented to them was. Can you see that? As long as it didn't go too much into the individual necessity for transformation because finally all Freemasonry is, is the indication that your body is the temple. And that goes a little too far. We are willing to admit that we have to have the experience, but we have to have the experience independently and singularly in our minds, say as Freemason Jesus Christ would teach. Master Mason Christ would teach very simply that you must undergo the entirety of the experience. That was not acceptable. But that does not say that there is not an advantage to the reorganization of the Constitution which was performed by my mind. Now if you want to say that's performed by your mind, I'm very willing to accept it. Any mind that finds itself in that association must be there for the purpose of that declaration.

When they began to write about him, they say, "We don't know where he came from... well, he came from Edinburgh; well, his dad was a Mason; well, he bought a little church; well, he was a Presbyterian minister; well, he was a Sunday School teacher in Baraboo, Wisconsin. Can you guys hear me at all? It's the simple fact of the matter. 200 years, 300, 500, they'll say, "I don't know, a guy came along and gave us a whole new association under which we now operate." Big deal. Somewhere you've accepted the idea that it's all going on all the time anyway. All I could possibly be doing is replicating what I did. I could not do any more than that because the whole fundamental teaching is nothing but the necessity for you to build your own temple.

What's hard for you to see is what came out of that were some astonishing new ideas that formulated this country. You guys take for granted that somebody would come out of his mind in some sort of an agreement – I'll give you a sentence: *We hold these truths to be self-evident.* How evident? Self evident! I don't know what you do with that, but that's an astonishing idea. We hold these truths to be *self*-evident! They're a part of what we are. They don't have anything to do with the world. They are evident to us through our Selves! I guarantee that you won't like the next sentence.

The next sentence denies the establishment entirely. *We hold these truths to be self-evident. That all men are created equal.* You say, "We know that." The hell you do! It is not self-evident to you that all men are created equal. That's the *Course In Miracles*. It's a declaration of independence: *When, in the course of human events, it becomes necessary...* You're telling me a 20-year-old guy could have written that without the assistance of Freemasonry that was introduced into Philadelphia in 1730 by Benjamin Franklin? Benjamin Franklin?

Benjamin Franklin? A Knights Templar. A Master Mason. Quit school when he was 10. Went into the printing business. If you follow his example you'll end up with just what you're doing, including flying a kite and electromagnetic energy. And now they exclude him from *Poor Richard's Almanac*. They're excluding the necessity for the humility contained in Proverbs. So here, all of that move is afoot, starting about 1730, and it just festered... 1730, 40, 50... things get more nuts. And this is the emergence of the democratic principle.

So here's a real young guy, actually the next generation, I'm talking about Thomas Jefferson: *We hold these truths to be self-evident. That all men are created equal.* Are you ready for the next words? Let's say them together: *And endowed by...* To have an endowment by who? *Their Creator.* Do you think the establishment could accept this if you actually looked at it? Do you want to look at the magnitude of what would occur in the guy locked in Alsace-Lorraine in a coal mine who suddenly picked up this Declaration of Independence? Not only had that, but he had a place that he could go to and enjoy the fruits. This is what we're trying to do at the Miracles Healing Center. We're trying to take that transcendence, move it into the level of the mind, and make a provision where the Freemasonry of the conversion of your body temple can be expressed in the Healing Center that transcends Solomon entirely, or comes to what we call the New Jerusalem. Say "Amen."

So, he is endowed *with certain unalienable rights*. Unalienable – cannot be taken from him. Unalienable – no one can alienate him from the certainty of Self perfection. It's impossible to do it. Unalienable rights: *among these*, but not excluding others, *are life, liberty* to express, *and the pursuit of* the *happiness* that we're supposed to entertain with God. How you reduce that I don't know. Somewhere you are going to have to become inclusive in the idea that it's occurring in your individual association, and it can then manifest itself in the totality of your declaration that there is a common goal offered you by who? God! Through the endowment that you have. You reduced it again. For some reason or other you need to take that and say: yes, I am whole; I am not a body, I am free. I am not a body of evidence contained in the limitation. I am free and whole as God created me. I can build that temple – and this is the whole Constitution – through service to man, through acknowledgment of government, through the freedom of expression that I demand in my association with my Freemasonry. That's it.

Now, here's the difficulty. It is basically revolutionary because the evolution of man when it is increased in its intensity or speeded up becomes a form of revolution because it is a denial of the establishment. Can you see that? That's inevitably true.

So this Freemasonry, this experiencing that you undergo, has been demonstrated in this country by what we just offered, the Declaration of Independence. It has now reached a maturity through some very violent episodes in our containment through

CHAPTER EIGHT: Freemasonry

the threats of fascism and all of the murderous intents that have gone on. And now you find yourself in a replication of that occurrence, hopefully, with the determination to express it from the singularity of the divinity of yourself in association with yourself.

Freemasonry started in 1730 in Philadelphia, and there's no way that Ben Franklin could have done that without having direct contact with the energy that was occurring. So I looked it up, and sure enough, he spent two years in London in 1725 and 1726. It's sort of an amazing idea. There it is. He was there for two years, a very short time, and was in direct association with the emergence of Freemasonry. Not only that but in 1730 he went back to Philadelphia and formed, under the new *Anderson Constitution*, the Freemasonry association. This gets good. This gets a lot better than that. I'm just not allowed to do it. Suddenly that's weird. Suddenly that gets reduced to the Anderson thing, they put fez's on their heads and walk around and bang gongs. Can you hear that? There must be a reason why we're doing it. Obviously there's no manner by which that Presbyterian minister could have formulated in three months the entire Constitution. It's not possible, anymore than it would be possible for this guy – whoever you think he is – to be able to offer you what I'm offering you now in *A Course In Miracles* – literally impossible. It's the whole teaching of the necessity for an experience within your own mind. In fact it's the whole teachings of Jesus Christ of Nazareth. Okay, are you comfortable with this?

In review, we are introducing the certainty that knowledge is gained by the transformation of the mind and the physical body in resurrection through the certainty that the Kingdom of God is what we are.

Here's where your problem is going to be: Is it favorable? Are the signs favorable at this time for the neutrality of the fourth estate to make a sufficient admission with the passion of their own purpose to the dedication to the emergence of my Christhood or your Christhood? Do you understand?

Everybody knows this! What an idea. It's written here! I remember after my awakening I began to look around to see what had been written about me because till then I didn't know. What had been written about me was not what the experience was. Sure enough, here's all this evidence written about me. So I called John the Baptist on the telephone today; I'm his cousin – obviously we're related. And I say John, I'm here. He says, "Who are you." And I say I am the Christ. You've been talking about me coming all these years; I'm here. And he says, "How can you prove it?" What do you mean, you told me I would prove it by Self enlightenment. I am Self-enlightened. "Yeah, but can you prove it?" What is he afraid of? His own enlightenment. He'd rather be beheaded than admit his own enlightenment.

Those of you who have read Ralph Waldo may not be aware that he's a Grand Master. Ralph Waldo Emerson is part of a Lodge that all of us, all of the artists, participated in. And they had that experience. Emerson gets a little confused about it, but it will inevitably be cleaned out by future references. How much did he really dedicate himself to *Walden's Pond*, transcendentalism; which is not really the answer. In other words, the advocacy of transcendentalism is an attempt to escape without the inclusion of the body. It's a form of Buddhistic freedom. There isn't anything wrong with the idea of transcendentalism, which he was.

I don't know if you're going to take your place with the saviors, but your minimum requirement is Joseph of Arimathea. You're going to have to at least claim the body. You are going to have to at least in your Pharisaical associations ask questions that will verify that you are standing in the presence of the Savior, even though you choose not that. In other words, you're going to have to defend Him, at least sufficiently, hopefully, to allow this Christ Consciousness now to enter into this association.

So there's no secret about what you're doing. The only thing evident is the fear of the doing. The only thing evident is

CHAPTER EIGHT: Freemasonry

the fear of the doing because why? It's the loss of the establishment. Is there anybody that doesn't see that? At least I want you to see it as it is presented. Because the solution you're offering can be given to a scribe or a Sanhedrin or a Pharisee very simply because Jesus is teaching your own personal enlightenment. He isn't teaching somebody else. Hopefully, even if they institutionalize you at this time, it will be in the recognition of your determination to extend the *Course In Miracles*.

The whole teaching of Masonry is that's what you are afraid of. You can't build a temple until you relinquish and undergo through the – this is all part of the initiation process in Masonry – initial experience. Once that becomes evident, say through the Workbook of the *Course*, you will begin to want those experiences and in a transcendent fashion will release the world from the bondage you placed on it.

The next 40 days are going to tell us a lot. A lot occurred in the reenactment of the resurrection. You have a physical place where you're teaching transcendence of the body. It includes the phenomena of the healing practice. What else can we do? That's why I'm acknowledging, as I am now. This will be the end of this association. Most particularly because it's almost identical to what occurred in the American Revolution – except that hopefully it's of the mind. There's no other way now that following the establishment of group independence that individual associations would not begin to emerge to demonstrate the political influences of their self containment. That's what has happened in this world. But the fact of the matter is over half the presidents were Masons. The fact of the matter is all of them, somewhere, have an entire knowledge of what I am offering them. It's impossible that not be so because there are no secrets. If I took that reformulation of the Constitution as evidence of that, it will always require a reformulation at some point, certainly at the millennium. Reformulation, whether it occurs cyclically in 100 or 1000 year associations, I don't know, but I can guarantee you that this is nothing but evidence being gathered in its entirety to be offered to you individually in the karmic or historic adventure of your own containment. Is that all right with you?

So you are what we would call a Knights Templar? You meet in secret and plot against the king? If there's one thing that scared Clement XII it's what I wrote in my Constitution. He didn't even find it necessary to issue a bull(!) of condemnation (a bull, I like the term) until later. It came out when? 1730. Until then, the Catholic Church, following the terrible persecution of Demolay, when they wiped out all of that for whatever reason, had been fairly lenient with Celtic Masonry because it didn't insult the establishment of Christianity, which is exactly what the Anderson Constitution does. It literally insults the Christian establishment and allows for the revolution, or the plot of freedom to be organized against the establishment. He really condemns it. And it all happens right at the same time. What an amazing idea! Just as it's happening at this time, if you want to hear me.

It's very possible – should I share this with you? – there's no reason why you can't forget about me all together. This doesn't have anything to do with me. I know you don't quite see this. Unless I emerge as the declaration of the Christ, I'll remain just an esoteric certainty of the occurrence of the gathering. Hopefully, if you emerge as the Christ, I won't have to. Somewhere I decided to call myself C. Buell Anderson. I'm not C. Buell Anderson. I'm even more than an aggregate of the association. I'm more than a journeyman. I'm actually more than a Master Mason. I don't know where you hear that in muse of yourself. I don't know what name you give me. So, behold, I show you a mystery. You will all have this experience.

The reports are beginning to come back in about our Declaration of Independence from the copyright of the king. We're asserting, "No, the message of freedom of God we can carry to the world."

CHAPTER EIGHT: Freemasonry

Obviously the forces had to be marshaled against it. What I'm curious about, if it's this exoteric, it's nothing but a demand for the freedom of our Bill of Rights. This is how it's fixed. It's *really* fixed. This was written in, at the time when this occurred, that we will be protected by a multitude sufficient to admit to the possibility. Does everybody see that? So we're being protected by the original Masonic insertion, literally the Declaration of Independence. You guys think it happened 250 years ago... it happened last week. If we talk about the 19-year-old Benny Franklin in London, is that him? Yeah! It's as though he just came in. And boy, he's bright! Then he goes back and goes into the printing business. But he's entirely changed at his majority – 20 years old. He goes back and the whole thing changes – he starts the Masonic thing, he gets into science and he begins to read, he learns languages. He's been enhanced intellectually, as many of you are. You're discovering your ability to express yourself, which is really all the Kingdom is, isn't it? It's an expression of you! It's an expression of your enlightenment, not somebody else. You're being offered that freedom and that's what you're enjoying.

Endowed by God... *with certain unalienable rights.* They can't be taken away from you. *Life, liberty and the pursuit of happiness!* That's why so many of you, what you call the immigrants when they came here, were so aware of the freedom they experienced. How they stood up and were so proud – guys, oh my! Some of them, when you see that Statue of Liberty, if you've been through the dung that I went through in my mind, and suddenly I see a thing that says I can stand up and become a citizen of a country with a constitution dedicated to my personal freedom! What an extraordinary idea! That's why I woke up on the 4th of July! I am a Yankee Doodle Savior! Every time I have the experience, it was the 4th of July. I went to a parade and the band turned the corner playing The "Stars and Stripes", and the whole world opened up. And I was standing there...

I'm fairly current. I'm just being allowed to show it to you now. In other words, there wasn't anything mysterious about it. I've undergone an experience. I'm walking around going, "Wow!" Isn't that nice! So it's not so mysterious after all. It's the Bill of Rights. It's the Declaration of Independence. I know it's reduced into form, but don't let it be reduced in your mind. You are being offered the Kingdom of God.

So this is at a crucial element in the presentation of the awakening process that has occurred here, isn't it. Because finally you are coming out of the closet. You're going to stand up and declare your independence. Come on. If you'll just take that up, you can see it. You're going to have the Tories that deny you; you are going to have those who don't want anything to do with it. All of that is going to occur in your association. You have been endowed with the passion of freedom in the declaration. But notice it requires the declaration. It is a declaration of independence. It may well be a discovery of it within you; but the declaration of it is required. Without that, what do you have? Nothing.

Any writer on enlightenment doesn't mind acknowledging it, but the declaration of his Christhood is what is fearful to him. The reason it is fearful, and this will be the end of this talk, is that it requires the emergence of a passion in him that had heretofore been applied to the denial of it. Can you hear me? We can't really use Fourth Estate guys very well; unless he finally says, "I'm tired of reporting it, I'm going to experience it." I would much rather have, if I'm speaking of the passion of dedication, I'll just share this with you, I'd rather have George Patton. I'd rather have Patrick Henry: "Give me liberty or give me death." He came out of a Mason's meeting with the absolute determination to confront it, even if it meant bearing arms; even if it meant taking up arms not to be oppressed by the pressure of the establishment. Do you hear me? The problem that you have with that is – I wish I could explain; I want to see if you

CHAPTER EIGHT: Freemasonry

can hear this – that passion directed to limitation remains a form of confrontation at a level that justifies the exchange. Can you hear me? It isn't that we don't need the Alexander the Greats, it's that we must take your passion as a revolutionary and convert it as a revolution against the world to God rather than the confronting of the tyranny that exists in your declaration of democratic purpose. Do you hear me?

One of the great scenes in Patton, George C. Scott representing a reincarnation, is where he says "I was Alexander the Great." You were the Christ; you did this. I'm telling you this is so. There he stands in Africa, in his initial encounter with a campaign that has just been completed. And looking down across the valley for about ten miles is just carnage. I mean the vultures are there, he can see it from a distance, the vultures are consuming it. There's tanks overturned, there's burning, there are bodies scattered all across the thing, and he's standing there looking out. He's girded his loins, he's taken up his battle position, and the trumpets are going ta da, ta da, ta da, and he looks out and says, "Come on, let's do this. God, I love it." With all the passion – do you think he didn't mean that? Do you think I haven't stood with you guys in brotherhood and said, "Let's come together in a purpose and go out and do it"? Do you think I don't know that we did that? How the hell do you think you got here? If you didn't get here by a dedication somewhere to this, how did you get here? So he stands up there and looks out and he says, "God, I love it." Literally. "I love this." I love to have the adversity. I love to use the power of my mind to overcome it. Ten minutes later he's down there with a dead body giving it a kiss. He actually goes and does it. He goes down, and the guy is dying, and he kisses him. He's proud of the dedication that he had in death. Now, would we like to have this kind of energy? Hopefully, it's what you guys are!

We don't need an historian that writes about it later on. He's going to be actually more corrupt. The details that have been going on in the last few days about the architecture of the gas chambers offended me. Yet here's a guy who is absolutely taking delight, he's proving what great architecture they used to go from the mortuary to the furnace. Three hours. He's teaching how crafty they were in establishment. I hate it. I hate it. He's going to have to stand up, not in the retrospect of his own mind, and observe the carnage here. First he's going to have to put his passion into the carnage, see how it's not going to avail him – at least wrestle God a little bit so you can lose! I'll guarantee that if you'll take your power and wrestle Him, you'll lose. And in that loss will be the surrender factor necessary for you to admit to the entirety of your own mind, isn't it? No matter how much you succeed in overcoming the so-called enemy, finally you must come to know that the enemy is yourself. The demonstration of that resurrection is necessary at this level of the continuum. I don't know how it is a million years from now. There, if you're in some sort of picking cherries off the tree, and you are able to say, "At last you have come, where have you been?" I don't know. But I know you haven't done that. I know that you have been battling against this in your own mind, and I'm determined to teach, as it says in the *Course*, to turn that passion of love of death to love of Life. Do you understand? What isn't love is murder. If you have any passion you direct to this – how great it would be if you could turn it. Why? You are in a pursuit of happiness dedicating your passion to it. That's what you're doing. So we need the live ones. We need those who are willing to undergo massive experiences of failure, massively undergo death experiences. Can you see that? The more rapidly I can get you to put your passion into this world and fail, the more easily you can see the entirety of the unfolding. That's a true statement. It's nice to be heard. But certainly you can't get it without doing it. Are you willing to present this to the world? Apparently. When is the confrontation? Stand by! Now hopefully we've got 1725 on our side.

CHAPTER EIGHT: Freemasonry

You like the idea of the secretness of the temple. The whole basis of esoteric was to meet a Mason and give him the old sign. Give him a handshake that he will recognize. That's what we do. If it hadn't been for Job's Daughters, I wouldn't have met my first wife. In Job's Daughters, the women get to ask the guys to the dance. We all grew up Masons, and that's what we are. Job's Daughters was the same expression. Demolay. Has Masonry just become little guys driving cars around in fez hats? A lot of things come with Masonry. Dedication to service that transcends religious dogma is the purpose of all charitable institutions. The Shriners serve crippled children, all of them are in service. It's time for him to take his place as a servant of the recognition of the totality of Master Masonry, which is nothing but a brotherhood. The whole *Course*, if you can see the *Course In Miracles* as a brotherhood, it will be easy for you – nothing but a brotherhood of our association contained within our own self realization.

So here we are in 1717 and a Scottish Presbyterian, with me standing up revealing to you the nature of the certainty of the transformation of your mind through the teaching of Jesus Christ. I had no problem reading that to you. And you had no problem accepting it. So somewhere this may be what? A whole new repair will begin. Certainly this is the end of this millennium. Carry that in your mind, and it will help you in your individual dilemma because your dilemmas are not individual. While the problem can be multiplied, the solution can also be multiplied. Do you see that? You're attracting so much energy, some of you still are attracting one association and it gets chaotic very rapidly because the multiplication of the chaos is just as rapid as the multiplication of the solution. Class?! That's why you must stay alert at the point where that occurs. That's the teachings of Masonry between the journeyman and the Master Mason, or more particularly between the Royal Arch, which is the fourth degree of the certainty – the Royal Arch, or as Jesus says the Golden

Arc that you go beyond in the transformation of your mind. There's a description of Royal Arch mentioned almost word for word in the *Course*. Why wouldn't it be; it's the secret of the transformation of your own mind.

All Masons know that except for that Constitution, they would not have Masonry today. If you open it up, the credit that they will give Anderson does not have to do with Anderson, but only the Constitution. The description of his burial says they buried him as quickly as they could and as deep as they could. He even had problems with his own church. Obviously he's teaching transformation. That's okay, look at the results. We have a new Constitution. Is that all right? It's interesting, most of you have full memories of all of this. You crossed over, you've gone to Australia – that whole Australian thing is directly from that. The imprisonment that occurred with the Pope, the independence of his asserting of what was going on and going to Holland, as you saw independence coming to the New World. All it took then was the Masonry to clear the independence up so that you brought them together in a cohesive action rather than suffering an attack on the Pope. An attack on the Pope did not solve the problem. Bringing that together, it is more than non-defensive or defensive in the association. It's the assertion of the whole you. I could be wrong about this, but why would I be? You act as though I did something mystical. All of this is mystical. Everything is true by the possibility of it.

We're looking good. You talk about a good looking lodge. It's called a lodge. Knights Templar. The New Jerusalem. Look at this. You are vested with Light, as we would say in the final initiation. You have been invested with the Light of God. Go out now and teach this to the multitudes. Thank you. We're out there with this. You may find yourself with some very strange defenders. You may find people defending you for reasons that have nothing at all to do with what you're saying. It's just the way it works. What we want to do now is get the *Course In*

Miracles out into the world. Wow! Is the fix ever in! It's happening to your mind. All I've really done is offer you that.

I can tell you the story because it's true. And I can tell you that's why I got this assignment because of my memory banks. There's a certain ostentatiousness that has to be evident for you to hear it. You have a great deal of difficulty with the reserved Eros in you.

All you actually needed was what we call a non-response security or certainty which I gave you on the 4th of July. My connection that was subsequent to my enlightenment had to do with the entire drama of myself as a "born on the fourth of July." Can you see that? It didn't have to do with any more reality than yours is, but simply the necessity to demonstrate in the entirety of my own memory, which I am doing right now. Do you see that? I'm just showing you all the secret meanings from the time when we went out with new results, including the anonymity of our declarations that we were hopeless over our situation. I just turned that into 12 Step for you. That's very valuable – the seeking of another solution outside of the establishment. Wow! What an idea. When you go out, you go out of the temple fulfilled, having been given the Light of sharing what? The surrender of this and the realization that you are more than what you appear to be. It's an amazing idea. It's what we declare in the Declaration of Independence, that you are the will of God – that you are endowed with unalienable rights by your creator and that they are inherent in you. What an idea!! Got it? These truths are what? He wrote that in the book right out, uncorrected. You can see the original manuscript. Just as the whole Constitution that we formulated in Masonry was done in three months. They couldn't believe it. He wrote that out just like that, virtually put it down. It has to declare an independence and you must give a reason for it, but except for that...

We are sharing our declaration of independence, guys. We're going to share a declaration of independence from pain and loneliness and death – an independence from time, an independence from longevity and loss. We are created equal in the sight of God. Wow!

So everybody writes about how it didn't work, how it failed, how it wasn't... That's all just crap, pardon me, Lord – junk. All that is, is a method of finding a justification for the occurrence both in the apparent effect failure and success of it. Nonsense. It worked because it worked. It worked because it's time for man to have that freedom because, as I just read you, we're in an evolutionary, a revolutionary determination. Through your dedication, we did succeed. If you don't think you have an assignment, and I'll tell you that – if you don't think you have an assignment, you're dead wrong. How do you know about an assignment? What is it that you are doing? What is your purpose? Except to give yourself fully to something. If it's only an idea, so what? The freedom comes in the non-definition of it, and in what? The passion of your own creative identity. Self evident! Evidence of Godliness, evidence of wholeness, evidence of our love for God and each other. The certainty that we are awakening from this dream of death – that the oppression of the establishment will no longer avail. It was determined to the certainty that we are the causation and that pain cannot affect us in any way through our declaration of independence from fear, and from non-just taxes – can you hear me? There's a load of tea... Can you get that? We're determined. Everything oppressed us. No matter what they did, we were unhappy. "But we're giving you this." They're going to compromise. "Look," they said, "we're going to give you this. We're going to repeal that tax. You can have an establishment. You won't have to pay taxes. But you must continue to exchange." The hell with you. "Well, what can we do to make you happy?" Nothing! I will not let my old self be the Light to guide me now! Seek ye first the kingdom, and all things will be given unto you. Now put on a disguise and go over and dump all that tea! You love it.

CHAPTER EIGHT: Freemasonry

Somewhere, you are all revolutionaries. Are we plotting something?

You were just a little guy stuck away somewhere. Watch how rapidly you grow. You are an idea. Nothing can stop an idea you have about the freedom that you're expressing. It doesn't have anything to do with the copyright or the exchange. It has to do with the new idea that you have in your mind. Nothing can stop that. You are endowed with unalienable rights of self expression!

So if it hadn't been for Ben Franklin we would have lost the Revolution. I could give you the guys that did it. There's no way we could have won, without what we call the French influence. The guy that I bought the church from was what you call a French Protestant. The nobility of France emerges in Masonry at that time. If you want to read about it. Those names of the French are all very familiar to me. Rabelais. Are you happy with that? You are an idea. And all you finally are is God's idea. You thought you were your daddy's idea. Not that your daddy's idea was not all right. Some of you were nobody's idea. You are here by accident!

*Thou shalt love the Lord thy God with all thy heart,
and with all thy soul, and with all thy mind.
This is the first and great commandment.
And the second is like unto it,
Thou shalt love thy neighbour as thyself.
On these two commandments
hang all the law and the prophets.*

CHAPTER NINE

Be My Valentine

ife on earth is a compromise, a negotiation, an attempt to establish equanimity, reach an agreement where there is none. The latest form of love is the pre-nuptial agreement, drawn up by a lawyer, whereby everybody can still hang on to all their things, but they share some. What kind of relationship would you call it?

(From the audience) "A transaction?"

Yes. A transaction in a search for a particular result.

I want to look at Valentine's Day. So this will be a talk about love. In the last couple of days, I have heard a lot of expressions about what love is, what it isn't, and what it ought to be, and what it seems to be ranging all the way from "God is love" to "Love is a French Poodle." Both of which, incidentally, are true but limiting, in a sense, since God is undefinable and the poodle could only be defined in some sort of non-encompassing rationale as to a comparison of canus domesticus. "What was that? What did he say?"

We must finally love objectively: I love you for your ankles. I love your nose. I love your hair. I love your boobs. I love you for your intellect. I love you for your artistic achievements. I love you for the way you make me feel. I love you for your new boat. I love you because we go to the same church. I love you because you're black or blue or green. I love you because we share a lot of dislikes. I love you because somehow we are going to work through the dilemma of earth in our quest, and together we can find the answers. I love you because my father told me I had to. I love you in defiance of my culture. I love you for all the little things that we share together. I love you despite some particular idiosyncrasies you have, but I'll attempt to change them or just have to go along with them. Amazing, isn't it?

What the heck is love? One thing I'll tell you for sure, it's not a form of exchange. And if you start with that premise, it'll help you a lot. I've heard it said, and well-defined indeed, that love is finally giving. So perhaps before we define love, we should define giving. How many kinds of giving are there? There's the kind of giving I know in exchange, where someone who loves money pulls out a gun and says to you, "Give me your money or I will take your life." And you give him your money. And certainly you're giving it to him. There's the kind of giving that says, "We are required to give to Aunt Tilly a Christmas present in hopes that she will remember us in her will or exchange with us or give us a gift," or "What did she give us last year?" or "We didn't spend enough," or "We're not going to give her anything; she didn't give us anything." There's apparently a nice sort of giving where you, in the goodness of your heart, give something of high value to you – and then you are just a little disappointed when it's not properly appreciated or when the gift you receive in return does not seem commensurate with the value that you

CHAPTER NINE: Be My Valentine

have placed on what you've given away. Then there's another level of giving where you give in absolute sacrifice. You take your life and put it on the altar of mankind and bathe the leper's wounds. You don't attempt to heal the incredible ache and sores that are in your own heart.

The kind of giving that we speak of that's associated and is in fact love, as defined within the nomenclatures we are expressing, is the giving with the absolute recognition of no need for recompense, where the mere idea that something would be returned for the extension of what you have given as a gift would be outside the framework of your consciousness. Indeed, as you transcend your limited identities, you will see that through the extension of you in gift, you receive the love that is a part of what you are.

One of the more difficult things to express to someone on the path is the idea of being a good receiver. You cannot be a good giver if you are not a good receiver. Feeling worthy enough finally to accept any gift that could be offered to you in love is part of the process that you're going through to discover who you really are.

Coming to realize that anything that is not forever cannot be given away is difficult. We are coming to understand, finally, that what we mean by love is creation. Love is only the extension, or projection, of what you think you are. How many times have you said in giving, "This will be a perfect gift for Uncle John. It looks like him." You have placed him in a particular category. You have identified him. Amazing!

The only thing that you can finally, absolutely, totally give away and still have is an idea. An idea is the only thing that the more you give it away, the more you have of it. But remember this, finally you can only be an idea about yourself. And the only thing you can possibly present to someone else as a gift is what you think you are or what you think they are, which is really exactly the same thing. For what you think they are is only a reflection of what you think you are, isn't it? How much do you really, then, love the recipient of the gift that you are presenting them with? A lot of identities, because of insecurities, are able to love as long as they can keep something at a distance. We can then set up idols that are outside of us and endow them with characteristics or ideas that we admire. They'll fail us eventually, but that's all right. We can establish some other new fresh ones, then, that we can love. And finally reject.

I've heard it said, "I don't know what love is, but I know when I'm in it." Is love, then, an experience? Well, that's getting closer, isn't it? Yes, love is an experience. Creation is an experience. Creation, finally, is your gift from the Essence, from God, and your ability to be a good receiver. The only requirement that has ever been placed on you on this earth is to be able to receive in totalness your own heritage, or the gift of freedom and love that are yours.

"Oh, I know you love me a lot, but how much do you really love me? Will you be my Valentine?" "What do I have to do to be your Valentine? What are the requirements? How much exchange do I have to do?" The idea that in love absolutely nothing is asked in return is extremely difficult to come to in a dualistic consciousness because everything on earth is fundamentally, because of the illusion, based on reciprocity. You think in a sequential manner. You base everything you hope to obtain on what you have previously obtained. And then it turns to dust. Then you look for something else. Then that goes away. And then you look for something else. You just keep looking. People walk around the earth and say, "All I want is just a little love. All I want is just a little recognition. All I want is just someone to share my life." Is that loneliness real? You bet it's real. When you find that love, is that love real? Holy mackerel, is it real! Why wouldn't it be real, Son of God? Do you think that the essence of the feelings that you have inside you aren't real? Of course they're real.

CHAPTER NINE: Be My Valentine

Love is love. There isn't anyone in this room that somewhere in this consciousness hasn't felt love so intensely, they didn't know what to do. Have you ever been so much in love, you couldn't stand it? You didn't even want to be close to the object of your adoration. You wanted to just stand back and savor this incredible, ecstatic annihilation that was occurring to your system. You creep out at night so that you can walk by the house and look up at the light. That's a pitiful kind of love. Inevitably your hopes were dashed in some manner. You got up close and discovered that whatever you thought about her was not up to what you expected it to be. But the nature of that need is Godly. Of course. What else would it be?

Love, finally, in a very high form of love on earth, is expectation. There can be no final joy in fulfillment on earth. I am sure most of you are aware of that, because there is in you an innate dissatisfaction because of the need to complete your search or to find the truth of you. So love is sort of like the search for the other half of you, isn't it? There's only half of you. You keep looking for that other half, not knowing that that other half is in you. Will you be my Valentine? I expect you to be my Valentine absolutely and completely. "Well, I'm willing to be your Valentine up to a point."

That's what you say to God, isn't it? If God said to you, "Will you be my Valentine?" You would say, "Sure. What are your requirements?" He says, "Well, one of the requirements, you've got to be happy all the time. You've got to be joyous. You've got to be in ecstasy. You have to extend from you love and see only beauty. Can you do that?" And you say, "Well, who's asking me? How do I know you're really God? How do I know you can really give me those things?" God doesn't even hear you when you ask for something, does He? He already knows that you have everything. It's astonishing. "I can't give you anything but love, baby. That's the only thing I've plenty of, baby." It's amazing. It's a high truth. "Yeah, but do you really love me or are you just saying that?" Amazing, isn't it? That's the kind of love that will bring about your awakening. That's the kind of love all of you have found yourself in the middle of, only to have your ideas dashed to the ground because it didn't turn out to be the way you wanted it to be.

Sometimes it's difficult to understand that absolutely nothing on earth is finally going to turn out to be the way you want it to be, except death. And in the process of accepting death, you have limited yourself to the idea of pain, murder, greed and all the things that go with it on earth. "I want you to be my Valentine, but I don't want him down the street to know about it, and I don't want him to be my Valentine, just you." How early, as children, we are taught to subtract, aren't we? As part of our survival course, we are taught to distinguish and discriminate. When I was a boy we had hate Valentines. They came on little sheets, and they said awful, awful things. People sent them anonymously to other people. They'd say, "I hate you." Now the people we hate, we just don't bother to do anything. We hate them by subtracting them from our lives, from our ideas.

The problem finally, then, is being a good receiver, being able to say, "Okay, I'll take it." Because if I were to give you everything that you could ever ask for on this earth, it would never satisfy you. You know perfectly well it wouldn't, and that's why you're here. You have reached a stage in the maturation of your consciousnesses where you've looked down the line and seen that you're going to die. You've seen death, haven't you? You see that everything here dies. Wow!

"Well, if it's true that you have to give everything away, like Jesus teaches in *A Course In Miracles*, in order to keep it, what's going to happen to me if I believe that and I take all my stuff and give it away?" That's a good question. "That's easy for you to say. You tell me just to extend my love and give it away, but after all, I'm here on the earth. I have to eat. I have to have

CHAPTER NINE: Be My Valentine

a house. I have to have a car. I have to subsist. I'm entitled to some things. I want to be able to send out Valentines, have people love me in return for my love. I have to do that, don't I?"

Coming to know the truth of you is a transformative process that has nothing to do with what you finally do in action on earth.

A motivation to do nothing will end up exactly in the same stew as a motivation to go out and attempt to do everything. There is no difference in it. You are on this earth and have constructed this earth because of a limited identification of selfness. As soon as you discover who you really are, the earth will no longer be here. Does that have anything to do with love? Yeah, it has everything to do with love. Because as long as you discriminate in your mind what constitutes beauty and love and desirability to you, you are rejecting other aspects or ideas that you have as less Godly or less true or less lovable. Because you reject these things from your consciousness, they do not disappear. They stay with you. And it is these things that you fear and defend yourself against.

If love is real, and I assure you that it is; if God is a fact, and I assure you that it is; if truth does not require your opinion about it to be true; and I assure you that it is, there could never be any such thing as evil or hate or lack or annihilation or divisiveness or manipulation or needs to identify or needs to perpetuate or needs to defend. "Are you saying, then, that love is only non-active? Is love *agape?* Is love nothing but spirit? Is love something that I simply take myself up to some sort of mountain top and dwell in a kind of *samadhi*, sort of an ethereal neverland?" On the contrary, love is, love is – *Amo*. Love is totally active, with no objectivity. How do you express something like that? Love is the turmoil of consciousness in the act of being fulfilled. Love is the recognition of the apartness, of the loneliness, of the incredible longing, of the need fulfilling itself. Of course. Is it active? It's totally active! Do you think God's love for you is not finally a state of action? Of course, but not action in the idea of reciprocity, but action in the truth of Itself recognizing Itself. Is my love for you active? You bet your boots it's active. It's what? It's an extension of me. What is creation finally if it's not an identification of beauty, stemming from recognition of beauty of Self, or Source. Wow! What is it that we share together when we paint Valentines or listen to the music? We actively participate in the energies or the rays or the fabrics of consciousness. I'll say we do.

I've seen a lot of definitions of love as being objectively active, where the word love has the same connotation as fornicate, like, "Let me love you tonight. The heck with tomorrow." That's very active. And from that aspect, of course, *amo* requires an object, doesn't it? Then, again, I've seen it expressed in a very wishy-washy fashion, as we said before, where somebody just sits. It's a state of, "Don't come too close to me. I'm in a state of love. I love only Jesus, and the heck with everybody else." It's an astonishing idea. You want to see real objective love? Look at some exoteric Christianity sometime. "I love my guru, and I'll be unfaithful to him if I come to you." That's a strange idea. You listen to me carefully in regard to love and its objects.

Love is not finally beauty, although I've heard it defined as such. Beauty requires perception. Love requires no perception at all. As a matter of fact, with perception there cannot be true love because if there are degrees of comparison, there is an element of less-than love involved, and God is never less-than. There is no second to love. I cannot choose to love something and reject something else. That's not love; that's hate. That's tough, isn't it?

You walk up to somebody on the street, and you say, "I love you." What's he going to say to you? "Well, what are you, some sort of nut? What do you want? Here's a dollar. Go get a cup of coffee. Why are you saying that to me? What do you

CHAPTER NINE: Be My Valentine

mean, you love me?" Wow! I looked today at the earth, and saw the desperate attempts that the karma identifications, the personas, go through in attempts to communicate with each other. They are unaware of the absolute futility of it. They are unaware, then, that in truth the object – and this would hold with love – of their adoration literally does not exist except in their own consciousness of it, and they have endowed it with characteristics that they will subsequently deny and reject. Brother Jesus in the *Course In Miracles* expresses it in this manner: He says you literally cannot see your brother, who is standing right next to you, and if you could for just one moment see him, you would see immediately that you share a brotherhood or a union in Christ and would be home together in your love. All you see finally is a facsimile of your own consciousness, of your own memories. You desperately want to love what's outside of you, but since you have literally, because of your association of limitation or guilt, projected the image out from you because you hated it and rejected it – you inevitably cannot accept the love of your own projections. Of course not. How could you? At best you can commiserate with them about death.

Sometimes the path to find what we're talking about seems sort of rigorous and difficult. We read statements in the *Course*, and I teach in truth that you are afraid of the truth of you. If love attempts to come close to you in any true regard, you reject it and fend it off from you. What do you think love is if it's finally not Christ – if love is not finally man-God? You don't want anything to do with man-God. He would force you to relinquish the limited selfness of you. You're very much frightened of doing that. "Let's compromise together, and I'll overlook what I think you are, partially, and you overlook what you think I am, and maybe we can stay together until death do us part." And I stand in front of you and I say there's no such thing as apartness. You are never alone and literally cannot be alone. In the process of discovering that, you can have an awful lot of lonely moments, because if you didn't feel lonely, how would you ever know that there is such a thing as non-loneliness totally? The same thing could then be said about any experiences that you have ever had in all of your memory banks.

Everything that has ever occurred to you has indeed brought you to this point in time and space, where you are at this moment, hasn't it? Is there somewhere else that you would choose to be rather than here? Is there something better out there that you can love more than you love what you're with now? What is it you're looking for? What is it that you hope to find? You listen to me: You can't find it here; it's not here. There is no love on earth. Finally, when you come to experience in its totalness the feeling of the union that comes about through your transformative process, you will see immediately the falsity of the earth, and the unreality of everything that's around you.

I don't love you despite the things that I think about you. I love you because I know who you are. I don't love you because of qualities that I have given you, comparisons that I have made with you in regard to other personas that are apparently outside of you in this confusion. You are incomparable. Could the Son of God be compared with anything? What would you compare Him with but His Father, of which He is the same? It isn't that you think too much of yourself, finally; it's that you don't think enough of yourself. You limit yourself, don't you? You limit your capacity to love, through inability to accept the idea that contained in you is all of the essence of the consciousness in the universe.

Couldn't the universe love itself totally? What else does it do? Wow. Just look at what love really is. Because love apparently in the illusion of separateness appears to attempt to sustain itself, which indeed it does, does not make it less lovable. Does not God sustain Himself through you? I say to you in truth that there are finally no degrees in Godliness – that the state of beingness, the dharma, that God's will is the unity and the singularity – that there is as much Godliness in this pencil as there is in

CHAPTER NINE: Be My Valentine

anything in the universe. The universe is not the sum of its parts. Nor is my love for you the sum of adding up the various qualities that you have in order to arrive at the conclusion that you are desirable to me.

How nice it would be if you could finally figure out on the earth that everything would either be totally desirable to you or not desirable in any regard. You would then have eliminated all need to judge anything and would only love. Wow! We then finally give to each other the only Valentine that can ever really be given, and that's ourselves. As long as I hang on to any portion of my Valentine, I cannot love you completely, can I? So I give you love, and I ask nothing in return because there's nothing that you could give me in return, because it's only through the giving of my love to you that I may keep it and be loved.

How could I love if I just sat, separate from something, and allowed something to be outside of me? Indeed, love is active and it is creation. When you come to your final truth, Son of God, you will discover that you are a creator. As I stand before you now, I am actually creating you, am I not? Do you not see that it is your conception that is bringing about your perception? Are you, then, creating something hateful? Are you making something that you don't like, that you want to get rid of? Strange. Jesus in the *Course* says nicely, *protect anything that you value by giving it away.* Wow! "Well, I tried that, and it didn't work. I went out and I gave a lot of things away. I wasn't appreciated for it. The world's simply no good, and there's nothing I can do about it, so I'll get along the best I can."

The process, finally, of totally giving, or giving of self, is a process of surrender or subtraction - or *death* is a nice word for it. I am bringing about in you a death process, and you'll still be here after its completion. Isn't that astonishing? Boy, that's a fun idea. There is no death, brother. If there were such a thing as death, how could there be love? Would you simply love something then until it dies? Then find something else to love, and struggle in turmoil. Wow.

Where do you find unity then? Where do you find this truth? In you. The universe finally is only your idea about it. How much do you finally love? What did you reject today as not desirable? How much did you protect yourself today from the projections, from your illusions? *The quality of mercy is not strained.* That's very nice. Sounds familiar. It's here all the time. Are you, then, a good receiver of the gifts? Be my Valentine. "I'm not going to give you a Valentine this year. I gave you one last year, and you didn't give me one back, and I'll always remember that." All of your grievances, everything that you're holding on to in the past tense – none of it is real. None of it!

For the first time – and I don't mean to think of time as sequential, but in this particular fabric or in this moment, we are attempting to teach the "illusion," and perhaps that's a word we'll use in this regard – the Atonement or the changing of the mind or the resurrection is totally subjective, and depends absolutely on you to bring it about, and that there's nothing outside of you that'll cause it. That's a very difficult idea for you, isn't it? The idea that you are responsible, finally, in your state of consciousness for bringing about peace and glory and heaven and the subtraction of pain are very difficult for you. But you stop and think just for a moment. If you're in a state of consciousness – and I assure you you are because you say you are – I believe that you think you're you, but you can't tell me who *you* are – it is going to become more simple for you to accept the idea of maturation, that you are awakening from a dream, that you are coming back to an original origin. There's absolutely nothing new about this idea. It's as old as man and always occurs in revelation.

I'm going to express this to you: Any attempts I make to teach you what occurred to me in revelation are forms of corruption. I say to you that there are quotes in *A Course In*

CHAPTER NINE: Be My Valentine

Miracles that are virtually identical to the great Pagan mystic Plotinus, neo-Platonism, or the Christian mystic Meister Eckhart, or more directly Meher Baba – Meher Baba has some quotes in *A Course In Miracles* – or me. It should finally begin to occur to you, on a direct intercession of consciousness that has occurred through scribeship from a different level of consciousness contained in *A Course In Miracles,* that there's one heck of a lot more to you than you have allowed up to this point. For goodness sake. That's what we're bringing about here. It's kind of difficult for you to understand that the only requirement there is, is that you come to your truth. There are no other requirements. Wake up! Wake up! Your creations await you. The tear in the fabric has been repaired. You're dreaming. This is all over.

It is difficult to feel love when you're being attacked by someone, isn't it? I just looked at the dilemma of consciousness where people who want to love are in villages where it seems like they're being constantly attacked and misunderstood. It requires a certain endeavor or determination. Faith maybe is the word. Trust. Make the commitment to eternal life or to the idea that there is no death. It is impossible for you to fail, so you be of good cheer.

Do you know something? As you get further and further along on this path, rejection won't bother you in the slightest. That's tough. It's very difficult to teach an initiate this, particularly when they get to a point where they're very sensitive, and they really want to love and they can't understand why they're rejected and why there's so much greed and corruption on earth. For me to say to them, "That's because that's the way that the world is," is difficult. They keep thinking that there must be something outside of themselves that will finally commiserate in totalness with the conclusion they have temporarily arrived at about themselves.

Finally, when you wake up, you will discover that you are absolutely, totally indifferent to what anybody on earth says.

Why? Because you know it's not real. The intensity with which the identifications protect themselves is insane. Of course. I'm going to tell you something though. Once you discover the truth for yourself, and it doesn't make any difference to you, you will then begin to extend from you the truth of what you are. You discover that you are me. Who do you think is standing up here doing this? What do you think Brother Jesus finally means when He says in the *Course In Miracles* that God only has one Son? No wonder I love you so much. No wonder I give you everything. Why wouldn't I? What would I hold onto? Nobody can give completely as long as they have a feeling of lack in them.

It's impossible for you to love anyone absolutely until you are love yourself. But you've all had your beautiful moments. The moonlight shining on the lake, the bark of a dog in the distance, the wind rustling through the pines, the pungent smell of mustard plant in the meadow; discovering just a tiny wildflower growing out of a crevice in a rock, a big swallowtail in the morning grass, the incredible feeling of lonely nostalgia when an ancient melody plays in your heart. What else would you finally be but divine? Those moments that you feel of completeness and ecstasy and serenity are part of your heritage. They are the real you. So it will be with you; so it is each moment that you allow it to be – not in preparations for tomorrow or next week or next year, a continuation of a limited idea about yourself, rather coming at this moment into what you really are, discovering through your surrender, through your non-defensiveness the invulnerability of the power that is you.

The species man has a covenant that has been fulfilled, and awaits your return to complete Heaven. That's the only requirement. Happy Valentine's Day! How good a receiver are you? How well can you finally see that it's the giving, and not the object. Sometimes it's a nice process when somebody does something thoughtful in their love for you – and I assure you that you're loved – you look very quickly at the thought that

CHAPTER NINE: Be My Valentine

went into them doing that and how they went out and bought it, and thought about it, and planned to give it to you, and looked forward with the expectation of you wanting it. That's the beginning of it, isn't it? True receivers are always very humble because they understand that a giver finally gives through love. That's very lovely.

I accept your gift when you give it to me because I recognize you as the Son of God. I see you creating me in your gift to me. And in my acceptance of your love have I extended mine to you. And indeed there is no difference between giving and receiving, or ever could be.

"I give to you as you give to me, true love, true love." How beautiful are the words that come from the mind of man. Where else in the universe would words or ideas come from except from the mind of man? Are you mindful of your divinity today? Did you act as the Son of God today? I'm teaching a review at the end of the day. Run a quick tape of the day in your mind and say, "I didn't get it quite right this time, but hang on, am I forgiven?" And a big voice will say, "Oh, yeah, you're forgiven." Why don't you go out and make some big mistakes? I'll forgive you for those, too. But you remember this: You can't fool me. I am the truth, and I say that you can't fool me. I have no rationale. I will not finally reason with you. What would you hide from me? I know you. When you begin to do that, you'll have a feeling of cleanness about you. It isn't necessary that you go out and make reparations for things that you have done or imagined wrongs. Forgiveness is of the heart. Are you then afraid to go to the altar and reveal what you really think about yourself? Of course you're afraid. That's why you're here.

You take my hand. We'll go together. I'll take you right up there. When we get up to the last spot, I'll give you a shove and push you right through, and your dream will be over and you'll wake up Home. And you'll go, "Oh, I was dreaming." All of you have had intense dreams that seemed so real to you, and then suddenly you awaken and they are very vivid in your mind, "Oh, I was dreaming." That's what will happen to you when you discover the unreality of the earth. It'll be just like that. You'll go, "Oh!" For many of you, that's occurring now. The more you come into that, the more it comes about. I'd like to have some quiet time.

Good morning. This is another day. It's actually two days after Valentine's Day, but Valentine's Day is every day that you allow it to be, isn't it, through your giving of your Valentine. Somebody said that they felt foolish, and that's what we're going to talk about just for a moment here, because when you're in love, you act in a very foolish manner, don't you. There's nothing finally practical about love. The moment that you make love practical, it's like trying to make God practical. There's absolutely nothing practical about God. How could there be? God is totally impractical. Everything that genius finally teaches, or master recognition teaches, will always be foolish to natural man, and that includes love or the idea of total love. The idea of total love implies abandonment, or the giving up to the one that you adore – the extension of your total self to that so-called object or that so-called image or that perception.

There is no practicality, there's no rationale in God, finally. He's a burning fire within you that needs to be expressed. That's what you do, all day long. You walk around, attempting to express this joy, this incredible abundance that's in you. What is love, then? Well, we've looked at a lot of things that love isn't. Obviously, love is never a form of exchange in any regard, is it? Love is never objective; it cannot be. Love finally is never exclusive, and cannot be. So we have arrived at a lot of ideas about what love is not.

Now, what is love? Let's come a little closer to it. Love, obviously, is an experience. You agree with that. Would you then agree with me that God is an experience? Since we are in a fundamental agreement that God cannot be defined, that truth

CHAPTER NINE: Be My Valentine

cannot be circumscribed, that love can only be experienced, shouldn't we then be about experiencing it? At what point have you, in these three days that have passed since the last talk, gone out and been very exclusive in your relationships? Remember that you suffer from a fatal disease called LP. That's Limited Perception. You are going to die because of it. I saw in the paper this morning that one of the Russian leaders is terminally ill. Everyone on earth is terminally ill. Did you think that? I mean, everybody on earth is obviously diseased. They have acknowledged, through their limited perception, the incredible, insane idea of termination. So obviously what's going to occur to them? They're going to be terminated. And with that termination will go their idea of love because their idea of love was limiting. And by limiting themselves, they have limited their innate ability to create, which is really all that love is.

Love is finally my total recognition that I'm making you up, and, by gosh, I better love you. To the direct extent I do not love you, I obviously could not love myself. The greatest admonition that a Christ can ever give is *Love the Lord thy God with all they might and thy neighbor or thy friend or thy brother as thyself.* Exoteric Christianity and being-born-again saviors to the contrary, you cannot love Christ without loving your brother, and the idea that you can is absurd. This is the whole basis of what we teach in *A Course In Miracles*. Of course it's much easier to love God from afar. It's easier to love, to respect, to idolize a guru in a white sheet sitting on the top of the mountain peak, and you can go and visit him, but you don't have to totally identify with him. With your brother you must totally identify. That's why until you find the Christ within you or in your brother, you can never find Him.

Is love, then, a search? Oh, yes! Ah. It's a delightful anticipation of fulfillment, isn't it? Sentences like *I am love* are very true. *The Father and I are one. I am that I am.* Of course. When you have experienced that moment – and all of you here have in moments of fulfillment – they are indelible in your consciousness as peak experiences. We teach in truth that when you transcend or change your mind or resurrect or are saved or are enlightened, you will live and extend from you a constant state of ecstasy – but ecstasy not defined as the opposite of pain, but only as truth or love. Did we get that? That's pretty much there. Which is much the same thing as saying, when you reach that state you will accept everything totally.

There's a point I want to make here. I understand very well that in your projections, when you look at something beautiful, you must judge it as more beautiful than something else. This is an inevitable process. Following your transcendence, what you experience is total self-love, or forgiveness of self, or non-guilt, which gives you a parameter by which you judge everything and love it subsequently. For example, if somebody said, "Do you see a poisonous viper as beautiful as a bouquet of roses?" they are speaking from a position where there is an implication that beauty is not finally a single thing. You remember this in consciousness: Everything is perfect unto itself except you. Can you hear that? You're the insane one. Do you think that that rose is not perfect unto itself? Do you think that that snake is not filled with total self love? Of course it is! Is the leaf on the tree not adorable to itself? Does a rock not churn with the molecules of identification of itself as granite? Of course it does! It knows perfectly well who it is, and it is fulfilling itself. *You* are the fault. You're the one that's schismed. You're the one that doesn't know who he is. Wow! Wow! You got that? Good. No wonder we teach: *To thine own self be true*, you dummies. If you can't figure that out, how could you ever go outside yourself and find it? You can't.

Now, the subtle difference that occurs in consciousness if you allow for hierarchies is this: The rock knows it is a rock, but it does not know that it is you. You may know that you are you and also the rock. For, indeed, if you are not the rock, you

CHAPTER NINE: Be My Valentine

are nothing, because there is nothing outside of truth, which is totalness. Do you see? There is only a state of consciousness. There is nothing else. That's why you can only define yourself as "I am I." There is nothing outside of you. You are the rock. You are the plant. You are the sunset. You are the rich brown earth that we will harvest from. What else would you be but those things? And I don't mean that you feel like a tree. I mean that you *are* a tree. A little difference there. You know, people walk around and they will feel this energy come up into their throats and they'll glance and they'll see a large porker in a pig pen, and say, "Oh, I can feel that big sow rooting around in the mud. I feel just like it." And that's a great truth. Or you'll talk to the trees, and you feel as though they're talking back. And that's a very real thing. After your final transcendence you have no identity as being separate from the pig, so you can't possibly identify your pigness. Ha! Ha! Ha! I wish I could express this. Do you understand? You become the tree and the pig. That's really what love is, isn't it? Those of you who have experienced real union in mating, when you come together, you can't tell the difference in each other. Of course not. You mate – I'm not recommending that you necessarily mate with a pig! Excuse me! See, everybody immediately tries to go out and act within the limited frame of reference. No. No, no. Love does not have to do with what I'm speaking of; love has nothing to do with that. All that is, are attempts to sustain limited consciousness.

Love defined in limitation will always attempt, after self-identification, to perpetuate a degree of consciousness. That's what the survival of the fittest is; that's what cause and effect are, isn't it? When you overcome that, you will see that indeed you are love and nothing but that. That's pretty much our Valentine's Day talk of love. So how do you feel today? Lovable? Is it possible to feel unlovable for a moment and still be in grace? You bet your boots! In fact, feeling unlovable is exactly the same as feeling lovable. Can't teach that. We'll try. At a particular stage of perception, in order to feel lovable you must have a moment of unlovability. Do you see? I feel totally lovable now, but just a moment ago I didn't feel lovable. When you become totally lovable, you can't distinguish between unlovableness and lovableness. Of course, because you can't judge it. That's how I know that I love you totally. I don't judge you at all. Wow! That's great highs. Get this, and you'll understand what we teach.

I cannot love you because of your qualities. In my own mind in schism, if I allow lovableness to be a quality, there's an obvious insinuation that there is something unlovable, and that's a fallacy. Everything is lovable. Finally you come to know there are no degrees of love. When you come to know that, you'll remember everything. You'll return to your creative posture. Jesus in *A Course In Miracles*: *Your creations await your return*. How long have you been gone? Just a second. You were gone and you're back. You're not really gone. You haven't really left. You haven't really gone anywhere. This is Heaven. Where would you go? Where can you go to find love? "I'll journey across the universe. I'll climb the highest mountain, go to the deepest valley in search of my true love." Everywhere you go, you are. If you stay here, you are everywhere.

I think finally we might say that love, like truth and God and completeness, cannot be described, but simply *is*. Sort of like when you're in it, you know you're in it. All we really teach finally is eternal love, because everything that is not eternal is not real. That's what we teach. Fear is death. If you believe you can die, you cannot love. You will simply commiserate. We are here to tell you that you cannot die and must finally be total love. That's all.

You listen to me carefully. We're adding another word to what love finally, really is: It's freedom. All love on earth binds. Because of your limited state of consciousness, you look for protection in relationships of love and bind yourself to that because of fear. So what you really have is love/fear, or love/

CHAPTER NINE: Be My Valentine

hate. If you want to measure your degree of love for someone who apparently is outside of yourself, judge the extent to which you release him. To what extent do you hold on to them because you think you can *have* love rather than *be* love? The highest truth that I can give to you is that you can *have* nothing because you *are* everything. You cannot finally *have* love because you *are* love. If you want a so-called love relationship on earth to be absolutely successful and absolutely perfect and without deviation and without any elements that are untrue, all you need do is give yourself to it totally. Anything that ever could be lacking in what you construe as a love relationship is what you do not bring to that relationship. Period. Does that answer your questions about relationships, dear brother? That's why all love relationships on earth are compromises, aren't they? You don't know yourself, and they don't know themselves, so you get together and don't know yourselves together. How close is love to hate on earth? Right next to it. How close is love to fear on earth? Right next to it. How close is life to death? Right here, brother. Amen. Thank you.

Why wait for Heaven?
Those who seek the light
are merely covering their eyes.
The light is in them now.
Enlightenment is but a recognition,
not a change at all.
Light is not of the world,
yet you who bear the light in you
are alien here as well.

CHAPTER TEN

The Bright Lights Are Heaven

All of the so-called spiritual teachings or religions will only be this. They will literally be nothing but *A Course In Miracles*. The teaching will attempt to get you to look at your impossible situation of perceptual self-identity and to undergo the experience of the transformation of your mind to the reality of what you are. That's all that religion is. Does everybody see that?

What we are doing here is attempting to communicate with reality. Listen. This is not a real place. There is no communication going on in your mind, in your perceptual associations. The Zen of this is to distract you sufficiently from your frigging past and future to allow you to undergo the Holy Instant.

I'll read you a little bit of one of the great Zen masters, who helped with the first 25 lessons of *A Course In Miracles*. He's right here! You see, Zen is the Buddhist communication with God, which is the active participation of the existential consciousness coming to his reality. Right? Mohammedanism is called Sufism – it's all the same. It'll be exactly the same. I want to show you that you ought to start communicating with God. Throw the book away. It's doing you no good at all. It's nothing! It'll only just keep saying the same thing, over and over and over. Do you see? That's amazing.

This is a lovely little enlightened book, *The Enlightened Heart*, that the Dallas Church gave to me. Listen to this. About the Sixth Century. Seng-ts'an: *The Great Way isn't difficult for those who are unattached to their preferences.* It says it's not difficult for those that are not attached to their preferences! *Let go of longing and aversion, and everything will be perfectly clear. When you cling to a hairbreadth of distinction, heaven and earth are set apart. If you want to realize the truth, don't be for or against.* This is the first 20 lessons of the *Course*. He wrote this. *If you want to realize the truth, don't be for or against. The struggle between good and evil is the primal disease of the mind.* He says it's a disease. It's a schizophrenia, isn't it, the struggle in identification of judgmental association. There are no neutral thoughts, so you're in this struggle of self-identity and you hold on to it. *Not grasping the deeper meaning, you just trouble your mind's serenity. As vast as infinite space, it is perfect and lacks nothing.* That's Jesus' definition of the mind. *But because you select and reject, you can't perceive its true nature. Don't get entangled in the world; don't lose yourself in nothingness. Be at peace in the oneness of things, and all errors will disappear by themselves.* Really?!

If you don't live the Tao, you fall into assertion and denial. Asserting that the world is real, you are blind to its deeper reality; denying that the world is real, you are blind to the selflessness of all things. Wow! *The more you think about these matters, the further you are from the truth. Step aside from all thinking, and there is nowhere you can't go.*

CHAPTER TEN: The Bright Lights Are Heaven

It's one of the most beautiful sentences there ever could be, because stepping aside from all thinking doesn't drive you into some sort of "Mmmm." You step aside from all thinking, and there's nowhere you can't go because you can go anywhere in the universe. You see? That's the teachings of the *Course* and of this. *Returning to the root –* Atonement *– you find the meaning; chasing appearances, you lose their source. At the moment of profound insight you transcend both appearance and nothingness. Don't keep searching for the truth; just let go of your opinions.*

For the mind in harmony with the Tao, all selfishness disappears. With not even a trace of self-doubt, you can trust the universe completely. All at once you are free, with nothing left to hold on to. All is empty, brilliant, perfect in its own being. In the world of things as they are, there is no self, no non-self. This is like there's no Holy Spirit and ego. *If you want to describe its essence, the best you can say is "Not-two."* This is the whole *Course In Miracles*: Not-two. That's as close as you can get to it. That's what the *Course* teaches, not-two, single. You can't get it by a declaration of singularity because it contains the perceptual observation. The beginning and end of the first 25 lessons of the *Course* are not-two, "There's nothing outside of me. I don't know who I am. I can come to know by examining myself because there is only one." *In this "Not-two" nothing is separate, and nothing in the world is excluded. The enlightenment of all times and places have entered into this truth.* Holy Instant! *In it there is no gain or loss; one instant is ten thousand years. There is no here, no there; infinity is right before your eyes. The tiny is as large as the vast when objective boundaries have vanished; the vast is as small as the tiny when you don't have external limits.* Ready?

Being is an aspect of non-being. Notice it doesn't say that not being is an aspect of being. Once more: *Being is an aspect of non-being.* Because you are not being now. But not being is not an aspect of being. *Non-being is no different from being. Until you understand this truth, you won't see anything clearly.* You'll keep trying to judge it. All it's really saying is you can only be you, no matter what you do. You understand?

One is all; all are one. When you realize this, what reason for holiness or wisdom? The mind of absolute trust is beyond all thought, all striving, is perfectly at peace, for in it there is no yesterday, no today, no tomorrow. That's nice stuff. What is this teaching? This is the teaching of the Workbook of the *Course.* Stop associating with yourself. You continue to do it. Somehow you think you're going to figure this out within your own association. It has nothing to do with reality at all. Why? The world isn't real. There's no sense in discussing it with me. The whole teaching is, if there is a wholeness and perfection, where you are in this association is no-thing. You're just caught in your own drama of self-exposure. You're just walking around, teaching your-self your own associations. Do you see?

Don't you see, it has to be transformation? The teaching is to the transformative mind that will be more inclusive in its self-identity. What part of this becomes unacceptable? Two things. First of all, it's the Jesus Christ declaration of non-establishment. That's not acceptable. Secondly, it will be a declaration of physical awakening, literally – that's what's happening here – which will cause an assertion, particularly in Christianity, of Whole Mind Christ identity. If there's one thing establishment is not going to tolerate, it's you having a mystical experience of Christ Self-identity. It will cause what? A transcendence of your association with the establishment. Now, once you begin to experience this awakening of your mind, you will find verification for all of the efforts to hide the illumination that is actually occurring all over the world.

There's a concerted effort by perception to deny illumination. That's why you're here. This is why you burn them

CHAPTER TEN: *The Bright Lights Are Heaven*

at the stake. This is why Jesus says if you can find the Christ, you'll kill him. That's literally so. Why? Because with that experience you lose your fear of God. And you'll begin to say very strange things, like Meister Eckhart, standing in the pulpit, "God needs me as much as I need him." He's liable to say, "God's eye is my eye." He sees his own wholeness. He admits to his own holiness. He isn't caught up in himself.

One more poem – this is a Christian poem. There's a guy – it's right here – named Symeon, the New Theologian, about the Tenth Century. He was Greek, and an Abbot. He taught experience. Listen to what he says here: *We awaken in Christ's body as Christ awakens our bodies, and my poor hand is Christ, He enters my foot, and is infinitely me. I move my hand, and wonderfully my hand becomes Christ, all of Him (for God is indivisibly whole, seamless in His Godhood). I move my foot, and at once He appears like a flash of lightning. Do my words seem blasphemous? – Then open your heart to Him and let yourself receive the one who is opening to you so deeply. Course In Miracles!* For if we genuinely love Him, we wake up inside Christ's body. If we can really love Him, we wake up inside Christ's body... It's an astonishing sentence! ...*where all our body, all over, every most hidden part of it, is realized in joy as Him, as He makes us, utterly, real, and everything that is hurt, everything that seemed to us dark, harsh, shameful, maimed, ugly, irreparable damaged, is in Him transformed and recognized as whole, as lovely, and radiant in His light we awaken as the Beloved in every last part of our body.*

The last 13 years of his life, he was exiled to a small seaport by the Archbishop. And you like this place? You think that he would be allowed as an abbot in the Christian tradition to teach what he just taught? Don't be absurd. It's a very fearful idea that you're undergoing a transformation of your mind, that Christ is in you, that you will have the mystical experience of the awakening at Gesthemane of the coming into the resurrection of you. It's frightening. It frightens everybody here. You're afraid of it.

    Why? You've been taught it's death. Quite literally, you've been taught, if you part that veil, you'll die. Remember in the *Course* where Jesus says that? "Don't look up. Don't do that." (Chapter 19) You'll protect yourself from that. Why? This is the experience of illumination. This is experience of awakening. And it's fearful to you. Yet what alternative do you have to it? I've told you about it now. You can go gnash your teeth if you want to, but it's too late. All you're going to do is defend your own death. And you'll walk out of here, and next week you'll be standing there, doing something completely futile, it will have absolutely no meaning, you'll be caught up in your own junk, and you'll say, "Why the hell am I doing this?" Then you're making progress. And everybody around you will say, "That's okay, stay here and fight with us." And you'll say, "I don't see the sense in that. This is becoming less and less sensible to me." It's not a discipline. "I'm just beginning to look at it for what it really is, and I've never done it before. I sat here and I said that 10,000 babies starved to death last night, and there's absolutely nothing I can do about it, and something is wrong with that. I'm in a place where these terrible things are happening, and I have no control over them, and I'm frustrated by it. I want to know what the answer to it is, and everywhere I look, there is no answer to it. I have become convinced of what? The answer isn't here." Now you're making progress. Why? How in the hell would the answer be here? If sickness and death and pain are real, who the hell is going to answer it? Come on. This is the whole teaching. If it's real, you're just caught in the dilemma of that association. Don't you see?

    Look at how unequivocating the teachings of a master mind are in regard to mortals and eternity – if you really did Lesson 76. You don't like it. There's no part about Lesson 76 you wouldn't

CHAPTER TEN: *The Bright Lights Are Heaven*

defend yourself from. That's why you're here. Now, I know you're going to do that, but I want to show you that through the practice of the release of the necessity for your thought form experience in time that you can undergo this transformation of mind. That's the miracle, isn't it? That's the change of your mind in regard to the perceptual death associations that you have established outside of you. Do you see? All teachings of religion are teachings to the experience of the transforming mind. Know ye not ye must be born again. (John 3:3) Without exception. Anything except that, if you'd care to look at it, would only be a perceptual association in time and death. I don't understand why that's hard.

The vehicle of communication with God is prayer. The teaching of the Workbook is to pray unceasingly. We were in a high condition of prayer when we played the Lou Waters Jazz Band. You have a tendency to doctrinize prayer, which is pure crap. You have a tendency to demand specific associations with God in regard to the benefit you will derive in your limited existence, and you wonder why God doesn't hear you, when the whole teaching is to listen to Lou Waters. But somewhere you're going to reject that as not a part of your own domain of ecclesiasticism or whatever you're determined to do in your self-assertion of telling God what He is, rather than what? Let Him be! You're very determined that you're going to bring your perceptual associations with God here. And you're wrong.

You know what's strange to me? The manner in which you prove you're right. Did you ever look at that, ex-Lieutenant Colonel, whatever the hell you think you are? You bring your credentials in to me, and I just laugh at you. Any credential you could possibly give me would only verify your heart attack, you dummy, which I'm just trying to keep you from having here. Don't have one. You guys are determined to have heart attacks. You're taking all sorts of stuff. Preventative medicine is one sure way to die. Whoops, be careful here. You'll say I told you not to take your pills. I did not. I'm telling you that cause and effect aren't apart. Nothing describes the disease better than the remedy. Seems strange, but obviously it would have to. So don't get sick anymore, all right?

If you can't die, there's no sense in getting old. There's no sense in what? Holding on to your self-identity. Sure in hell you're going to have a heart attack. Why? George down the street had one and you didn't. Weird. Weird. "Well, I'm not going to have that, I'm going to get cancer instead; I'm going to die of something else." You're determined to hold on to the existence until it falls apart. You love death. You love sickness and death. You are absolutely dependent on it. It's the one thing you can be sure of here.

And I'm coming to tell you the one thing you can be sure of is eternity and God. You insist that the one thing you can be sure of is death and disease. One of us is wrong. Isn't that so? One of us has to be wrong because if there is a God, eternal, there's no such thing as termination and disease. Why is this hard? Is it too simple? Of course. Why? Because the perceptual mind *is* the conflictual association. It has nothing to do with you being mad. It is madness that thinks that. And that's what's difficult for you. You think that you can choose between being mad and being sane, and you're wrong. Choice is madness. Could you hear that? Could you hear what I just said? This is *A Course In Miracles.* Choice is madness. The idea of choice is what madness is. You think there's a thing that can actually choose between good and evil, and you're dead wrong. This is the whole *Course.* It has to start with the impossible assumption that you can choose. It says in the first page of the *Course In Miracles* we are dealing with an impossible association because perception is not real. It says it in the first sentence. The condition that you are in is impossible. We have no alternative because decisions of the mind provide perceptual mind with choice. So we must teach you that you have a choice. Is the thing that

CHAPTER TEN: *The Bright Lights Are Heaven*

chooses real? Don't be crazy. How could a thing be separate from whole and be real? You never ask that question. What is it that makes the choice? Is the nothing the thing that must choose? The *Course In Miracles*, the Atonement, says yes. But then it must choose once. And did. The moment that the idea of separation entered your mind, I came and told you it was crap. *I* did. I came and told *you* that you're in your dream and you're not going to get away with this because I was here with you in time and it just doesn't work. That's what I'm here to tell you. Isn't that so?

Who else is going to tell you this? No one. Do you understand this? It has nothing to do with who's telling you. Can you hear me? I don't know whether you guys hear this. It's the principle of the declaration of wholeness. It doesn't have to do with being an ex-Lieutenant. It has nothing to do with perceptions at all. Do you think that I have credentials to teach you what I'm teaching you? That's the craziest thing I ever heard. I know you think I do. Somehow you're going to give me an identity. I watch you do it. The teaching is the relinquishment of identity. All whole minds teach non-identity, for goodness sake. Isn't that so? Sure!

You're tired of being little. I was tired of looking at the stars and being told I could never go there, or that I would have to suffer pain and death, to live a thousand lifetimes in order to get it. That's crap to me. My question would always be, if I know about it, why can't I do it now? "That star is 100,000 light years from now, and this one is 3,000 million years away, and you can never know about the myriads of civilizations in time because you're confined to a body and can never get there. And millions of years are past and your life span is only 70 years." You like that? Then you be that.

You know where I got caught? When I saw there wasn't any more than that, I kept killing myself. Which is what you're doing. But I couldn't get away with it, finally. It didn't solve the problem. Everyone who comes here is only suicidal. Is there a question on this? Obviously, you came here to die, and you're making that choice. You may do it in a lot of different ways, but you're choosing it. Sometimes in this association it gets so frustrating, there's no purpose in it at all, you cut your wrists, and you are standing right there, doing the same damn thing. I'm encouraging you to have that experience right now so you can be here doing some better things, so you can be doing some whole things. Why? You can never leave here. This is Lesson 131. You can never leave here. This is the only thing you'll ever do. You say, "Oh, yes I can. I'll prove to you you're wrong. I'm going to get up and go out and stay with all the other things I've been doing." Well, that's nothing. That's no-thing. The closest you can ever get to doing everything is doing it right now, as we sit here, isn't it?

Can you actually come together and bring all of your thought forms into this, which is what this "body" is, a bag of memories, into a reassociation and spring to a new reality? That would be a miracle, wouldn't it? Who is it that observes it and denies it? There's a lot of phenomena going on in this room right now that I could show you, but I don't want to because you'll just take it as phenomena. You see? It's hard to teach this.

The resurrection is going on right now. Literally. Missed it again. Literally, it's going on now. Listen to me. It's all that's happening. No matter what you do with the thought forms in hell, nothing is happening. You can organize it in a thousand different ways. You can take all the separate parts of it and put it together, but you will never get the whole. It's impossible. You've already separated it. Come on. You're in perceptual mind and somehow you're going to fit this together and get the solution without including yourself? You can't. You call it objective reality. I'm teaching quantum here. You're caught in Newtonian Physics. You've got to include yourself in the equation. But if you do, your perceptions will disappear, and you'll be nothing.

CHAPTER TEN: *The Bright Lights Are Heaven*

It's what I'm trying to get you to do – be inclusive. "Well, how will I know who I am?" You won't have to. You'll be everything! That's what I'm trying to get you to do. You stay outside your own Akashic Record. Why? If you went into your record, you'd be lost. Space/time would disappear. So you hold the tension of your thought forms and feel the pain of it. You're crazy. That's the whole teaching. Don't do that anymore.

You think that somehow you have to have qualifications to have that experience. So you will inquire of me, "What did you go through in order to get this?" There's no way that I can communicate that to you because you are designed not to communicate except by your own limitations of self-identity in order to verify what you think is your own awakening. Isn't that so? That's exactly what you're doing; that is exactly what happened when Jesus Christ rose from the dead and is in Heaven. You immediately question the method by which He did it. That's why you're here. It took the admission of the resurrection rather than the manner in which it occurred, because religion is a teaching of association of perception with God, and that's a manner of self-expression which is not real.

It's the judgment of the temple, isn't it? It's the judgment of the association of the laws of man. You are under no laws but God's. From the very beginning you've been taught an infinite number of laws that you must adhere to you in your own mind: right and wrong, stop when the light is red, go when it's green. Don't jump in front of trucks. Don't hold firecrackers. Don't touch the stove, it's hot. What is associated with it? Your self identity in the body. "Protect the body and you'll be free." Jesus says protect the body and you'll be dead because at no moment is the body real. At no single moment is the body real.

Each moment you hold the body together by an association of a past frame of reference and a future conclusion in time, based on that association. Where is the now? Great perceptual left-brain mind, where is the now? You're just generating stuff out of this brain, holding it together in the thought form, and have literally covered reality, which is all around you. See? You see this? *A Course In Miracles*, Chapter 13. You actually take time, which is an association of thought forms, make it linear, and give it sequentiality. Time is not sequential. Once more: Time is not sequential. You may make it that way in your mind, but – I'm doing the exact sentence – do not believe then that it is true because it is delusional. Things that are past are past, and basing your reality on a thought that is past is absolutely meaningless. Why? The thought is past. So all you have sitting here is your past associations – since they are already gone, each moment *you* are only gone.

Come on, why is that a problem? Every moment that you're standing here in this memory, you're nothing. In order to protect your nothingness, which is already gone, you project it into a future. You lay up stores to protect what you didn't have before and had died with in order to assert your reality in sequential time. Everybody got that? This is Lesson 76, and Lessons 131 and 132. That's *you* that's doing that. It's not somebody else, you dummy. You're the one that has stored up the association of time in you, and you hold that, you identify your past with a future frame of reference. Now, can you not do that? No. Of course you're going to keep doing that. All I want you to do is have all of the thoughts at one time. That's the At-one-ment.

There's got to be something besides a beginning and an end. Why? You say there's a beginning and an end. Isn't that so? If there's a beginning and an end, there has to be something else. You can call that nothing, but it doesn't make much sense. You can say, "God and everything is nothing. Anything not in space/time is nothing." Or you can say, "Everything not in space/time is everything." If you say it's nothing, it must compare to something. If you say it's everything, it doesn't need a comparison. Pythagoras. It will simply be, won't it? You can't be non-something. It's impossible. You can't be negative. You

CHAPTER TEN: *The Bright Lights Are Heaven*

can only be totally opposed to something, and if you're totally opposed to it, you'll become it.

What's the difference between the Devil and God? Time. The Devil is time. What did you think the Devil was? Come on. It's linear time. The Devil is nothing but the idea of possibility not fulfilled, which is the self-expression of the determination to formulate yourself in your own mind. That's the Devil. That's the evil one or the separate one. What I want you to see is you don't have to do that. All around you is the reality of what? *You* in your own mind. Why? Power is singular. "Not-two", the Zen says. It doesn't make any difference what it is. It's only one. Jesus calls that forgiveness.

It makes no difference what it is – it will still be you. The acceptance of that must force you into a non-guilt association with yourself. You discover you can only give to yourself, you give everything away to yourself, and you're in Heaven creating. Do you want to analyze that sentence? All God does is give. How else does He know who He is? He doesn't give to something. He gives Himself, and that's you. You are God creating. He doesn't have a storehouse of thought forms that He creates and puts together in some sort of ingenuity of contraptual self-identity. That's what you do. Ingeniousness is not worthy of a whole Son of God. That's a nice sentence in the *Course*. (Chapter 3) Isn't that nice? You keep building better mouse traps. There's no mouse and there's no trap. Throw them away.

This is funny. You've always got a way – invention. You're going to invent something to solve an insolvable problem, because the idea of the problem is what the non-solution is. Quite literally, if the problem is real, it's not going to be solvable. You give it a reality and solve it within the method of your false association. Therefore, the problem and the solution are actually the same. In the third Chapter Jesus says, "Remember, though, that the problem cannot exceed the intent of your solution." If you seek an answer, you can only get the answer you're seeking by your definition of problems, and you don't ask the right frigging question. You keep finding the solution in your own limitation. Cut it out! Then you verify that solution in an attempt to share in a non-communicative association, since there's really no communication going on, a verification for your own limited mind construct.

These eyes do not see. All they see is memory of themselves. They cannot see anything but that. So they keep adjusting the effects, continually looking for a solution to something they have already acknowledged is outside of them. Amazing! The problem cannot be solved.

When I was really young I looked at: If dualism is real, we're screwed. I would sit down. "Let's crack one and sit together and decide if we can really communicate or not." We reached the conclusion we couldn't, except occasionally we would enter into transcendental associations. And we'd have another one, and then you really begin to transcend. It doesn't solve the problem, but at least it brought a temporary solution to the certainty the damn problem can't be solved. "Let's play darts." Play darts or something. Do something because this problem is not solvable. Or, "I'll solve it in the only fashion I can see, and die with it. I will become an old man and a grandfather, and they'll put me in a nursing home and I'll drool against the wall and die. Because that's what I did to my father."

I couldn't stand the guilt of this place. Do you know that I tried to remedy the guilt? Most of you guys that are with me do this. I couldn't stand the guilt of it. I would do everything I could; I used to go in a nursing home, "How can I help? Let me do something." You guys that are professional healers – professional meaning that you think you can exchange; you are unhealed healers – are really trying to aid the effects of your own mind. I know you are. That's how you got to me.

Somewhere you had to figure out that there's no justice here, because all I ever did was try to find a reason for this that

CHAPTER TEN: *The Bright Lights Are Heaven*

I could verify in my own mind. I wanted justice. I wanted the punishment to fit the crime. You ought to be able to hear this. I was told in jurisprudence that through the use of precedent we can arrive at a reasonable conclusion to justify the association. That's crap to me. The whole teaching of the *Course* and what I'm declaring to you is that if there's any judgment at all involved, you can never know everything about the situation, and this is what frustrated me. One guy gets 30 years for smoking pot, and the other guy pays a $100 fine, and all you say to me is, "Don't get caught smoking pot in Texas." What the hell is that? How the hell does that solve my problem? It has nothing to do with right or wrong. It has to do with the laws of man in association with the justification of the crime that's committed. It's frustrating to me. Remember this, though: Everyone must be guilty, and on this is jurisprudence based. These are the laws of man. Somebody has to be responsible for this. This can't be right. Something is wrong with this.

Here's the answer, and this comes from Jesus in the *Course*: This place is totally insane. Any justification of the association is crazy because separateness is what craziness is. The laws keep changing all the time. The laws of sickness, the laws of nutrition, the laws of companionship, the laws of love, the laws of defense. And here you are, forced to hold this together in your mind. Not any more. Don't hold them together. I came to tell you: Stop holding them together.

I went through the experience of trying to hold it together and it doesn't work. They all fell apart, and now I can sit and tell you that it doesn't work. That's how I do it. I'm not here. You ready? Nothing is here. I'm not here. You're not here. I am sure that you're not here. You are not yet quite sure that you're not here. But I want to guarantee you, I'm standing in front of you as your Master, as your Teacher in Enlightenment, to tell you that you're not here because nothing is here. See how easy it is? If nothing is here, you don't have to be concerned about it.

Jesus says, "You brought these thought forms with you to verify yourself in your association with this." Yet they all get sick and die. Do you understand me?

We all know each other perfectly well. When we come into associations, I become your teacher by the assignment of your associations with your thought forms, but it would be impossible that I don't know you perfectly out of time. How could I not know you? We are all the same associations. Some of you guys I look at and you seem real familiar because I know you. Obviously we're all genetically alike, but what am I showing you? What am I showing you to do? Remember our future association. Jesus in the *Course In Miracles* calls this the reversal of temporal order. Remember our future associations because they're just as much gone as these are. If we're out of time together, we can mount a campaign that you call saviorship and insert our light associations into the fabric of consciousness. This is what the *Course In Miracles* is, incidentally. You understand that? That's what the *Course In Miracles* did. We did that with the *Course*. And you sat here for 1000 years or 2000 years and did nothing with it. Nothing. So that's why I got this assignment. Come on!

I couldn't get one of you guys to undergo your process, quite literally. This is my occupation. It's what I do. There's nothing hard about it except the attempt to communicate with the dead ones. And that's only as difficult as the conflict itself. Remember that everything that I say to you is inherently conflictual. Because you are inherently conflictual. Don't you see? Any judgment is only conflict. And if there's one thing you can't stand, it's altruism. If there's one thing you can't stand, it is that truth is true and nothing else is true, and that there's a God and He's real and perfect. But you're going to have to accept it. You'll do all the alternatives you can to keep from knowing it, but you're going to have to accept it because it's true. I can hold you in this association – I mean literally, in my mind – if

CHAPTER TEN: *The Bright Lights Are Heaven*

you will come into the harmony of the declaration of our mutual thought forms in time. This is the whole teaching of the *Course In Miracles*. And you're right in the middle of it now. We're generating a lot of energy. See, this isn't due yet, and you get disruptive.

Think of time as a piece of cheese, Swiss Cheese, nine dimensional, and there are compartments of time, worm holes we call them, or black holes, going on all at the same time in different thought form associations, simultaneously. This is how you travel through time, incidentally. I'm not going to give that talk. I'm doing it with my head now. But see, when you hold together a particular association, you bring into that all of the thought forms, and if you get disruptive or start to leak through, you'll leak through to your other identity. Remember, you can only have one identity at a time because each identity includes everything. I want you to stay in this dream with me. Stop switching your dreams. Dream this one. I'm not talking about the experience of the observation of perceptual dream, "Oh, I remember dreaming this." Remembering is not the same as dreaming the dream in that sense. Those are thought forms. I mean that some of you undergoing this enlightenment will literally enter other associations of your mind and become other selves. Obviously it's still you. Why? There is only one such thing as you. Can you hear this?

Everything is always only you. But you can only have one thought at a time. And you can only accumulate so many thoughts in this association in time, can't you? We want to hold you in this dream, which is obviously the only dream you ever really had. You do all sorts of memories with past time, but that has nothing to do with reality. Reality is this one single memory of you, as identified, being asleep and waking up. You can define that in all sorts of ways, but your sole purpose now is to wake up and remember that this is a dream. I am here to tell you that – it is impossible that you will not do it now with me, literally.

You gave me the assignment. It has nothing to do with all the peace and joy you'll get from it. But there is a lot of peace and joy connected with it. But I can't let you escape into your own death wish again, and that's conflictual for you. But somewhere you must have told me to tell you this. Right? Well, I'm telling you. I just won't let you off the hook.

You keep saying, "Well let me off the hook with this." No. No, no, no. You're at the end of time. Do you see? If you want to get off, obviously nothing can keep you here. You now can see very plainly that you have a choice between getting sick and getting old. For you to get old is really insane. You're about as old as there is already. This consciousness is 3500 years old before it even starts. Its original experiences are very Egyptian. Should I show you that? Now it wants to know about that. I don't have to tell it about it. What it is now with those memories is very clear in my mind. We had a lot of association. I don't teach that, but this is all part of how well we know each other. And why would we not? Can we remember doing this together? Perfectly! This is all that really happened. Once you start this, everything that you look at will verify this reassociation that you're undergoing. Everything. It will become a giant allegory. It will become a giant passion of your participation in memory associations that will literally turn into a parable of enlightenment. Then all the stories that I tell you about how we came to earth together and broke our communications, which is what really happened, will make sense to you, because you're entering in totally to the reassociation of your mind with reality. Come on!

The reason that I do this better than anyone else is that I have no self-identity. I am only your self-identity as you're determined to hold me in my place. That's why I'm here. I'm giving you no doctrine at all. I'm giving you no discipline, except you ought to sit still for a minute and go to God. I'm not offering you any advice about our associations. I'm not giving you nutritional advice. I'm not doing anything. I'm reflecting back

CHAPTER TEN: *The Bright Lights Are Heaven*

to you what I know that you are in the certainty of my own mind. That's the miracle.

In the *Course* Jesus says that the most advanced teachers know that He's everywhere. I'll use that sense. Obviously I know I'm everywhere because everything is everywhere. That's where we are, everywhere. By freeing your mind, you can go anywhere. I just read you that from the Zen. Anywhere you want to go, you'll be. Now, at that point you might say, "Gee, I think I'll stay here. I'm very grateful for finding this out and I feel the need to tell somebody about this." Perhaps you'll do that.

This is not a real place. What does Jesus say? You relate to these shadowy figures – this shadowy figure. That's not a shadowy figure. That's a big, bright light. See that? Was that a healing that occurred there? Sure. It was perfect. Will that be observed by the consciousness in its new association? I don't know. But it's whole. The reason that it can't die is that it's only here for a moment. You see? This body is nothing but a total association of an accumulation of Holy Instants. It's what I'm trying to get you to do – bring those together in your mind, and you'll just stay here until you vault out of time. It's what you're doing. See, we have to hold you at this jumping off place. Isn't that so? When you decide you want that, you'll put away your toys and you'll say, "Hey, I'm going to climb the hill. I'm going to wait on the Lord."

The reason Dayton is hearing us so well is there's a lot of Quakers there who taught, "Wait on the Lord," and underwent the experience of quaking, for which they were persecuted and condemned and all the other things that go with physical awakenings, which are not tolerated. But many of them have pacifistic attitudes – so many of you do – or nondefensiveness, which is the whole teaching of Jesus: Don't defend yourself from your own associations. That's the whole teaching. In other words, don't have an opinion about it. That causes what? If you're in this mandala association it will cause enlightenment, quite literally. This is the same idea as, "Hang around the Old Man." If you're dumb enough not to see that there's light all around you, just go on out and do what you were doing. I would suggest that you hang around the source of your energy association. Your denial of it is not going to avail you. But you will not do it until what? As Jesus would say, until you have the experience. Once you begin to have the experience, which is the whole purpose of the *Course In Miracles*, you will begin to want it and you will begin to teach to the mind transformation. You're not going to go around and present yourself as an ex-so-and-so who knew the dead scribe. That has literally nothing to do with the *Course In Miracles*. The whole basis of the teaching is: Become non-perceptual in your associations. Isn't this so?

Are there any *Course In Miracles* groups teaching the *Course?* Not until you start doing it. Don't be absurd. They're just studying their associations with it. That hasn't anything to do with the *Course*. The *Course* is a course in enlightenment – *your* enlightenment. What's your sole responsibility? Accept Atonement for yourself. The reason I got away from the *Course* a little bit is that you guys get your butts tied up with specific personalities that apparently teach the *Course*. They have nothing to do with the *Course* at all. Why? The earth has nothing to do with the *Course*. It is not that they are specifically in non-accord. It's that they are not real. That's the whole teaching. That's the basis of the teaching. Jesus says, so succinctly, we get out of concepts as soon as we can. The whole idea is that the concepts are what are causing the problem. Now, they will look you right in the eye and say, "This conceptual association of forgiving my brother and forming new relationships is very valuable to me." That's good, but it has nothing to do with reality. Nothing. It only has to do with their determination to structure in their mind their own death sequence.

Whenever I mention names you have a tendency to think that I am giving that a specific sense of value and you are dead

CHAPTER TEN: *The Bright Lights Are Heaven*

wrong! I am just showing you the source or the association of that form and giving you identity of where it occurs. All identity is false. You have a tendency to separate the cause and effect and believe that somebody, through a perceptual genetic association, can inform you better about what you are. Watch them do that. "How long have you been doing the *Course?*" Well, I've been doing it for forty thousand years. How about a million years? How long can you really do the *Course?* Just a moment! If I do Lesson 131, it will literally say, "Today is the day that you went out of time." Now, if you get to 132 it obviously means that you didn't go out on 131. You hear people say, "I've been through it five times, and it doesn't give me as much benefit as it used to. So now I'm seeking something else." Isn't that funny? In parsecs it would be about 2948 – at that time, all we ever got to read was the preamble of the Text, and everybody springs into Heaven. Do you understand that? They're ready to hear it. We could do it with sky-writing: "God is Love" in all languages. And everybody goes, "Oh! God is Love!" Wungo! They're gone. Not, "What does he mean by God, and what does he mean by Love?" Which is nothing but your own thought form associations, isn't it? Where? Deeper in memory, deeper in potential that needs to be fulfilled. Earlier in time.

When did the great reversal occur? Instantaneously! To you it seems like time. So I give you the term reversal – I'll give you three, I'll give you in, being there, and out. You're somewhere in there. The deeper you are in your potential, the more time it's going to take for you to use up your own black hole. Do you understand me? To become a quasar. Each galaxy has a black hole, which is nothing but potential of that galaxy, which is this. All memory is nothing but a black hole, a female, isn't it – an unfulfilled potential that needs to be what? Liberated from its self-associations as it returns. Why? Because no matter how much you impact staticness – this is the way Jesus teaches it – it still will contain the whole thing. It doesn't make any difference. It's a glitch in eternity. But the glitch, which is nothing but what you're doing now, must have in that potential all of the enlightenment of eternity. Time is nothing but the fulfillment of your potential. That's discussed as Mother Earth, the impregnation of the Virgin, the coming of the Spirit, all the things that go with the theology. But obviously earth is potential, or cyclicalness, or evolution, isn't it? What am I doing? I'm teaching mutation – revolution of mind.

This is *A Course In Miracles*. It's impossible to get this too early. Now, granted you're at a very minimal association of space/time, that is, you're deep in crap, aren't you? You think you have a lot of potential still to use up. What am I really doing? Getting you to use it up by activating your creative potential mind. We are not equal in time. There's no reason why you can't write a symphony at five, but you think there is. Do you understand me? You call that "genius" and say, "I cannot do that," because you're held in your perceptual self-identity. Do you see? Obviously, when the symphony appears to Mozart, it appears as a whole thing. He doesn't delineate it in his necessity to hold his perceptual mind together. A creative mind is only self-expression. Isn't this so? I am teaching you creative self-expression. Now, if I declare to you you are the Christ or Whole Mind Savior, and you believe me, you will begin to create as a Whole Mind. Did you know that? How would you not? You are a Whole Mind.

You have a tendency to disassociate it because your passion frightens you. Jesus says, "Let's face it, you're afraid you'll kill yourself with your own mind." And you will. And you do. I'm telling you that's okay because it's only your own mind. Do you hear me? This will release your capacity to formulate, to self-express. Really, that's what you experience around these high teachers – the release of your own mind. That's what I want you to do. I don't want to take anything away from you. You are ashamed of your own self-associations. There's nothing more immoral than the passion of coming to God. Nothing.

CHAPTER TEN: *The Bright Lights Are Heaven*

There's nothing more immoral than unconditional love. Why? It doesn't have any moral conditions. It doesn't have judgmental associations. This is why you crucify me.

You are First Covenant weirdos. I understand that you have to pass through a self-identity, "I don't know who I am. I will establish laws of man in reciprocity with what appears to be projections outside of me." This is literally the Covenant of Abraham. This is the First Covenant. Do you understand? This is Genesis, Exodus and Leviticus, particularly, where you're literally taught, unlike a baboon, to associate with your mind in a cultural attraction of cause and effect. That's what a human being does. Do you understand me? Jesus says there has not been a lot of progress in the relinquishment of an-eye-for-an-eye, or projected associations. The New Covenant is nothing but "Lay down your arms. You are only in conflict with yourself," which is nothing but the Sermon on the Mount. Don't resist evil. Be poor in spirit. And you say, "How dare you say that! How dare you threaten us with our heritages of mutual self-identity!" Of course.

Remember, though, that you're the chosen one, obviously. You're chosen to know this and can make that choice. You just haven't made it. Being chosen is nothing but the capacity to choose. The Atonement Principle has to do only totally in your mind with Jesus Christ of Nazareth. I'm teaching you the Atonement Principle. Do I need Jesus Christ? It hasn't anything to do with Jesus Christ, except in a full sense of your memory of being at the crucifixion. But hell, you're at the crucifixion right now. I mean, it's going on just as much as this is. Why? You're crucifying, as Jesus would say, in your own mind. You are the anti-Christ, denying your own resurrection.

The reason I'm trying to stay out of perceptual thought forms is you want to doctrinize that and say, "Well, I hear that's what a particular sect of religion teaches," and that's not what I'm saying. You are the passion. This is your resurrection. This is how the world ends. This is Armageddon. How does the world end? It's just gone. This is the going out of the world. That's what I came here to tell you. This is not a real place. And you know this now because we're sharing this. And now you're going to go out of time. You are not under any laws here. God is real. I assure you God is a fact. Never mind what this place is. God is a fact! It's real. It's eternal, and It's perfect, and It's forever, and you are included in That. You are That. You would stop justifying this instantly if you believed it. There could be no possible justification for an earth.

The only justification you could possibly have here is you think you can get sick and die, that you're suffering. And you can't. How many times will you have to go through a death experience before you come to believe me, before you can remember it? I don't know. Jesus says, "I'd like to get you to your fear threshold. I need to force you to look at your own associations with yourself." Quit teaching. I'd quit teaching, if I were you. I mean, you're going to have to undergo that experience. I'm really not teaching. I'm just declaring myself. You think we're exchanging, and you're dead wrong. I'm not exchanging anything with you. Because you think I am is why you're here. If you would accept that I speak from the truth, you would immediately enter into the association. It's called a healed teacher. Why? He's only declaring his own Self. He is not saying that's true, isn't it? I don't say to you that's true. That's nonsense.

God is real. He's a fact. I don't know whether that makes you unhappy or not. I know you feel very threatened by that, but that will not make it so. Why are you threatened? Because the manner in which you come to do that is relinquishment of yourself. Right? Lesson 76. Could it possibly be that this is really happening here? You have no idea of the momensity of it. You are so little. You reduce it into your thought form associations. That hasn't anything to do with it. There's one dreamer of the dream, and there's one association that awakens from the dream.

CHAPTER TEN: *The Bright Lights Are Heaven*

And that's *you*. This is the whole teaching. Is that fearful to you? It would be. You're all alone in the universe. But there's a God. Otherwise, how do you know that you're all alone?

In *The Obstacles to Peace*, the greatest one is the fear of God. You're afraid of being whole. You're afraid of hatching. You want to stay in the womb of potential. Yet it's impossible because the potential has to be fulfilled because the idea of potential is what fulfillment is. Is that so? Are you with me? Cause and effect are not apart. You keep them apart, and, as Jesus says, you call it potential, which is absurd. You think there's places you can go and gather things in your mind and assert them. Not so. Everything is activated by the thought of it. Can you hear that? Maybe. There isn't any such thing as staticness.

When Jesus teaches this – I'm into the *Course*, because it is so beautiful – He teaches that mind is only totally active all the time. You hold it in little chunks, don't you? But it's not. It never sleeps. It never rests. It's just full. That's the description of the Holy Spirit in perception. Whatever you bring in that association to this light factoring will be made whole by the definition of yourself in the reflection of eternity if you'll allow light to be an aspect of total consciousness, which it is. Isn't it? That light, fractured consciousness, is light, or an aspect of eternity. The Great Rays! That moment of the schism, the little peek-out. Now that comes back to reality.

Is this all over? Is it? It has to be all over. Do you know why? I'm telling you. It's all over. Look right at your death. You are saying to me, "No, I'm going to die and have another experience." What's your alternative to this being all over? Death? You can't get away with it. Let me see you die around me. You can't. The only way you die is if you are absolutely rejecting me, which you've been doing. Well, then, go away. How long have I been telling you this? Since the beginning of time. How long do you think I've been telling you? How often would I have to tell you? You only hear me once. It has nothing to do with the manner in which you hear me. Don't you see? I keep circling this. It's so obvious that there's one problem, one solution. One anti-Christ, one Christ. One unreality, one reality.

Can you teach this? How do I know? I don't know. Sometime back when Jesus taught, He used to teach, "If you go into a village and you're not heard, put dust to your heels and get out of the village." (Matthew 10:14) It simply means that there's no one who has fulfilled the necessity of hearing you. When I woke up, I couldn't find any village. There was no one who heard this. I had to put dust to the whole earth. It's taken this long for you guys to hear it. Isn't that amazing? You lost your savior. The one who was supposed to be doing this flunked the final test. That's a fact, incidentally. You understand me? He fell off the truth wagon. Everything is designed to bring about a particular association, but everything is always by chance. Everything happens by chance, and the accumulative association that would have caused enlightenment didn't work. Can you hear that? And it rang a little buzzer on a board and it said, "Uh oh, Quadrant X4710 lost Jesus, or what you call the Second Coming." So you didn't have an identity, and I was passing over in X742. I was on a furlough. I had a furlough coming, 1000 years furlough. And they said, "Would you mind stopping by?" I'm speaking to you from my alien association. And I said, "Yeah, how long will it take?" And they said, "Oh, just a second or two." So I keep telling you, "Oh, it'll just take a second."

So what did I do? I made a covenant. I made an agreement and entered into this. But it has absolutely nothing to do with our mutual self-identity, except I have a good memory of it. In fact, I have a perfect memory of everything here. Obviously, that's what I do, I bring that memory in and reassociate it. In that sense I'm an instrument, and I'm teaching you to come into your own light associations. Was that a dramatic experience for this human being? Ha! I wouldn't even attempt to describe it. I like people who say, "Well, I underwent an experience; a

CHAPTER TEN: *The Bright Lights Are Heaven*

little voice told me." That's not what my experience was. My experience was different than that. Was I prepared for my experience? No. But obviously I had fulfilled the necessity. The frustrations that I expressed as a human – like being unable to solve the problem, like not being able to stand this place – got me just to where it might work with me. And it was really touch and go. Do you see? And it worked, obviously. I'm here. But there were some major adjustments that went on at that time. You weren't even scheduled for this association. It was an Eastern teacher. You wouldn't have got it. We jumped ahead 1400 years. That's why I'm so early with the *Course*. The *Course* doesn't have an awakening schedule. But it's too late. It's already here. There's no reason you can't take the *Course* and wake up. I remember when they delivered the *Course* to me. It arrived in a box at my house for no reason. I looked at it and I said, "Oh! Look at this. This is the truth. Everybody'll know this. My problems are solved." I said that all they'll do is pick up this and, Wow! In fact I said, "Geez, what am I even here for? All they'll do is pick up this, and they'll see it immediately." And it was not so.

What's happening to your mind since last night is you actually read it differently. You have undergone a transformation. I never could understand why anybody would do what they're doing to the *Course In Miracles*, ever, because I was awake before I looked at it. Obviously, that's why I got the assignment. But the way the mind will cover itself up in that association is astonishing. It will look right at it and read it and what? It can't see it. In the *Course*, Jesus teaches natural man does not know of spiritual man. He cannot know that. I can't understand why you don't see this immediately. You can't understand how I can be teaching this to you and not give you rights to your own associations. There is no communication between us. This is Paul's great teaching after his Damascus experience. (Acts 9) Natural man does not know of spiritual man.

Jesus says it over and over. Doesn't he? Jesus says, "John the Baptist is the highest among humans and below the lowest of the angels." (Matthew 11:11) He literally says that, that the mind has to be awakened from the prophecy; from the messenger to becoming the message, which is what the Christ is. Do you see? Is John at that time beheaded? Of course. First he baptizes Jesus, who goes to enlightenment.

So this is your course in enlightenment, and it's coming about in you. And that will make you very happy. The problem I'm having with instruction, is your energy pitches are so high, I can't get my energy down to low, perceptual association. The group is too mixed. What happens is, the mandala, as it gets closer to the Light, will formulate. In the Christian tradition this is called principalities and thrones or orders of angels in association with the pure Light. As these associations in brightness come, they are actually undergoing their own transformation – Jesus calls it the revelation. I am teaching now into your own vision from revelation. But as this begins to succeed, this consciousness is undergoing its own enlightenment. That's the whole teaching. That's what I want it to do, isn't it. It loves to come listen to me express, but when you run into associations that are limited in their association, they literally keep the vortex of energy in a constricted association. This is why you get out of the village.

This is why people are coming to God's Country Place, just incidentally. Whatever they're doing, they want to be in association with that, and that's nice to do that. Need you come there geographically? No. There's no need for that. There's also no need for you not to. I can't give you direction on that. But I can give you the direction that you can't get out of time without going out of time. That I must tell you. And I don't think there could be anyone that would be around this that goes out that first will not benefit from it by their reassociations. They will subsequently have another death experience that

CHAPTER TEN: *The Bright Lights Are Heaven*

will show that their associations were false. Obviously. That's my whole teaching.

See, at this depth, the assertion of real bright, what you call true energy, will not avail because it will just throw you into an ecstasy, or into a fear thrashing. The basis of the teaching is to get you to reason with your mind, which is really all there is, to see that love is reasonable and that hatred and sickness and death are not reasonable. Love is finally only communication, which is full reason. I would get as close to that as I could. That's Light! But when you've got them identified as Gladys, who you've known since you were a kid in high school, it's a little tough. A prophet is not without honor except in his own home town. Jesus had a little problem working miracles in Nazareth. Isn't that nice that that survived in the Bible. (Matthew 14:54-58) That's nice. It shows you how much that teaching is true. "Isn't that Joe the Carpenter's kid? Doesn't he have brothers and sisters? Why does he say he's a healer?"

Jesus was just undergoing his own human-to-God experiences. What's He say in the *Course?* "I just did it a step ahead of you. I'm a little more willing to do this." He's a great guy. There He is. He wasn't around long enough, really. But He's accumulative in the icon of your associations. He's everything that ever happened – every time a martyr was turned on the spit, every time the King James version sprang into light – you have all of those associations with you. I assure you. You're the guy that turned the thumbscrew, and you're the guy that had the thumbscrew turned on him. For goodness sake. You have suppressed this information in your own determination to stay here a long time. It's out now, though. It's out! You're afraid to teach it, but it's sitting there.

That's a trick. Talk about a miracle! You guys talk about miracles. You don't even look at the miracle of the *Course In Miracles* even getting here. We really lucked out. That takes a particular capacity of self-identity to even scribe that. You give that reality, which we don't. All we're talking about is the configuration of thought forms. This, being able to do a whole light insertion into this thing, is wild. It wasn't due. It worked just fine. Look. It's working.

Is it an operational process? If I took all the religion out of it altogether and all of your sacred ideas, I would teach you directly that you're undergoing a metamorphosis. I have just as much energy in the certainty of the spontaneity of physical awakening as I do in anything because my awakening was spontaneously physical. It had nothing to do with spirituality at all. It had only to do with my necessity to find an association that was true. I had to get to that point, of course. But that being said, I had no voices saying, "I am the Lord," until my final revelation. In fact, I was denied any spiritual, doctrinal associations. None. I had none. That doesn't have anything to do with me going to church. I remember the first time I discovered this was spiritual. I actually wrote on a napkin, "This whole process is a spiritual process." I was undergoing a physical awakening. I was astounded. I mean spiritual in the sense that it was going to be a whole undertaking. I was amazed that that's so and that I had no control over it. I'm teaching you the spontaneity of the occurrence. Let it happen. It'll be bizarre.

You keep needing to identify it. Remember that each moment you're actually rejecting in your self-identity the natural pressure of enlightenment that's all around you. And it's very scary to you because these strange things begin to happen. Wow. Are those miracles? Sure. But they're nothing compared to the big one. I'll show you how that feels. See, this is mine. See, this causes this association of energy, and that's why if you come into this new association you'll be able to take full advantage of this. As of now, you may look on that as very strange and say, "I wonder why that's occurring." Like you always do with physical awakenings. You didn't even let the Methodists in until they calmed down. Come on! Somehow you're going to keep that separate. You want some orthodoxness here. "Let's keep our

CHAPTER TEN: *The Bright Lights Are Heaven*

value systems intact. Let's not be making this declaration of Pentecostal association." How the hell do you think the spirit got here, except by Pentecost. Do you think it got here by observing man with man? It doesn't have anything to do with that. It has to do with your communication with reality. That's what this is. And that's the identity that's occurring. This consciousness is in all sorts of mandala associations with lots of stuff. But it's going to get it this time. It'll get it.

See, you're all coming from all over, different places in time. The forgiveness is only the forgiveness of your perceptual association with the guy who appears to be separate from you. We're all the same. Not only are you that way, but the different centers of your association in your microcosm are all in different places in time. This is Revelations. This is the teachings of "your churches don't know each other." Your own associations in your chakras are not familiar with you. You do not have instantaneous communication. The enlightenment of the body is nothing but the whole communication of the body association. For goodness sake. And that's what enlightenment is. Is this, then, the universe? What did you think it was? Everything is the universe. Every cell is the whole. That's fun to do that!

Don't put any value in your sickness here, guys, and I'll take care of your diseases. Stop valuing it. You guys really suppress this, but you have to look at the alternative to this in order to get it. Is that okay? Would you care to let go and make that contact? "Oh, that's scary. Everybody here would think I'm crazy. All my dead ones would say let's not go off the deep end. We don't talk about that sort of thing. That's for the fringe lunatics that talk about God. Let's stay here in this time. And look at all the lovely results that we're achieving." In the *Course*, Jesus says that they'll threaten you, they'll do everything they can to keep you from looking up. It's one of my favorite passages in the whole *Course*, it's in Chapter 19. It says don't look up. All of these things that you value will disappear.

Look at this. Is it all right if I go to enlightenment? Is it all right? See, some of these guys are saying the heck with it and going to their light. You think there's judgment involved in this. You actually look for balance in what I'm teaching. All balance is to death. Do you understand? No matter what I come to teach you, you always look for the other side of the association, which is nothing but judgment to death. Quite literally, the other side of this is what the crucifixion is. If there is a reporter here, she will report that people underwent experiences. The side effects are not too good because some of them lost contact and couldn't go to work at the bank the next day. And that will be presented as the negative association. The mind needs to balance itself, doesn't it? And that's okay. But all I'm really saying is that it's not doctrinal. I'm teaching only to the experience. It isn't that the reporter would not want to be non-prejudiced, but the idea of opinion is what prejudice is. It's the idea of the possibility of balancing your mind, and, of course, that's not what I'm teaching. I'm teaching a release from that.

Is this disruptive to your relationships? Sure. Nothing could be more disruptive than what your relationship is, however. Nothing is more chaotic than a tightly delineated thought form association, as Jesus would say. Nothing is more unstable than staticness. And you're just desperately holding it together, aren't you? This is Bell's Theorem. You hold it together because you believe in the Second Law of Thermodynamics. "If I hold this together, it won't fall apart." The whole idea of Bell's Theorem is that through the release, through the chaotic release, it will go into a higher association of the mind. And it does.

Really, all the *Course In Miracles* deals with is your confrontation with these apparent images of fear that seem to be outside of you that keep you from seeing the wholeness that is all about you. This is all the *Course* really says. It's all any tradition really says – that you must be born again, that you must undergo this experience.

CHAPTER TEN: *The Bright Lights Are Heaven*

What is the strangest obstacle faced by this perceptual association in coming to enlightenment? Fear of God. But you have to realize really what we mean when we say "fear of God." If there is a wholeness and the truth of you is constructed on a bondage of association; your freedom literally depends on bondage to that identity. And you call it freedom. Do you understand what I'm saying? You literally call it security. And to you, security represents freedom. Isn't this so? Money in the bank. Anything you want – children, possessions. Having things binds you through identification to that association, and you literally call it freedom. A whole mind calls it bondage automatically and does not want to be possessed by the limited association. You depend on eating, you depend on sleeping, you depend on clothes, you depend on family. You depend on all of those things to what? Express your freedom. You call that freedom. I know you do. You have the security, then, to exercise love and happiness when you take off for a weekend. But you've evolved the security of that limitation to guarantee you. You believe that you've earned freedom.

Those of you who have had the Friday feeling, that I want you to have all the time, say, "Hey, I'm free for a whole weekend. I have fulfilled my obligations. I am now entitled to feel happiness." I'm telling you that you're entitled intrinsically to happiness all the time. And it doesn't depend on what you've brought into that association of bondage to declare yourself.

Here's the problem: The only way you can possibly come to know that is to relinquish the bondage that you're identifying as freedom. And that's a threat to you. Why? You'll lose your self-identity associations. Jesus Christ of Nazareth teaches nothing but "give up your stores." All he has ever taught is, "Consider the lilies of the field." (Matthew 6:28) Don't lay up the stores of your self association, and you'll discover your own reality. Isn't that so? Now, you're obviously afraid to do that. Now, when I say "stores of your own association," I'm talking of the idols of your self-identity. Do you think you know what an idol is? An idol is any thought, any association, any identification that holds you in the bondage of this selfness. You are literally afraid to be free.

Here I am, telling you that this freedom is directed to the reassociation of your physical contributions to reality, that you will actually undergo an experience of enlightenment that will free your mind. And since your mind is projected onto the world or is the world, it will change the whole world in your association with it. That's the miracle, and that's the truth of this.

Now, I want you to hear this. That bar that you will cross is very real to you. And ultimately it's the only thing that you ever do. You got that? Now listen. Chapter 19: *What would you see without the fear of death?* Which is what you call this. *What would you feel and think if death held no attraction for you?* By attraction, that means you resist it in order to have it. You and I get our biggest kicks out of not dying together. We always have. I've stood with you on battlefields. I've been with you guys. We have our most camaraderie in adversity. We are literally attracted to peril and death so that we can experience the passion of our own love. Do you know that? The passion of love and passion of death are actually the same passion. Obviously, passion is passion. Isn't that strange? Sexually, too. Our real passion comes when we overcome a threat together, when we overcome death together. All relationships of so-called love here are based on existing, or overcoming death together. That's what this says. That's literally true.

What if death did not hold that attraction, if you didn't need to share existence? What if you didn't need to have possessions of a family and yourself, which is nothing but the attraction of death. The attraction of existence is what death is. Can you understand me? The idea of death is what death is. You're not really alive if you can die, are you? But you're attracted to that existence in your own association with yourself. You

CHAPTER TEN: The Bright Lights Are Heaven

can realize how really insidious this is. And you love it. You love death. Of course. It's the one thing you can absolutely depend on. That's amazing! How do you teach this? Try this: You are what you defend yourself against.

What would you feel and think if death held no attraction to you? Are you ready? *Very simply, you would remember your Father.* You'd remember your Creator. Why? You'd release it. *The Creator of life, the Source of everything that lives, the Father of the universe and of the universe of universes, and of everything that lies even beyond them, would you remember.* Ready? *And as this memory rises in your mind, peace must still surmount a final obstacle, after which is salvation completed, and the Son of God entirely restored to sanity. For here the world does end.* Now you're beginning to feel all of this lovely peace. Now you're beginning to feel this release of yourself. And all of a sudden, unh! Like that. It'll hit. Uh oh. What was that? That's your fear point. Most of you haven't even gotten that far. Well, a lot of you guys here have. You come up to that, and you go, "Boy, I better not do this. I'm going to lose this association." Those of you in meditations have begun to experience the opening of this new association of channel energy. Fear will enter that immediately unless you are prepared for the onslaught of your own defensive mechanisms.

In the Eastern tradition this is taught as a premature awakening of the *kundalini* energy, where if you demonstrate through *pranayama* and suddenly you will awaken this energy, if you're not prepared for it, it'll fry your head. It'll throw you into a schizophrenic panic. You're not ready to do that. All right. My instructions to you, obviously, are this: You are ready to do this, or you wouldn't be here. Remember that the teaching of the *Course In Miracles* is the teaching of the direct route to enlightenment. Do you understand? It doesn't have twelve-fold paths. It doesn't recommend various ways of yoga. It says, release your own identity and come home, which is nothing but a *kundalini* awakening, where you just simply take all that you have and abandon it to that reassociation. That's what this says. That's what's happening to you now. Listen.

The fourth obstacle to be surmounted hangs like a heavy veil before the face of Christ. Yet as His face rises beyond it, shining with joy because He is in His Father's Love, peace will lightly brush the veil aside and run to meet Him, and to join with Him at last. Ready? *For this dark veil, which seems to make the face of Christ Himself like to a leper's and the bright rays of His Father's Love that light His face with glory appear as streams of blood, fades in the blazing light beyond it when the fear of death is gone.*

In the text of Christianity this is called "being washed in the blood." Remember that the red association of energy is the passion of war to you, or death, rather than the passion of love, isn't it? So when you're washed in the blood you become as pure as the lamb. That's what that means. You take this red, or passion, association and instead of dedicating it to the planet Mars, to war, the red, you dedicate it to the passion of eternal life and it becomes that. Many of you will have the experience of seeing this final contortion of your fear express itself as gargoyles or weird things that come into your memories when you're exercising the awakening process. It's very common to have. And you're very fearful of it. Nightmares and dreams of horror. There's nothing to be afraid of. Remember that this is at your direction. And all of these constructs are parts of your own mind. There's nothing really that could ever threaten you or hurt you in this awakening process.

This is the darkest veil, upheld by the belief in death, and protected by its attraction. It's upheld by death and its attraction at the same time. You want to die and don't want to die at the same time. That's the friction of self-identity. *The dedication to death and to its sovereignty,* inaccessibility, *is but the solemn*

CHAPTER TEN: The Bright Lights Are Heaven

vow, the promise made in secret with human beings, with egos, with self-identities, *never to lift this veil, not to approach it, not even to suspect that it is there. This is the secret bargain made with the self mind, with the humans around you, to keep what lies beyond the veil forever blotted out and unremembered.* This is, in the tradition of Christianity, called primordial guilt. He's talking about the original sin, where you actually share a guilt of disassociation from reality. With everyone you meet on the street you are making a tacit acknowledgment that you can set up a defense against reality that surrounds you. Listen. That's what you're doing in your own mind.

When you ask somebody, "How ya doing?" you're literally asking him how he's doing in attacking and defending himself from God. Quite literally. Well, you might as well look at it. That's what he's doing. "How good are you at existing in separation and sharing death with me here? You're a lot better at it than I am. I see how much stores you've laid up. You must be very happy, laying up the stores that are going to keep you from getting cancer or dying." See the ambivalence of this. You want him to die so you can have his wealth. All based on scarcity and separation, isn't it. "How we doing with this?" you say. "Oh, we're doing pretty good. I'm managing to exist." Remember in Milton's *Paradise Lost*. At the end of *Paradise Lost*, as Adam and Eve walk off, away from Paradise, he turns to her and says, "We'll get along okay." That's the final sentence of *Paradise Lost*. "We're going to be able to struggle okay with this." And that's what you're doing with it. And there is no power in heaven or earth that can stop you from doing that if you want to do it. But there's no sense in being afraid of God. And if you're not afraid of God, what are you doing here?

You must be afraid of everything. Actually, being afraid of God is exactly the same thing as being afraid of everything, isn't it? Wouldn't it be true, if you're afraid of anything, you're afraid of everything? Of course! Eventually anything will become everything. It would have to. Any fear will be all fear. Ready? A fearful thing is not real. It has nothing to do with *having* fear. It is simply fear itself. It holds itself for just that moment in its possessed thoughts and is fearful and then it disappeared to reality. What you are doing here is holding together fearful thoughts. But they're not real. They share one thing: fear of union with God.

Here is your promise never to allow union to call you out of separation; the great amnesia in which the memory of God seems quite forgotten; the cleavage of your Self from you; – the fear of God, the final step in your dissociation. Disassociation is impossible. If you stop and think about it, if you're disassociated, you must have been once associated. What you're saying is, "I'm afraid of total association." No question. *See how the belief in death would seem to "save" you.* See? "I'm going to die." *For if this were gone, what could you fear but life? It is the attraction of death that makes life seem ugly, cruel and tyrannical. You are no more afraid of death than of the* no-mind that you are. *These are your chosen friends. For in your secret alliance with them you've agreed never to let the fear of God be lifted, so you would look upon the face of Christ and join Him in His Father,* which is what you're doing now, if you're not afraid of God. Isn't that so? I know this may seem like a silly question to you, but are you afraid of God? Well, obviously you must be. It's very reasonable that you're afraid of God. Staying away from the word *faith*, what we're saying is, you don't trust your Creator. Perception is inherently suspicious because it's separate, it's dualistic. You want to know what God's credentials are so you're not afraid of Him. That's the way you make idols, isn't it. Golden calves. Can a fearful thing become not fearful? No. No, it can't. Scarcity cannot come to wholeness.

Every obstacle that peace must flow across is surmounted in just the same way; the fear that raised it

CHAPTER TEN: *The Bright Lights Are Heaven*

yields to the love beyond, and so the fear is gone. It's the only way it will work. *And so it is with this. The desire to get rid of peace and drive the Holy Spirit from you fades in the presence of the quiet recognition that you love Him. The exaltation of the body is given up in favor of the spirit, which you love as you could never love the body. And the appeal of death is lost forever as love's attraction stirs and calls to you.* The appeal of death, which is nothing but what the earth is, the attraction you have to time, to being here, to your self-identity, to proving how powerful, how good you are, your credentials, your identity, will give way as the system of your association becomes more whole. Your judgment of self-identity changes. How does it change? By your commitment to this process. How else would it?

From beyond each of the obstacles to love, Love Itself has called. And each has been surmounted by the power of the attraction of what lies beyond. Your wanting fear seemed to be holding them in place. Yet when you heard the Voice of Love beyond them, you answered and they disappeared. This is past tense. It's impossible that you did not do this. You will never be happy until you create. You can't be. In your limited identity you are creating, or mis-creating, in association with yourself. You can never be satisfied with that. The call of love is only the call to totally create with your own mind. Do you see? That's this. This is what you're doing. Here's where some of you are going to come into right now. Here's what happens.

And now you stand in terror before what you swore never to look upon. What happens? *Your eyes look down, remembering your promise to your "friends".* These are the people around you, incidentally, that say, "Hey, don't do this." You think I'm kidding? They literally are going to tell you, "Don't go to God." I'm speaking from deep experience in this. I was obviously in special relationships at the time of my awakening. Not only will they not tolerate it, in the sense that you have conflict with it – obviously it's constructed in your mind – but they will do everything they can to direct it to temporal associations. And this is the way you guys are teaching the *Course In Miracles*. And that's obviously not the answer. They will redirect it to perceptual harmonious associations that better benefit you. My associate at that time, my ex at the time I underwent the experience, did not object to the spiritual association, she objected to the non-identity of it. She called up the Episcopal archbishop and decided that I could go for a year and become an Episcopal priest, because I had decided that I was going to do this. And she did not understand that I had no intention – that I didn't know what an Episcopal priest was at that point – that I was not seeking for any identity in my associations. I didn't want to be *A Course In Miracles* teacher. That's absurd to me.

Do you think I'm *A Course In Miracles* teacher? That's nuts. I'm teaching what I am. I was undergoing the experience. I didn't want to have credentials to verify what was happening to me. I could see that I was losing my credentials through turning my will over to God, and was having an experience of reality. Any way they can, they'll direct you. The thing they won't accept most is they can't give you a perceptual justification for why you're doing it. That's very difficult. But that's really where the test will come. They must find you guilty of a perceptual reassociation: "You're going to find another relationship that's better than this one." Don't tell me. I know. The idea that you would just simply make a commitment to God is absolutely not acceptable here. "Oh, you're just going to associate with other friends." See? It's going to come down into a re-illusion rather than the passion of that commitment. That's what they can't stand. "Tell me you found another woman. Tell me anything, but don't tell me you're doing this." Do you understand? "That's crazy! Don't do this. Nothing could be worse than what you're doing. I can't understand it. I don't understand what's happening to you. This is very fearful to me. Why did I see light in your room? What's going on in there? What's happening?" This is

CHAPTER TEN: The Bright Lights Are Heaven

fearful. And it's very fearful to you. And you will justify the previous associations you have, not to go through this experience.

The whole teaching of the *Course* says that this is the spot which you always come to, which you always do, and always turn back into your own karma. Why the hell do you think you're here? You keep reassociating in time rather than undergoing the transformation of your mind. Come on, guys. The whole teaching is existentialism – that this is only in your own mind, that all of this is just a protective device of your perceptions to keep you from seeing God, from coming whole. Does that seem outrageous to you? Too bad. What's your solution? What solution are you offering to the problem of sickness and death, besides putting it off? There's got to be something outside of this. And that's what's happening to you.

Your eyes look down, remembering your promise to your "friends". The "loveliness" of sin, the delicate appeal of guilt – how much you like to find the other guy guilty of this, not yourself. How lovely is your opinion – all opinion is slander. Stop it! In my awakening I couldn't stand judgment; I still hate it. People will constantly use the tongue to murder. I'm not sure you understand this. It's a million-fold greater than simply shooting somebody with a .45. All of these consciousnesses around here, by their opinions, literally slander and kill things that are outside of them. I assure you that's true. How dare you? By what right do you judge that? What temerity! To judge them in association with your crapful mind. Cut it out. I used to try to teach it this way, and nobody wants to hear it: *Judge not lest ye be judged.* You haven't walked in his shoes. How the hell do you know how he feels? Cut it out. That's what this is, the attraction of guilt. All of your associations are attractions of guilt. You can hardly wait to talk about somebody else that you're not or want to be. Don't kid me. I look at the soap operas. And that's what this is.

The "loveliness" of sin, the delicate appeal of guilt, the "holy" waxen image of death, and the fear of vengeance of the projected mind *you swore in blood* – literally – *not to desert, all rise and bid you not to raise your eyes. For you realize that if you look on this and let the veil be lifted, they will be gone forever.* Who will be gone? *All your "friends," your "protectors" and your "home."* All of these lovely things you have will vanish. *Nothing that you remember now will you remember.* Is this too uncompromising a statement? No. This is what I'm leading you gradually up to, so that you'll stop getting this authentication of your own fearful identities.

It seems to you the world will utterly abandon you if you but raise your eyes. Yet all that will occur is you will leave the world forever. This is the re-establishment of your will. Look upon it, open-eyed, and you will nevermore believe that you are at the mercy of things beyond you, forces you cannot control, and thoughts that come to you against your will. That's one of the toughest sentences in the *Course In Miracles*. You actually believe that there are thoughts that come to you against your will, and you use them in your play of passion, of anger, in order to keep your own self-identity. Who are you kidding? You love to hold on to the passion of anger and war. Your reality is based on it. Isn't it? Entitlement, it's called. Do you like to teach it this way? Can you take this or not? It's impossible to be unjustly treated. You nod your head, but then why do you feel unjustly treated? Somewhere you feel a justification for what you're doing here. Somehow you don't accept responsibility for this. And this is the process that I'm trying to get you to look at. That's what this says.

...you will nevermore be at the mercy of things beyond you, forces you cannot control and thoughts that come to you against your will. It is your will to look on this. No mad desire, no trivial impulse to forget again, no stab of fear nor cold sweat of seeming death can stand against your will. For what attracts you from beyond the veil is also deep within you, unseparated from it and completely one. This is

CHAPTER TEN: *The Bright Lights Are Heaven*

Chapter 19, which is literally what's occurring here. This is the lifting of the veil.

Where did this come from? You want to look at the context of what I'm reading to you? Do you understand that this is coming from a consciousness not associated in a body? Do you want to look at that for a minute? Do you want to see how close this Guide is to you when you listen to this in this direct statement to you to lift your veil, to undergo this experience?

Forget not that you came this far together, you and your brother. And it was surely not the no-mind *that led you here. But first, lift up your eyes and look on your brother in innocence born of complete forgiveness of each other's illusions.* We want to get you to this point without having you panic, which is what you'll do if you get here too quick. This becomes very fearful to you. I'm very fearful to you. I would have to be. I'm asking you to look beyond this veil of sickness and death and see that God is real and is a fact. It's embarrassing to you, if nothing else, that all of this is futile. Everything that you're really doing didn't mean anything.

No one can look upon the fear of God unterrified, unless he has accepted the Atonement and learned that illusions are not real. This, again, is the premature awakening. Preparation for that is what you have been going through, because in your mind you have had this experience. This is already over. Prepare ye the way of the Lord. This way has been made straight for you now and you can see this very clearly if you're ready to do it. Why? This is the time that you did it; this is the time that you looked on this.

No one can look upon the fear of God unterrified, unless he has accepted the Atonement and learned that illusions are not real. No one can stand before this obstacle alone, for he could not have reached this far unless his brother walked beside him. And no one would dare to look on it without complete forgiveness of his brother in his heart.

Okay, here's what we do. We know that it's very difficult to teach you complete forgiveness. When I told you that we were tempting you with this or fooling you with this, I meant that we're bringing you closer and closer to this veil, even though you're not totally forgiving. And suddenly all your unforgiveness will hit you. This is literally true. And some of you may cave in with this. Suddenly you become terror-stricken by what? The parting of this veil. This is the awakening of the crown chakra. Quite literally, this is the final demonstration of your own whole-mindedness. Everything in the universe was constructed in perceptual mind to prevent you from doing this. And you never know what it is until you're beset with it.

You remember this, I understand perfectly well that when you are fearful, you are fearful. You guys sit here and talk about fear. If you're alone, and you're undergoing this change of your energy associations, and you suddenly feel this fear, that's a very real thing to you, isn't it? It's paranoia. Somebody's going to pop out of the closet suddenly. Why? You're expanding your thoughts. Your mind is expanding. You're experiencing the schizophrenia of this real identity of you. You are on the mania side of the awakening of your energies, without the depression – the depression of fear that will cave that in for you. This is really what the human mind does all the time. When you get to this point I want you to say, "Hey, it's going to be okay. I will not be afraid. I will not defend myself from my own thoughts. I will simply extend my wholeness to them and love them." This is called the Guardian of the Threshold, the Ring Pass Not. And this is expressed in a lot of traditions, how you are afraid to finally part that last veil. That's what we're doing here now. And that's what you're undergoing.

You will be ready. Stand you here a while and tremble not. Let us join together in a holy instant, here in this place where the purpose, given in a holy instant, has led you. And let us join in faith that He Who brought us here together

CHAPTER TEN: The Bright Lights Are Heaven

will offer you the innocence you need, and that you will accept it for my love and His. That's a lovely sentence from Jesus. What's occurring in here is what you call a circle of Atonement, where the consciousnesses who have reached this new level of the parting of the veil, through the purification of their memory patterns, stand as light identities for you to share at that veil point. They will literally say, "Don't be afraid, brother. This is okay." This is what you call the church.

The church is established to bring about communication with God through the relinquishment of the self-identity. In that sense it really is a church, isn't it? Because you have these light brothers who are standing here, saying, "Don't be afraid. That's okay. You can part this veil." And you look back out there and you say, "Well, what about all of these things?" And they say, "No, that's all right. That's all right. They will disappear if you will make the commitment. But you can't bring your sickness and death to the altar. You can't do it." All this said is that if you have something for which you feel guilty, go and make the amend for it. Clean up your act. You can't make it total, but you can sure as hell go out and satisfy yourself somewhere in a relationship with yourself. And that's the requirement.

Nor is it possible to look on this too soon. Obviously you think it is and that's what makes you fearful. Once more. It is not possible to look on this too soon. There's no such thing as a premature awakening of energy reassociations, except by the limited identity. It's too late. You already know about this. I'm telling you, you do not have to be afraid. A lot of your yoga friends will say, "Don't do that. That's a dangerous route." Why is it dangerous? Why is it any more dangerous than any route except you've constructed the fear in you to make it dangerous? I'm telling you to take the direct route. That's all I teach. Why the hell would I want you to go somewhere else? You can't go there without going there. That's what this says. All of the practicing doesn't really mean anything in that sense.

This is the place to which everyone must come when he is ready. A journey without a purpose is still meaningless, and even when it is over it makes no sense. Now we're ready. *To look upon the fear of God does need some preparation. Only the sane can look on stark insanity and raving madness with pity and compassion, but not with fear.* Wow. In other words, if I have a sane mind, I can look with pity on all the junk that you're doing here because it's really terrible. Otherwise what? I'll be a part of that and I can't stand that. *For only if they share in it does it seem fearful, and you do share in it until you look upon your brother with perfect faith and love and tenderness. Before complete forgiveness you still stand unforgiving. You are afraid of God because you fear your brother. Those you do not forgive you fear. And no one reaches love with fear beside him.*

Let me take this up a notch: The description of the veil is not what the veil is. This is the veil now that you're looking at. Your attempts at the re-establishment are your attempts not to go through it, and are your needs to keep your self-identity. It will suddenly occur to you that this is happening to you, really. Then look out. Then you'll get serious. I can tell the serious ones. There's a breaking point, where they suddenly say, "Uh oh." That's nothing but the attraction of love beyond the veil.

This energy reassociation is accumulative. These are Holy Instants, incidentally, and you're saving a lot of time with whatever you think you're doing now. All I want you to do is see how much is really happening to you. You have no idea of the power of your own mind. Jesus says in the *Course* that every time you have a thought, it's resounding in the universe. And when you begin to have thoughts of this energy association, it really begins to resound and it will attract like to like all throughout the nine-dimensional association. And the more you do that, the more the bell rings and the more the light shines. Do you see? They'll come from all over the place. And this can have a tendency to make

CHAPTER TEN: *The Bright Lights Are Heaven*

you a little fearful because they'll suddenly appear. And there's a lot of phenomena connected with it.

So I just stand here and wait. And you walked up with all your garbage. And I say, "Why don't you put that down and come home?" And then we associate. And I just keep saying, "Why don't you put down your garbage, which is nothing but your perceptual self, and come on home?" And you say, "What kind of teacher are you? I've got to try and find somebody that will verify my garbage." So you go out and you find somebody that'll verify your garbage. And that ain't hard to do. They're all around you. Come on. You can always find verification for yourself. Except from me. I won't give you any. You don't like that. But why are you here? Except that you have felt the attraction of love in the realization that your guilt associations are not availing you of anything. This is literally a process that you undergo.

In the beginning all I expressed to you, which is the same as the *Course*, is constancy. I'm absolutely constant. All whole minds are only constant. That's usually the way a perceptual mind will define you, "You're nuts. You're just constant. Everything I say, you just give me the same response. Give me a different response than that." And I say that there isn't any different response. "I've been listening to you for 2000 years, and you just keep saying the same thing, over and over again." Yeah. Go find someone else that'll tell you something different about yourself. That's what you do. They'll verify you in this regard. You actually think there's a spiritual path. I don't understand that. What do you do? Just construct one? You're constructed not to be with God. Any path that you construct would be what would keep you from getting there. You have no intention of going to God. If you did, why wouldn't you go?

Come on, great teacher, where's the obstacle to you being with God, except the spiritual path? Time. Variations in the manner in which you're going to present yourself to God. That's just craziness. If there is a path, it's only yours, and it's right now, and you can do it. Do you know the sentence in the *Course?* The only one on a spiritual path is somebody with their hands over their eyes. That's a direct sentence from Jesus. It would have to be. Because God isn't hiding. Why do you pretend that God is a secret, except that you're afraid of Him? Obviously you're afraid to find Him. Seek but don't find it. No matter what you do, let's all get together and pretend we're on a spiritual path. We'll keep our identities in various ways as long as we don't have to succeed. Is this the first time you ever looked at that? All of these teachers, so-called teachers, have absolutely no intention of going to God. They are specifically designed to keep their perceptions and protect themselves from reality.

"Well, isn't there value in the practice of relinquishment?" None! None. No value. "Well, at least you could give me a little credit." How much credit do you want? I'll give you total value, but what are you going to do with it? Just spring into Heaven. That was the lesson: Let go of your credentials! You don't mind the idea of letting go of the credentials, as long as you can make the separation real. In fact, you like the idea of coming back to God. It gives you a reason for living in death. That's why you don't like my teaching. This is not real and the separation never occurred. That's what's not tolerable to you. All whole minds teach the unreality of duality. All of your *Course In Miracles* teachers are teaching the reality of separation and the capacity to come to God. You ready? There's no such thing as capacity. This is in Chapter 3 – aspects, degrees and intervals. Potential. Any capacity is fulfilled immediately. What would prevent it except your own mind? Come on. You're going to get this, aren't you? It's nice to get it very reasonably because everything I'm saying is completely reasonable.

Do you really believe that something would prevent you from standing in front of your Creator and saying, "I love You as You love me?" What the hell would it be? You may think there's a Devil, that there's an evil force that's keeping you from going

CHAPTER TEN: *The Bright Lights Are Heaven*

to God, that God allows to be. That's a very common Christian idea, that God tolerates an evil force. Imagine that. Or He doesn't have power to control it. I didn't want anything to do with that God when I was about 12. I asked very literally to my parson at church when I was about 14, "How come God tolerates the Devil?" And he told me, "So that you can work through the obstacles of coming home, so that you have free will to choose to do it." And I said, "Well, why didn't God just make me perfectly?" Which is a very legitimate question. If He made me imperfectly, He must be imperfect Himself. There is no answer to that question, and at 14 I was told, "Don't consider that. We don't look at that part of it." Why? The dual mind requires the association of evil and good, or it can't be here. Do you understand?

This is the great paradox. It's not reconcilable. Thomas Aquinas could not reconcile it. If evil is real, good is gone. Do you see? How would you know which was good and which was evil? That's the problem you've got now. If there are separate things, wouldn't the Devil be just as likely to be God as God? Or is God more godly in some regards, even though He has some evilness about Him? That makes absolutely no sense. What am I really teaching? A nonjudgmental reality; that God doesn't judge. Isn't that okay? Then why do you? I mean, if He created you perfectly, why are there requirements for you to exist and judge in your own association? Relinquish your judgment. Forgive your associations, wake up, and be the creator that's going on right now. That's all I'm telling you to do.

You ought to remember me real well. You and I know each other perfectly. Some of you guys I'm communicating with out of time. Everything's going on all the time. This is a program of enlightenment that's happening to you. I mean, it's an astonishing thing when it begins to dawn on you that this program is designed for *you*, to happen to *you*. And that gets real exciting. It gives you purpose for life. Otherwise, you had no real purpose. In order to get that, most of you have used up your purpose, anyway. You say, "What the hell? This is sort of futile." Is this really all you're going to do, step out of time? Yeah. How long have you been here? Not very long. Forty days. Will you answer me something? What difference does it make how long you've been here if you're going out? What difference does it make what ordeal you've gone through if it's all over?

One of my favorite sentences in the *Course* is *when They have come*. Remember that passage, how poetic it is. When They have come, They have come. We've come! It's time for you to go home. Why the hell do you want to bring some baggage with you? Throw it down! It's time to come Home! Isn't it? See, Babylon is burning. See it? Now you're crossing the river. Don't look back. Just cross over. Let it burn. Don't keep going back down into the burning building. This is the teaching. Straight the way and narrow the gate. Come on home. Can you do that? Sure. Will you do it? Sure. Did you do it? Sure. The first thing you'll say in your enlightenment is, "I knew it. I always knew that." Yeah, you did. It's kind of a remembering.

Everything that's in your mind now is all there is. There is nothing but you doing this. Once more: There is nothing but you sitting there. Nothing. There is nothing outside of you. There aren't more thoughts than you're having. You have a new depth of thought now that is being creative in your minds – you're coming into this new association – where you are all that there is. There are not separate thoughts outside of you. This is fundamental to the teaching. There is not something out there, thinking separate thoughts. Come on. This was the great Aquinas association. There is no such thing as duality. That would be evil and good or good and evil. However, they could not communicate with each other. If they define themselves as separate, they cannot communicate. That is literally, Socratically, true. They could reach a communication of 99.9 to the millionth degree. And they would not communicate because

CHAPTER TEN: *The Bright Lights Are Heaven*

communication must be whole to be real. And anything less than that is simply not real. Can you understand this? It just creates thought forms of mis-association, or association in time.

Once more: Communication must be whole to be real. Obviously. If you know anything about somebody, you would have to know everything, wouldn't you? If there was something you didn't know, how would you ever know him? How could you trust him? Why wouldn't he be fearful to you? When would he turn on you? When would he decide that he suddenly didn't want that association any more? That's the fear you guys are living in all the time. Right in the middle of a lovely episode, the thing turns ugly on you. It's terrible. There's some nice sentences in the *Course* that talk about this. You can't trust anything. Of course not. You can't trust yourself.

Don't be afraid. You are under no laws but God's. That's a single power of eternity. The decision is yours. But no matter what you do, you will not be separate from everything.

For verily I say unto you,
If ye have faith as a grain of mustard seed,
ye shall say unto this mountain,
Remove hence to yonder place; and it shall remove;
and nothing shall be impossible unto you.

CHAPTER ELEVEN

Faith, Crop Circles and Chapter 17

"Yes, I know we're apart by thousands of miles, yet as I lie here you seem so close to me". I *am* close. When I get to Australia, I'll say it is very close. In that sense, it didn't have anything to do with distance at all. Yet our bodies were apart.

"Well, can I come and see you, so our bodies...?" Ah, our bodies in our situations can find a more equitable or loving correspondence in our relationship. Now, the truth of the matter is we are fundamentally in conflict with our relationalship associations. Many of us would rather talk to each other on the phone than be present together. In fact some of us would have nothing to do with each other. We have no intention of bringing our Cain and Abel... Can you understand this? We're not going to bring our separate associations together. All attempts at harmony in conflict are to organize conceptual associations that will give a correspondence, or a purpose, for us coming together. Is that so?

We seem to have a situation here. I'm going to tell you what I'm going to talk about for just a minute this morning. There is a very fundamental need after a graphic description of your objective possibilities of transformation and philosophy to look at how basic the psychology of this teaching is. This actually is Chapter 17. I'll back up just a little bit. It is impossible that as we come together as human beings we are not expressing a form of – and most of you who know me know I generally don't use the word – *faith*. I'm going to use the word *faith* this morning, because in the fundamental teaching, listen to me carefully, I understand that you consider yourself to be advanced in relationship of the manner in which you correlate data in your own self identity. That is, somewhere you have made the necessity for the very fundamental admission of causation. "I am the cause of this." Is that so? You have learned through the *Course* to look around and say, "I don't care what that looks like, I'm the cause of it. I'm not going to let it affect me." That's what you are working on. The fact of the matter is that from a very fundamental idea of correspondence, the word *faith* can be used.

The reason I don't use the word *faith* is that it is inevitably misconstrued to mean faith in relationships of separate organized thoughts – faith in some god that's going to help me do something. Can you hear that? That, of course, to me is not at all what faith is. Faith is what? A total relinquishment of the necessity for the expression in the situation, or in where you find yourself. Very fundamentally, faith in yourself is unfaithfulness to God. Well, you all say "right" to me, but remember, for that to be true, it must be uncompromising, and this is where it's rejected. This is true just because it is the fact of the matter.

If I read you the last three pages of Chapter 17... Did we do 18 yesterday? Did you guys read 18? Yes! It's kind of fun. In 17 it's going to say that you bring into the situation everything that there is. It doesn't seem like you're doing that. It seems as though you are bringing into it only the necessity for your own definition,

CHAPTER ELEVEN: Faith, Crop Circles And Chapter 17

and you depend on the other association to provide you through his own separate faith in his association, the correspondence that will express your faith in each other, using a reality that you refuse to accept in its entirety. Obviously you are going to make that application. But in the truth of the matter, the fundamental truth of the matter, it's a faith in your own association rather than a faith in the single reality of a creative God. It will actually say this on those three pages.

Whatever the purpose in our coming together, it can be directed to our faith in an almighty God, that if we will get out of the way, will show us a new way to look at each other and our relationship with the world. That's called *A Course In Miracles*. But it must be uncompromising in order to be true. If I walk up to an association on earth who is in a situational endeavor, he is serving the purposes of himself and the projections of his own dream – this is the fact of the matter – obviously when I begin to undergo, I suddenly feel the Light and begin to undergo the recognition of my innocence – this could go on to Forrest Gump, this could go on to Chauncy Gardner (The movie, *Being There*); when I come into a situation, I am innocent momentarily of participating in it because I have released my necessity to judge it in the association with my body. You got that? I am innocent of the necessity of the defense of the projections of my own mind. That's called the holy instant, if you let it be. At that moment, I have freed myself of the responsibility of the correspondence with the association I'm addressing in the release of the correspondence with myself, where I'm not going to suffer the conflict of my own association. Is there any question on that?

Let's use the word *special*. All relationships are special (I backed up to 16 here) if the purpose of the relationship is anything but to express the certainty of "we're going to get the hell out of here." Do you see that? That's really where you guys are now. Any other purpose will be totally meaningless. Now, how would that not be viewed as conflictual? I understand perfectly well. You call me on the phone and say, "I'm in this terrible conflict." Of course you are. There is a readjustment of the association that you heretofore established to determine the outcome of pain and death that you wanted, or wanted to overcome in your historic relationship. Inevitably there is a disruption that must occur. It's impossible that not be so. Does everybody agree with that. I'm going to sit down and read you this because it is there. There is no question that that will be viewed as painful and loneliness and rejection and distrust, because it is inherent in the nature of you not receiving the response you have demanded in recognition of the new you. In effect, this is nothing but a Gethsemane or a continuing crucifixion of yourself. Does everybody hear that?

    I don't know whether beginners can hear that, but the truth of the matter is the closer you get to this, the more conflictual it will be unless it's giving you peace. What you'll discover is either you seem to be in total peace or total disarray. Can you get that? That's when you call me on the telephone. Obviously you have been unfaithful to God. There is absolutely no question that it's true, but it is true in a fundamental fashion, not in the fashion in which you attempt to find faith in the limitation. Obviously you're feeling some conflict because you called on God to give you faith in the limitedness of your own association. Can you hear that? He can't do it; then you feel the frustration since you have followed His instructions. There's no question that you followed His instructions. "My Lord why hast thou forsaken me." Do you hear that? Jesus uses the word crucifixion at the end of Chapter 17. Because that's all you're doing. What's the truth of the matter that he will evolve right in that paragraph? He will say that you forgot that who you are meeting out there is you. He'll absolutely say it. Who in hell do you think, in your nightmare, you're meeting but your own self.

    This is why the *Course* is so valuable. Obviously you are meeting in a sharing of conflict of your own mind. The realization

CHAPTER ELEVEN: Faith, Crop Circles And Chapter 17

of that would be the complete Atonement, or the release – why the hell would you defend yourself? The conflict is obviously going on between you and the images of the projections of your own mind. You got this?

That's intensely conflictual. It could not *not* be. For many of you, especially in your Nazareth, the new you that is emerging cannot be recognized in the situation that you previously shared with the identity. The key to this is: "You are doing it to yourself." Do you see how I have to keep going back to that? Then at least you are given the provision of a momentary release of the defense from the attack that is coming into you. Come on! Could you hear that? That's a miracle, isn't it? Here everything is going along smoothly, you think the association is on the same page as you're on; he's not! He's just giving you a perceptual – I've dealt with this since my awakening – he's just giving you a perceptual response in his determination to continue to find an unenlightened correspondence to your relationship. Suddenly he'll turn and attack you. And it is inevitably sudden because until that moment he was justified in the faith of correspondence he had found by identifying you in a willingness to accept the new relationship you offered him. But remember, very probably, since he has not had the totality of the Atonement, that is based on a newer relationship that he intends to establish to justify your continued necessity to be unfaithful to God. And you're saying to him, "No, I am not faithful to this; I am faithful to God." I'm getting away with the word faith. That's what that says. Your unfaithfulness is why you're here.

The funny thing is you are teaching that is an objective emotional fact of the situation. That's actually happening in the situation and is formulated into thought forms that contain the emotions of the protection of your associations – "gimme that doll," "gimme that toy," "gimme that..." Can you hear this? You've already been taught to share the conflict of the association. Into this impossible situation come the teachers of God. Now you must be taught to dispossess the soldier, the doll. There's usually only two things, boys play with soldiers and girls play with dolls. If you want to play with soldiers, what's the matter with you! You can't even escape from the gender. It's just absurd. That being said, it's always an exchange of a possessive association. Isn't that amazing. And you like the variation of the association. And you are excited by the prospects of turning a crank and having a little doll jump out at you. You really don't like to know when he jumps out, but you want the final prediction of the inevitability of the correspondence of turning the crank and getting the result. I ask you to turn the crank and don't expect anything. Then you can always stay in the excitement of not having to identify, without getting a result of your own jack-in-the-box. It's finally only you that's springing out of the box anyway.

At the end of the chapter, Jesus says, "Of course it's conflictual; you're the conflict anyway." And the closer you get to it, the more conflictual it will be. It's a simple fact of the matter. Your solutions can be to attack it and die or to withdraw into your own illusions. Generally speaking, minds of the caliber – I'll use me as an association – will withdraw from the situation, both mentally and physically, into academia or teaching. I'll withdraw from the conflict of the situation and depend on previously-formulated solutions to the apparent problem that have broader ranges or implications of acceptance of the harmony that I am seeking. Can you hear that? Good. I know that this is the field many of us would have followed. We could have gone to our ivory walls and dealt emotionally and intellectually with attempts at communication within the civilization of the world. We could have taken spatial references and become geologists or musicians or whatever. But that's what we would have sought. Why? The conflict of our own mind in the ultimate solution became too intense for us. That's why you need a savior. It is impossible for you to deal with this without

CHAPTER ELEVEN: Faith, Crop Circles And Chapter 17

my mind. I don't care what you do in there; I am offering you the entirety of a conclusion to your apparent conflict that will be divine and take you out of this world because of my innocence of the situation.

I am not teaching you to find another correspondence; I am teaching you to be innocent of the situation. No wonder that seems conflictual. It seems that you are being disloyal to the previous situation. This is why Jesus teaches that everybody's going to get you. Everybody's going to say, "Don't do that. You are being disloyal to us in your own mind." You don't mind looking at that conceptually, as long is it outside of you. But when it happens to you, you don't like it. It's true of you because I'm telling you that there is only you and that this is your mind in relationship to the Universe. What's the sense in talking about this? This is real conflict. I'm going to get you to look at the real conflict that occurs in your mind when you try to resolve the condition which you're in with the true condition of what you are. They cannot be resolved. It's impossible. But at least you've got this far. You've admitted they cannot be resolved, and somewhere in your process of discovering through your own causation that it is not necessary for you to participate in the conflict of the world. Is that so?

It's kind of fun to see how much we can actually share this if you want to share it with me. I am very much aware in my new mind that physical occurrences or manifestations are actually antecedental purpose of the apparent situation; are actually spirit or mind, and that there's always an attempt going on spatially – spatially, mystically – to offer you a form of harmony that will best express the totality of you without the necessity for a conceptual association. This is Shankara, if you'd like to look at it. This is Beethoven. He's saying in the harmony, spatially and mentally, in the music of the spheres there are mathematical formulas of true relationships that will give you the joy of your own mind because it is what you are. And virtually, in the old days, every real mathematician or geologist knew that there were mystical forces involved in his objective association. This is the whole basis of any sort of scientist. But to the extent that he is willing to admit in his own mind his transcendental correspondence, he will escape the necessity to describe it outside of himself. This is Platonism; this become Neoplatonism. So what happens when we are faced with a geographic anomaly? *Science News* is an attempt to look at happenings in relationship to reasonable possibilities in what's termed the scientific community. Obviously it's dealing with what you call "cutting edge quantum connections" but always to the need to make the human connection. Now someone who is aware, say of the nature of what I'm going to talk to you about, is very much aware that much of the phenomena that actually happens in this relationship of separation cannot be really explained within the parameters of what's going on. I don't care whether you call it flying saucers, I don't care whether you say there's a big cover up going on, the fact of the matter is there's a lot of mystical phenomena going on around you all the time. Not only is that true, but since your minds in separation or aggregation are demonstrations of the search for the combination of the emotional or temporal configurations of harmony with the apparent objective associations, your attention somewhere is always being directed to your search for the harmony of your association, no matter how you express it.

  I'm going to try this with – get ready for this – I'm going to try this with crop circles. How many know about crop circles? Well you all know about them because somehow they were mystifying. They are logically mystifying because they appear to present concentric circles with various geometrical shapes in which there is no way that there does not appear to be an intelligence involved. Not that there's not an intelligence involved in everything that you're seeing, this is true, but in this case, it is so obvious that it requires an intelligent relationship between

CHAPTER ELEVEN: Faith, Crop Circles And Chapter 17

circle and line. The whole basis of the universe is circle and line. Can you hear this? That's all that's ever going to be involved.

I'm not going to give you this if you're not – I want to see if you can feel my energy in this. There could be nothing but a circle and a line. A circle is nothing but what? A dot. A circle is nothing but a dot. No matter how you express it, it's a single dot. A line is nothing but the distance between one dot and other. Big deal. Do you get this? My Lord, I'm going to present the string theory of the universe here! This is very clear in my mind. So all we really have are circles in relationships of the expanding circle in the correspondence from the original dot. Do you want to know what a *HolyInstant* is? It's a dot anywhere on the line in a totality of the relationship with the other dots, since all lines are nothing but dots. A line is nothing but dots with no apparent separation. But the truth of the matter is there is no separation. If you can take one single dot in your own mind and don't bbb———b—bb · —·———reak it up into all sorts of correspondences, this is called a *Holy Instant* or an extension from yourself. Can you hear this? So when this is accomplished in nuclear physics they call it the string theory; and the universe as they view it in space/time is a lattice of cross references of concentric circles in combination with geometric drawings. This is how crystals will come together. Isn't that fun. If you take a bunch of Bb's, physically, and you shake them all up, they will have a tendency to form into geometric patterns. What an amazing idea. Is my mind formulating them? Or are they being formulated by mind associations? I seem to have your attention. I don't have any distance in my dots. If you have a dot, you are forming a concentrical association with your own self. I'm doing the same thing. The distance between us will be the line that we are determined to establish in our separate circles of Atonement.

So suddenly here appears in these fields these big circular things and they're perfectly designed geometrically, in isosceles, in various triangular associations that are demonstrated. This is all Euclid geometry – in theorems of Euclid geometry. The reason I never really wanted anything to do with geometry, in the eighth grade it was obvious to me that the theorem established the quotient. The theorem was a response to what could be observed. Either one of them simply justified the other and did not explain how they came about. Now when they appear with no apparent human association, they must become an anomaly.

So here's what this says. I'll read it because it's kind of fun. This is "Theorems in the Wheat Field." This guy, and anybody, had no problem drawing Euclid theorems in correspondence with what was actually being drawn in the field. And everyone could see it – anyone who wanted to see it. The difficulty in seeing it was it didn't appear to be an author who had generated what this could be. He doesn't want to have to deal with that. He doesn't want to have to write an article that says that there's no way that those crop circles could be in the field. The truth of the matter is, and this is to share with me or reject, there *is* no way, it's impossible. He doesn't deal with that. In his mind as a professor, he's an astronomer in this case which is lovely, he is teaching from the academia presenting the objective association with the correspondence of the math of his own mind and the reasonableness of Euclid. It's so beautiful because for the human mind to actually bring this about in a mental correlation or a theorem, a theorem must express the relationships of the object within his own temporal association rather than objectively. This is the difference between algebra and geometry. The difference between algebra and geometry is what I just expressed. The correspondence of the missing numbers or the discovery of lines that do not appear to be evident to your condition, but are actually there.

I'll try it this way: It is impossible for there to be a duality without a third association. You express this as a triangle. Can you hear that? You must! It's expressed as a triangle. But the problem we have is we don't want the solution to our problem

CHAPTER ELEVEN: Faith, Crop Circles And Chapter 17

to be a massive conflict, so we set up an arbitrator who forms the triangle of our association. Class?! Not only do we do that geometrically, we do it in allowing a judge or referee to determine the outcome of our conflict. He's nothing but the third part of our triangle. Now the closest you could get to a harmony would be equilateral. We are laterally equal, which is nothing but a statement that all of our sides are the same. Therefore, all of our angles of resistance in correspondence with each other will find a form of harmony. Are they acute? The problem you have with obtuse angles is that they go more than 180°, you're faced with a circle, which is nothing but the expression of two triangles, which becomes the square. Put two triangles together – "if you build a diamond, I will come." If you give me that reference of the crop circles, I'll be able to land my whole association. I can put my spaceship down on your crop circle. Oh, that's way too far out. This is kind of fun.

"Since the late '70s, farmers in southern England looking out in their wheat fields in the morning have sometimes been startled to find large circles and other geometric patterns neatly flattened in their crops. How these crop circles were created in the dead of night at the height of the summer growing season remains a puzzle." He said some hoaxers went out and tried to duplicate it and it was absurd. It wasn't anything like it. It didn't matter; at least it indicated the possibility that they could have. They weren't concerned about it; there was no correspondence at all. Do you understand that? It had to be a denial of a perfection that could not be identified separately. It's like my weatherman story where the pigeon plops on the Bulgarian farmer. Remember *The Weatherman* (see page 308), the story that I wrote? It's the idea that that could be perfect – I did a pretty good connection. Those kinds of stories are historic. The man was crucified and torn apart simply because he was perfect for a moment outside of himself. "Several years ago astronomer Gerald S. Hawkins, now retired from Boston University, (he's really lovely, we'll get his book) noticed that some of the most visually striking of these crop circle patterns embodied geometric theorems that expressed specific numerical relationships among the areas of various circles, triangles and other shapes." All he really says is that within the circle there will be triangles that express correspondences in not only single circles but concentric circles. Most of you know this. There is a picture of it here, and you'll be able to look at it. Obviously, an equilateral triangle will do nothing but express a single circle, because the harmony is within that. I'm not going to get into that. All I really want to show you is first, that it's true; and second, the way his mind finally has to deal with it because it's kind of nice.

If you look at the original one, there's a pattern that shows a circle in the triangle. "In one case, for example, an equilateral triangle fitted snugly between an outer and inner circle. It turned out that the area of the outer circle is precisely four times that of the inner circle." I'm not going to explain that to you, but if you want to have some fun with it, that's a whole other talk. Listen, "Three other patterns also displayed exact numerical relationships all of them involving diatonic ratios." Does everybody know what a diatonic ratio is? Da da- da- da- My dog has flees. That's a diatonic ratio. I'll ask Michael R. Is that a diatonic ratio? Michael: That's three diatonic ratios. Yeah, okay. That's what I needed because one wouldn't have been enough! That's how we signal aliens. We've been signaling the aliens da-da-da-da. (*Close Encounters*) And here they are with their patterns. Sure enough this big ship is landing. So obviously they are constructing landing fields and are getting ready to land. Is that true? Yeah!

The problem you have with this is the same as you have with *A Course In Miracles*. Obviously there appears to be no way by which those crop circles could be there. That's not possible. It's impossible that the circles are there because they have no source that is here. It's nothing but a miracle of circles.

CHAPTER ELEVEN: Faith, Crop Circles And Chapter 17

But the thing is too damn reasonable. You don't mind miracles that are unreasonable, but miracles that are reasonable make you *very* apprehensive. We are offering you a broader range of your own association.

"Three other patterns also displayed exact numerical relationships, all of them involving diatonic ratios, the simple whole number ratios that determine a scale of musical notes." That's exactly true. Music of the spheres. What an amazing idea. "These designs," says Hawkins, "must demonstrate the remarkable mathematical ability of their creators." Thank you, Hawkins, for using the word "creator" because a mind can be afforded some creativity by its ability to demonstrate the harmony of the universe through the harmony of line and circle.

I spent an hour last night looking at this last association. I'll let you do it. And you will begin to hear music in it. "Hawkins found that he could use the principles of Euclidean geometry to prove four theorems derived from the relationships among the areas depicted in these patterns. He also discovered a fifth more general theorem from which he could derive the other four." That's the diagram that he's drawn here, and I'm going to let you look at it yourself. Suffice to say it's a triangle with one, two, three, four circles of varying arrangements, each one of which corresponds to the line and the circle as it grows. It's a lovely idea. But there was no theorem for it. So this is the challenge that went out to mathematicians: Give me a theorem for this diagram. It's really nice. "The theorem involved concentric circles which touched the sides of a triangle and as the triangle changes shape, it generates the special crop circle geometry. Curiously Hawkins could find no references to a theorem in the works of Euclid or in any other book that he consulted." Actually, it's pretty much a combination of all the Euclidean ideas. You can look at it here if you'd like to. "When he challenged readers of Science News and the math teachers to come up with this unpublished theorem, given only the four variations, no one reported success." He couldn't. It would involve the admission of his own association with himself. It would be if he suddenly found it, he's liable to just disappear all together. What reason would he have to see that if he found total harmony in the reference of the associations of his own mind? How are you going to handle that? "This past summer the crop circles makers showed knowledge of this fifth theorem, Hawkins reported. Among the dozens of circles surreptitiously laid down in the wheat fields of England, at least one of them fit the pattern that he was searching for."

So somebody is trying to tell us something. He doesn't know. Obviously he's already got his tongue in his cheek in regard to this. This is why he's retired from teaching at Boston University. He has no one with whom he can really share his certainty and reasonableness that no human made the crop circles. Do you understand me? Come on, stay with me. I don't care what you do with it; it doesn't come from a human source. That cannot be admitted to, particularly if it's reasonable. The fun we have with him here is he doesn't attempt to say, "Therefore it must have come from God." He's like the text of *A Course In Miracles*. He doesn't say, "Therefore I must accept that Jesus drew the circles." All he says was, "They weren't done by a human being." You say, "Oh yes they were." No they weren't. "Then I don't have to know about it since I can't identify it," is the rejection of it.

The admission that it did not come from here, that theorem, which is so reasonable, will allow me to sit for an hour with that circle and let my mind be freed of the responsibility to do the same friggin tune over and over. I was free to harmonize in my new mind various associations of the staff and the circle of the twelve notes, the association of myself with the dots of my notes, whole, quarter, eighth, or whatever, the distance between the notes and the staff of the line which I was finding between the space and the line. Boy is that mystical. A sheet of music is

CHAPTER ELEVEN: Faith, Crop Circles And Chapter 17

really mystical. What's mystical to me is that you can look at that sheet of music and play it in your mind, can't you? Not only that, but you employ a capacity to use prestidigitation – the magic of your fingers will find a correspondence of the black and the white notes based on the harmony that you find. What an amazing thing. Some of us can do that; some of us can't. But I can sure as hell enjoy you doing it, because I know there is no way possible, though you organize it in your own mind, that you can be responsible for the entirety of the creative harmony that emanates from that reference of sound and sight and all the other things.

Here's the way he does it. It's kind of fun to read the final part: "The persons responsible for this old-fashioned type of mathematical ingenuity..." This is before they thought they knew everything, it was the classic condition of discovery of at least various theorems within ever-expanding complicated lines and circles. "The persons responsible for this old-fashioned type of mathematical ingenuity remain at large and unknown." Obviously they are considered felons, and they're still at large and the establishment is looking for them. "At large" is such great wording. They came fugitively and then left. That's real subtle. No way does he say anything about that. He's just sharing our certainty of what the human condition must do with something that's so reasonably spiritual – reasonably creative. Isn't that lovely? So you not only hear the call, the music of the spheres, it's reasonable to you within the entirety of your own separate relationship, which is the universe, and the certainty of eternal life contained in each element. Sing Amen. All: Aaa - men ! It feels like I'm doing a mass; it's exactly what a mass is. It's an offering of the combination of beads on the – did you ever do the beads on the rosary? They express Euclid geometry in forms of the line of the rosary. I have no idea where that came from!?! Somebody told me they had figured out that the beads of the rosary are in a certain geometric pattern. Somebody's trying to tell you something. Somebody here is trying to tell you something.

Let's just finish this: "The persons responsible for this old-fashioned type of mathematical ingenuity remain at large and unknown. Their handiwork flaunts (I love the word) an uncommon facility with Euclidean geometry." It *flaunts an uncommon facility.* The guy that wrote this, at the very minimum it's an uncommon facility. It flaunts it because there is no way that it can be really explained. "...flaunts an uncommon facility with Euclidean geometry and signals (here's the fun) an astonishing ability to enter fields undetected, to bend living plants without cracking stalks, and to trace out complex, precise patterns presumably using little more than pegs and ropes all under cover of total darkness." That's all. That's the end of the article. What that is is just a nice dig at those who are determined that there's a human perpetrator. Isn't that nice? We should write to him.

Here you are in a construction of your own dots and lines searching for harmony in concentric circles that do not find line harmony. It's as though you are nothing but all small bubbles. This is the whole teaching. Each one of you is trying to find a definition within yourself. And it's within yourself. But the strangeness is as you begin to find the harmony of that correspondence, you will begin to blend creatively with the other bubbles that are actually part of the entirety of your own mind, and were broken up in your circles to keep yourself from seeing harmony. Are you all right with that?

So your circle is expanding. It's always running into the conflict of another organization that has found a correspondence within its own. I'm just looking at how this uncompromising teaching causes conflict. It sure does. This is more for humans.

I'll just read a couple of interesting sentences. This is Chapter 17, *The Call for Faith.* I want you to try and hear it because there are some real dramatic theorems in it. *The substitutes for aspects of the situation are the witnesses to*

CHAPTER ELEVEN: Faith, Crop Circles And Chapter 17

your lack of faith. Notice it says "substitutes." *The substitutes for aspects of the situation are the witnesses to your lack of faith.* This would have to be true if all of the aspects are contained within you. You are fearful of all of the aspects of the situation in which you find yourself. It's an indication of a lack of faith in the ultimate order of the universe in relationship with yourself. You do substitute because the relationship doesn't gratify you in your previous intention. If that's not lack of faith in God, what is it? What we're saying is that power is in your mind and there's no compromise in it. You are either being *un*faithful to God; you can't be faithless, so you must be faithful to the old association which is nothing but unfaithfulness to God. Okay, you've got it. What do they demonstrate? Past tense: *They demonstrate that you did not believe the situation and the problem were in the same place.* You did not believe that time and space were together. *...you did not believe the situation and the problem were in the same place.* Come on. Nobody here in this world does. Yet obviously they're taking their problem with them. And the situation in which they find themselves has nothing at all to do with their apparent problem. You're always deciding in other situations solutions to the problems that you brought with you in correspondence with the problems that exist in that situation. This is what the human condition is. And you continually resolve them in your own mind. What a lovely sentence. *...did not believe the situation and the problem were in the same place.* You always think they're outside of you. You always think that some other situation that you can correspond to has solved the problem that you want, so you're going to go and find them. So every situation you find yourself in is actually resolving the problem of what you think you are? You have faith, then, in your capacity to resolve the problem contained within the apparent situation. What an amazing idea. And you attempt to solve the problem of separation separately within your own associations. Guys, it can't be solved.

But what you're telling me, (I'm talking to humans for a minute), you're telling me that the problem is always solved completely. If you're saying that, you're saying that the difficulties encountered in the apparent relationship have nothing at all to do with the resolution of the problem? Who says that? You do! That's what you're teaching. Guys, that's the *Course In Miracles*. I'm staying with the word faith here because total faith in God would spring you into Heaven immediately because God is your Creator. I'm trying to stay in the vernacular of faith to determine how the human being must first fundamentally reject this entirely. Then as he has the experiences of his inability to solve the problem (AA Program), he discovers that the problem is solved. Do you see that? That could take a little time. I don't want to get into the teaching. I'm trying to see where a human would hear this.

The problem was the lack of faith, ("was" past tense) *and it is this you demonstrate when you remove it from its source and place it elsewhere.* You're always looking outside yourself to solve the problem. That's impossible. Nothing here can solve it. Did everyone hear that? Yes! Good for you. You guys are hearing it at a real good level. So there is no time where you and I could not come together where our problem has not been previously solved. Notice I said "previously" because the presentation of the problem is what the solution is. It's an amazing idea. I love it in regard to crop circles. I could teach the reasonableness of the harmony expressed in associations in my mind. And certainly you demonstrate it in your joy of assuming geometric proportions when you listen to music. Can you hear this? The sound of the music as you assume various geometrical associations is nothing but a demonstration of crop circles. I guarantee you that if I set up a big circle and you come in and begin to assume roles, you'll be generating energy. Do you see that? You're liable to get a ship to land right here. The reason that you reduce it with motions of rhythm and all that is to keep the energetic association going.

CHAPTER ELEVEN: Faith, Crop Circles And Chapter 17

But remember this, there is no such thing as static. Were you to demonstrate the entirety of the perfection of that static condition, you would simply disappear. So we must teach you to activate from that holy instant of correspondence concentric circles that reach higher and higher dimensional proportions. In the advent of coming to that, they will express ratios of relationship with the angles that you are establishing in your correspondence, in your holy triangle. Do you hear that? Obviously if you go past a particular degree, expressing degree as both passion of you – the degrees of heat involved in the hologram – as you express that association, you can come at it completely from the back side because it's forming a triangle behind you. But it's just as vivid within the degrees of the association. It's like having a vision of seeing the back of your head when you looked in the mirror, which is actually what you're doing. For some of you, it's an out-of-body experience. It's standing out of your body and looking at the whole association. It's nice.

As a result, you do not see the problem. You can't. You've already divided it into multiple problems in your own mind. Now you seek the solution of your existence by addressing that particular problem, because that expresses the dilemma that you had when you came in. Or the dilemma you had just a minute ago. This is the whole Workbook. You keep trying to solve that problem in the previous association. I'm talking about this as human relationships – this is a human relationship chapter. It's going to say that your special relationships are going to be very strange, and that's an understatement. I won't jump ahead; I'll read it. The strain is nothing but an unfaithfulness in God. I know you don't like that; that remains the fact of the matter. So go ahead and nod your head at me. "But I'd rather do it myself" is your problem. Your need to do it based on all of the new evidence you've gathered that I'm verifying for you in the new relationship we have found in a better circle. And it's more inclusive. And it makes more sense to you. If it makes sense to you, it probably has nothing to do with reality at all. I say "probably" in the sense that at that point I cannot know. But I can only tell you that it will either make total sense in the admission that God is your Creator or what? No sense whatsoever. It beats staring at somebody who's going "What the hell's he talking about." "You told me evil is an illusion." I'm trying to get you involved in the miracle of our mind. I'll tell you, as this is discovered, look out in this world. You'll see a turning of this world that will astonish you, because the regeneration of the energy of our minds will find a fine circle; it's called the Circle of At-One-Ment. Contained within that initially will be every possible combination of line and form, all speaking to the harmony of the universe. This is so beautiful.

As a result, you do not see the problem. Had you not lacked faith that it could be solved, the problem would be gone. I guarantee you that's true. And I suppose that's practiced somewhere. Fortunately, you can't fail at it because it's always gone anyway. If I can get you to release it, it will continue to solve itself because it always is solving itself. This is what you can't explain to a human being because his expression to you is what the problem is. But you can offer him the vision of the certainty of the correspondence with your wider circle of reference. If he will accept it, he will enter your harmony. You don't really care what he brings into it because it is at that moment he found, through the miracle or the release of himself, a new harmony. That's all I can tell you. "Father, into thy hands I commend my spirit." Or, "My Lord, my Lord, why hast thou forsaken me?" Which are the only two situations you need to know. "What's the matter with this, it doesn't work. Everyone's denying me." "I did everything you told me to do. It's not working." Now you're blaming who? Me for your situation. You need to blame someone else or you'd have to bring your whole situation in with yourself. And you don't intend to do that. If you did that, your situation would be immediately solved. What are you afraid of? The totality of your own situation. Did I get it right? It's that you are afraid. Literally, spatially, you constructed a body in containment because you're afraid of the world outside of you. What an amazing idea! Yet there is nothing in that little dot that does not contain every body association that there is.

And the situation would have been meaningful to you, because the interference in the way of understanding would have been removed. That's the quantum leap that would bring you to universal mind. You are using time to demonstrate your separation. *To remove the problem elsewhere...* That's to "remove" it elsewhere, not to "move" it, to "remove" it; to "remove" the problem, thereby retaining it. It is a *re*-moval of where it appeared to be. Now you have two sources that are unreal. *To remove the problem elsewhere is to keep it, for you remove yourself from it and make it unsolvable.* But the problem that remains there is your unresolved problem. So your associations of other humans are nothing but your own unresolved problem. And you have constructed a total unreality – that's what you call a body – it's a solution contained within itself. This will say that you are meeting yourself. Can you share in your unresolved problems? What a teaching. This is faith again, just for a minute, because I could teach this from the pulpit and it is taught. This is taught. It isn't that this isn't taught.

There is no problem in any situation that faith will not solve. God, I trust you, not myself. I'm making it simple so you can say, "I can't do that." So that I can say, that's true, you can't. I'll do it once more for you. When you say to me, "I can't do that," I know, you can't. But the statement that you can't do it is just a denial that God can and will cause the conflict that I can read about over in here. In other words, your statement, "I can do it" and, "I can't do it," if it doesn't give you instant eternal peace, is nothing but a retention of the conflict. Say "of course." Well, it would have to be. I jumped ahead; that's what this will say. Once you get trapped into that association, you can't get out. We call that crucifying your Christ. Or breaking your Christ into particles, your own body, that are in conflict in an entirety of the universe being held together by your mind in disharmonious associations where your parts of your jig-saw man do not correspond to each other. And you call that life, and it's not life at all. It's nothing but disassociations that you attempt to hold together. Got that? What a strange place. Instead of letting the harmony in each incident formulate a universal body of harmony. Do you see that?

There is no shift in any aspect of the problem but will make solution impossible. Your cues of references to the solution of the problem that you see are false. Any attempts to shifting the problem to correct it will result in a multiplication of the problem. You have been a liar from the beginning. You cannot resolve it because you have no true reference. All I really offer you, as what you call a miracle mind or an enlightened mind, is a true reference of yourself. "Well, that's based on the harmony of your mind." Oh, dung! What do you mean, "my mind"? It's based on your willingness to correspond to your own mind to the conflict you have set up with me in order to keep separate in your own situational identity. "If I defend myself, I am attacked." Obviously the ultimate attack would be me. This is why the community rejects you. This is the teaching that I cause conflict. I could not *not*. Jesus says, "I came to divide brother and sister..." He says it. I don't have to teach you that. You just make a situation out of that and come out with statements, "You told me I had to hate my father." I don't know what the hell you're talking about. "You told me that evil is an illusion." I told you Truth was an illusion, evil is very real. Is there a question about this? Somebody is saying, "We don't go to you because you teach that evil is an illusion." We don't teach that evil is an illusion. We teach that evil is very real. We teach that you're the cause of the realness of you. Obviously if you knew it was an illusion you wouldn't be here. That's the truth of the matter. You find in the *Course* where Jesus says the devil is very real. He doesn't say it's an illusion. He says you

CHAPTER ELEVEN: Faith, Crop Circles And Chapter 17

are! That's the truth. You have made a world of illusion, and it is evil because it's separate from God. Then you say, "Oh, you mean the separation is an illusion." Only if you are. If you are in your entirety, what are you concerned about? Here it is:

There is no shift in any aspect of the problem but will make solution impossible. For if you shift part of the problem elsewhere the meaning of the problem must be lost, and the solution to the problem is inherent in its meaning. Now you've just got nothing but unsolvable problems. That's why I always have taught you: one problem, one solution. If your problem is being a human being, your solution is not being. If your problem is an alcoholic, you have one problem. It's caused all your other problems. Sure enough, you don't drink any more and a lot of your problems are still there, but at least they go away to the extent where you're going to find more harmony. That's really what I'm offering you initially. But I assure you that as a mortalholic, you have a single problem, and that's the conflict you suffer from attempting to create not under the auspices of the totality of God. You are unfaithful to the certainty, which must make you unfaithful to the certainty of the solution because you don't know who you are.

Is it not possible that all your problems have been solved, but you have removed yourself from the solution? You search everywhere but where the solution is because you are fearful of the entirety of the solution. Why? Because you will discover that you had nothing to say about it at all. Do you see that? Which is what surrender is. At least I'm being heard. That's why I don't do this chapter. *Yet faith must be where something has been done, and where you see it done.* Both – where it *has* been done, and where you *see* it done. It has been done. At any moment it's always being completed. It's only that you recognize the miracle, not that you do anything about it. It's always there in its fullest – "Thy will be done."

A situation is a relationship, being the joining of thoughts. If problems are perceived, it is because the thoughts are judged to be in conflict. It would have to be. My thoughts are in conflict with yours. You tell me your problem; I'll tell you mine. And we'll find a resolution within the problem. At no point are we looking at what the fundamental problem is. We wouldn't dare do that, or the resolution would begin to occur. But the resolution must begin to occur in my mind and you will not understand the manner in which I am resolving the problem. I am obviously resolving the problem by not attempting to solve it. To you, that seems unreasonable. To me, it's perfectly reasonable because I've experienced the solution through not attempting. Not that I knew that the solution was somewhere else, but I stopped trying to solve it. Have you got that? "My Chauncy, you have such a demeanor of unconcern." Obviously. He doesn't even recognize it. Can you hear that? Forrest Gump is the story of innocence demonstrating power. It's exactly what it is. But it's also true. Not only that but you *know* it.

But if the goal is truth, this is impossible. Some idea of bodies must have entered, for minds cannot attack... Here we go. *Faithlessness brought to faith will never interfere with truth. But faithlessness used against truth will always destroy faith. If you lack faith, ask that it be restored where it was lost, and seek not to have it made up to you elsewhere, as if you had been unjustly deprived of it.* That's a resentment. Could you hear that? It's nothing but a statement of a grievance. I've been unjustly denied my rights in an old situation; I intend to get even in this present situation. What an amazing idea. Are you doing that to yourself? That situation is just your refusal to bring the entirety of the admission of your responsibility, projecting it outside yourself where it becomes a grievance. Is that what this world is? All: Yes. There's an important element that I asked in the fundamental psychology of this, the admission that you are the cause of your own pain. There's a value contained in that in your decision not to continue to foster resentment based on the old association simply because you say anything, including "it's not worth it." I don't mind you doing that. I always used to demonstrate it by the guy that cut you off in traffic and gives you the finger. It's so easy to see that you're carrying the emotion in your own mind. And a guy suddenly zooms by, forces you off the road, and then gives you that finger. How you would not feel the resentment about that is beyond me. You think that I am teaching you you're not supposed to feel the resentment. That's bulldung. How would I possibly teach you that. If you didn't feel it, you wouldn't need to be taught. You also wouldn't be here. Can you see that? You say, "Well, Master, as an evolved soul, he doesn't feel any resentment." Ha ha. I feel it totally about everything. I don't have to address them separately. That's what salvation is. Can you hear that? That's not really what I wanted to talk about.

I wanted to mention in this that you as a human can see that you are now feeling the resentment of that situation. Is that situation over? Yes or no? It happened to you. And you're going to hold onto it as long as you're in time. As long as you're in time, you will try to get even with the injustice that you think was done to you. I didn't mean to move it up that fast. But that's the truth of the matter. You are dealing with it on a specific basis so you can keep your problem solved. The fact of the matter is if you had simply forgiven that situation in its entirety, you would have had a *Holy Instant*. You can always pick it up later to examine it, twist it and sedate yourself because you can't get even with it. You sedate yourself because you can't get even with God. That's what the resentment is. You have very broad ranges of resentment because even in your apparent harmony you are able to find another imperfection in your own association that is going to cause you to grieve. You're a good candidate for Atonement, for salvation. That's true, isn't it. You are a likely candidate. But I'm not taking your conflict away from you. But I must tell you fundamentally that you are the cause of it, or there's no hope at all. Then, at the very minimum, when you feel this intense conflict, you can finally say, "Wait a minute..." What are you doing? You are justifying his capacity to cause you pain. All psychologists somewhere teach you are doing it to yourself. They don't take it to the next step that you are the cause of it. But somewhere they will allow you to be the cause of it sufficiently to relinquish the problem that you think you're suffering. Could you hear that? Yes! This becomes Freudian counseling, I guess. Let's salve the ego sufficiently so we can find some harmony within ourselves.

But that resentment is real, isn't it? And you're entitled to have it. Did he or did he not cut you off? Did he or did he not rape your sister? Did he or did he not do it? And the answer is "of course he did." And you intend to get even with him if it takes the rest of your life. You're going to search him out and kill him until you die. You're trapped in that resentment of your own mind. You can't teach this without forgiveness, I'll guarantee you that. I don't know where the hell you are with it in your own mind, but I guarantee if you keep it, it will be you. I can't teach you to relinquish it, but I can show you how you can experience the peace of God through the forgiveness of the necessity to demonstrate – the demonstrations of this world are nothing but an attack on God. It's nothing but an attack on the entire universe. It's nothing but saying "I want my will to be done in my spatial/temporal reference." Sorry about that. I took it up to the philosophy for a minute. But without applying the psychology, there's no hope for you. That must be resolved within your own mind. And it *can* be. The second step is difficult for you, and I'm teaching you if you resolve it in your own mind, it will be resolved out there. That's a step you don't want to make, that there's a solution contained in the entirety to which you can correspond in your mind. Do you see that? This is the offering that's always being made to you, that it is impossible that Universal Mind, Creative Mind, not be in harmony with itself. And all of your manners of bringing your own conflict in continuing reassociations of harmony are nothing but the lessons

CHAPTER ELEVEN: Faith, Crop Circles And Chapter 17

of crop circles. Can you hear me? Nothing but that. Everywhere you are being told to find the harmony because you are telling yourself, because there is *only* yourself. Obviously you are going to suffer more conflict because what you told yourself before wasn't true, and you're going to have to examine it under the emergence of your own mind that sees the unreasonableness of the conflict that you heretofore justified. I know you are listening to me; but I want you to see that the progress that you will make in this *Course* is based on your willingness to remain in the conflict and not resolve it. It's called becoming miracle minded. Because it is being resolved. That's why it's so valuable to have this here.

Distinguishing between conflict really doesn't make any sense to you, does it? Why do you want to separate it off? You have one problem with one guy. That's your whole problem. "At least you don't cause me as much problem as your brother and sister." What a place to be. This is nothing but a retention of the conflict of self identity which results in death. Has everybody got it? Good for you. And each of you, individually, is determined not to do that anymore? So you're entering into a new harmony with the associations of your mind. It requires the admission of what? This is my original teaching. Before I had the *Course* at all, I always taught this. Do you remember this? The first thing that I ever did when I went to Unity Church – I don't know why they told me to give the sermon – within the first five minutes I said, "Everybody put your finger on your nose." Okay, let's try it, put your finger on your nose. That's the problem. But it's also the solution because it's the total cause. You like it when I do that. That's actually what I teach. I don't know why, because I knew that the problem was there, not out there. One problem, one solution. I learned that on the 12 Step program, that I could relinquish my necessity to justify my grievance and let God solve the problem. That's all I teach. That's an action of your mind, isn't it? That's the joy that you experience called the peace of God. It's the admission that you evolved for me that the problem couldn't be solved. It isn't that I didn't know I had the problem, it's that I thought I could solve it. You can't. Now that evolved my ability to use aphorisms, like "in my weakness is my strength." Well, that's very true. In my total weakness is my total strength. "Don't analyze, utilize." That's *A Course In Miracles*. I got all the phrases for you. And you say, "You don't mean entirely." And I say yes I do. Never analyze, and utilization of the power of God will be immediately available to you. Say "of course."

Now that may very well be because you get sick and tired of analyzing. I don't know. But you can't escape it by stilling your own analyzations. But it can be simplified in the analyzation of – this is the accomplishment of a real mind. I just wanted to simplify it, so your analyzation must resolve possibilities. I want it to resolve the possibility of this or not this. *Then* you can begin to make choices not of your own making. Because I guarantee you, I am the guarantee that that other choice is available to you. That requires your faith that I have solved the problem. The more faithful you are – I can use me or use anybody, I don't care – he's only a projection of your own mind anyway. If he has in fact solved the problem, so have you. It could not *not* be so because he's a product of your mind. Now albeit I am offering you a solution you don't want to accept, but if you'll accept it, your problem will be solved. I'm the Savior telling you your problem has already been solved. You're not here and there is no world. But remember, having accepted that, you are also gone from here. The step you have arrived at is being gone from here and sharing momentarily the solution *and* the manner by which you come to it because it would be impossible to share the entirety of the solution without sharing the cause. But remember, I'm only speaking of you.

So I'm not going to bring my problem into the situation no matter what. Now many of you say, "Well I'm just going to have to do this." A little sacrifice. "I'm not going to complain about it. I'm going to keep myself wrapped up and I can always go to

CHAPTER ELEVEN: Faith, Crop Circles And Chapter 17

a psychiatrist or Aunt Tillie where I can share my problems that are in me separate from the problems that are out there." I suppose that's fine. You can always find someone who can commiserate with your need to do what? Inflict pain on yourself. While I'm willing to acknowledge it, I'm a therapist to direct your attention to your own causation. Many of you now like to hear that from me. The question is do you want to hear it in its entirety? That's called *A Course In Miracles*. Do you hear me? I'm giving you this realistically because it *is* realistic; it is a real problem that is the problem of this world. What? Unfaithfulness to God; the separation that you believe is real.

Only what you have not given can be lacking in any situation. The twists in his mind are incredible. The only thing missing in a situation is what you haven't given to it. Is that true? If you give everything to the situation, it will immediately resolve any problems that you could have with it. Is that true? You don't examine it at all? You don't set up objections, you simply give? That's very close to creating, because your situation will change in its entirety because by holding it in a grievance, you've prevented it from being resolved. The only thing missing in a situation is what you don't bring to it? Yeah, but if you bring your whole self, you'll be crucified instantly by the association. That's a statement of fact. That's what this says. They are going to find you and seek you because you are offering them harmony. I'm not going to take that away from you today, because many of you in this final step will feel that conflict. I can only offer you the entirety of the solution, not a partial solution, although you may make that application. *Only what you have not given can be lacking in any situation. But remember this; the goal of holiness was set for your relationship, and not by you.* Doggone you! If I can get you to at least teach this in the *Course*, you won't have a problem. You keep trying to perfect your own relationships with yourself, but all of your goals are designed to keep you from solving the problem.

Boy it would be nice if I could find a million people who could hear what that says. Obviously all of the teachers for the past 20 years have been teaching you to perfect your special relationships. It's exactly the opposite of the teaching. You can't solve your special relationship. That's why it says "remember," otherwise you'll try to examine together what your problem is through a relationship that's going to show you God. The separation of the problem cannot show you God. It cannot be resolved. God ends up as an arbiter of your problem, which is the condition of the human being. We'll ask God together in a parish, and then suddenly God solves the problem momentarily for the parish, which has nothing at all to do with the world; it's a resolution based on a continuing establishment that denies what the real problem is.

...the goal of holiness was set for your relationship, and not by you. You did not set it because holiness cannot be seen except through faith, and your relationship was not holy because your faith in your brother was so limited and little. Your faith must grow to meet the goal that has already been set for you. I am offering you the ultimate goal because that's the one that has been set for you. Your return from time to eternity. Wow! This is really something.

The power set in you in whom the Holy Spirit's goal has been established is so far beyond your little conception of the infinite that you have no idea how great the strength that goes with you. And you can use this in perfect safety if you will. You don't have to be afraid of the power of your own mind to declare it. I want to try this with you. I just want to show you how certain I am this is true. All you really have to do in your own mind is stand up and say, "The hell with it." I'm talking about you. I'm using the power to keep this – just stand up and say, "The hell with it." But that's going to be in you, isn't it? That may appear momentarily to be a conflict. But at least you've got the conflict in you. Now, the ultimate conflict will

CHAPTER ELEVEN: Faith, Crop Circles And Chapter 17

occur in your relationship with yourself and God. That's the truth of the matter.

I shook my fist at God a lot of times. I denied Him and said, "Go screw yourself." When a chaplain came up to me when I got through with combat and said, "God is this," I said get the screw out of here. Don't you tell me that that's the resolution of my problem with God. I'm giving you the fact of the matter. If this is the kind of world you made, I don't want anything to do with that guy. There must be another solution. Maybe I then rejected God and directed it to myself. Maybe then I began to employ the power of the freedom of that in my mind. I'm offering you all the possible situations that could have occurred to you to reach the ultimate conclusion that there is no world. And *that* requires the miracle of your confronting.

And you can use this in perfect safety. Yet for all its might, so great it reaches past the stars and to the universe that lies beyond them, your little faithlessness can make it totally *useless, if you would use the faithlessness instead.* I can't do anything about that. *Yet think on this, and learn the cause of faithlessness: You think you hold against your brother what he has done to you.* I guarantee you that you would not be here if you did not blame something outside yourself. And that includes the acceptance of the world in which you appear to be, as though you can't do anything about your physical association. If this world was here, you have every right to be resentful about the rain coming on you, the thunder, your crops being destroyed. After all, isn't that what's taught in the Old Testament? Doesn't God arbitrarily decide – that's nonsense to be trapped in that. Nonsense. *But what you really blame him for is what you did to him.* You don't like that. That's Sermon on the Mount. I don't care whether you like it or not, I'm just telling you it's true. I'm not asking you to practice manners in which you can not hold a grievance through blaming a guy out there and then trying to resolve it. I'm telling you it can't be resolved. If I can teach you to do that, you won't keep establishing sin and then trying to atone for it. If it really *is* outside of you, you're not going to succeed in doing it anyway. *It is not his past but yours you hold against him. And you lack faith in him because of what you were. Yet you are as innocent of what you were as he is.* This is the whole *Course.* Just listen to me a minute Actually we're all innocent of our human relationships which are doing nothing but denying us our own creative certainty. That's a true thing. There is no such thing as this. I have to speak to you individually because you're holding it together in the patterns of your own mind. I would like this teaching basically if I were you because I directed your attention to what must be the solution. I'll use the term "ultimate" if you want me to use it, but I assure you, from my certainty, that you are in your own nightmare or dream. Have you got this? Is that true? That at least gives you the capacity to suffer with the admission of self-inflicted pain. You are determined to justify your own grievance through projecting it onto the world. Is that so? Do you guys hear me? This is the whole teaching. The dilemma that you'll have in teaching this is always directing the association to the responsibility of the cause of it. He can't accept it. When he does, he won't be here.

Guys, if I had just 300 people here that had never heard this, would there be an advantage to what I'm doing now? I'm just curious. I'm just reading it. If you're going to take the *Course In Miracles* out in the world with your new mind, why can't you do this? That's an offering that must, hopefully, incur in our sharing of God, a harmony called a miracle, where we begin to share the love – I didn't mention that word – but faith in God is what love is! That moment of faith in God, is Love. You guys know this perfectly well. I wish I could teach you that. I don't know how to teach that. You're always only meeting me or nothing. I bet you can't hear me. There *is* only one situation. You're always only meeting me – I can assure you I can solve your problem. Do you see?

CHAPTER ELEVEN: Faith, Crop Circles And Chapter 17

At the very minimum you've decided to stay in the circle where the problem can be solved instead of refusing to bring the entirety of your problem to me. I don't care who you bring it to, if you brought the entirety of your problem to any situation, it would have to be resolved because there really isn't any problem. You come to me objectively and ask me to relieve you of your burden. If you'll bring your entire burden into the situation, it is very easily relieved because I have nothing to do with the relief of your problem except offering you the entirety of the solution because I am *A Course In Miracles* teacher. Obviously your problem is that you refuse to do it. Why? You'll lose the little that you have. If I give you everything, I'm going to lose all of my old thoughts. I would rather hang on to the little crap that I've got than surrender. That's the fact of the matter. You are afraid of the loss of your old associations, and that's exactly why you refuse to come to this Academy, because there's nothing compromising about our association. At the minimum we constantly demand your metamorphosis, your reassociation of the entirety. You don't object to the concept of it, but you object to it in its entirety because its entirety is an admission: first of all, that there must be an entire solution outside of it; and second, that you can come to it by a means not under your own direction. That's just the truth of the matter.

It's fun for me to look at the manner in which you come at this perhaps obtusely in your triangle identity. It's impossible that if two people are together there is not a third association. Stand up. You stand here, and I'll be here. This is a human's condition. There is no condition possible in duality without a third relationship. Can you get that? I could do this in the crop circles for you if you want me to. The question is not that, the question is where will I be in relationship to you? Is this a triangle? Look at it. Not much of one. Now let's stand over here. You're forming objective energy relationships with what appears to be a third object. See if you can get this with me. If you'll let the third object be a circle rather than another dot, this is called the

Holy Spirit. "Where two or more are gathered, I am there" because I am the entirety of the distance between you. Do you see that? That's why you form holy triangles. Without a triangle, there would be no solution at all – I'm not saying there wouldn't be, but all you would have is a straight line. You stand here. You stand here. I'm standing between you. Well, if you set me up as obstacles between you, by your own objective senses: "Hello, how are you?" "Hello, how are you?" Now you're studying me in relationship, and you're studying me, and you guys are talking about me. It's impossible for you to talk about me directly because I'm the conflict between your minds. Can you hear this? What do you do? You form a triangle. See? Now you can correspond with me and use the triangle as your reference point. That's called space.

So here I stand. It's also impossible for us not to form a circle in that. I won't get into that. Why? You are actually the circle and you will form a circle in correspondence with it. And you will define space as curves because there's no such thing as a straight line. If I stood straight with you, and you removed this obstacle, the line would become eternal. An eternal line is what God is. It never turns around. But a line that's eternal has no beginning and no end. If it has a beginning and an end, it must be circular; it would have to be circular because it has to come out where it ends. Otherwise, how would it know it is curved? Your problem is you can't know you're straight until you curve on yourself. That's a fact of the matter. You like it when my mind begins to do that. But that's true. Here we stand as a triangle. Now we've got three people trying to do it. Now we have what we call a human relationship.

Somewhere you must take sides in the association. This is called justice. I'm going to be justice. Why? You have made a sufficient commitment to me in your own mind where you are willing to share it with his mind based on my ability to arbitrate. These are called the laws of man. These are called the idols,

CHAPTER ELEVEN: Faith, Crop Circles And Chapter 17

aren't they, that you establish. This is the king, this is the authority that you give him, the covenant. Do you understand me? Now, you appeal your case to me, and you appeal your case to me. I am a conglomerate association of the combinations of you. I am able to see some of your problem and some of your problem, and you trust me somewhere with a sufficiency to be aware of your historic problem, and aware of your historic problem as an elder to make a more truthful judgment of your conflict. That's why you're here. I really don't know anything more about the solution than you do. I am nothing but an accumulation of your problem that you solve within the parameter of your individual abilities not to solve the single problem, but rather to resolve it within the limitations of your own mind. This is a good idea. This is a good reference. I wouldn't dare stand between you because you couldn't communicate at all. You must allow for some communication. But you're afraid of it in its entirety because it would resolve the conflict that you're experiencing with each other. Yet I must be that because the expression of the conflict is the expression of the solution. But you're trying to solve it here rather than including him in with your problem through your non-definition of the separation of yourself.

I'm a hell of an arbiter because I really don't see your problem. And I really don't see yours. But every time you ask for a solution you want it to be solved, at the minimum, under terms of yourself, at the maximum, under terms of the apparent relationship. First of all, you decide, "The hell with it, I can't solve it. This is going to be my solution." Now at least you have directed your problem to where your solution is. I assure you I will not arbitrate between your previous conflicts because they don't concern me. Just as certainly, I am offering you my Christhood, or your Christhood, which is nothing but the conversion of the great arbiter, the Holy Spirit, to the certainty of causation in objective association. In other words, our two Christs can come together. Isn't that nice? And just did! What are we doing? We're just demonstrating in our dance, in our singing, in our harmony.

I noticed this association wants me to bring a director from outside, who doesn't believe in us, down to do Godspell. I won't do that, dear one. Why would I want to bring a director who doesn't even understand what we're doing? You direct it! "Well, he's more expert." Crap. It isn't that I mind bringing professionals in, but I have no understanding of that. Why would I pay somebody to come in and direct us to the falsity of our association? That's okay, but I just wanted you to know – you keep looking for play doctors. The doctor of this play obviously is false as the Holy Spirit, not somebody who's coming in, or certainly the Christhood in you being shared in the new aggregation of the Great Ray association. The Great Rays will be mentioned.

Now, if I move over here, your ability to find harmony is nothing but a broadening of your circle association so that any triangle I present you with you'll not be concerned about, including what we would term the negative triangle, or the moment between 12 and 6, the moment where the angle does not exist. Salvation is actually in the circle at the moment, isn't it? – where the angle does not manifest itself, where the line is perpendicular. The circle then is demonstrated by the cross , which is going to be nothing but triangles, which will square the circle in the relationship with you. Do you see? Your solution is obviously a straight vertical line. It could not *not* be. The manifestation of the necessity for that is the cross, which will set up triangles of energy in the circle Are you with me with that? So obviously, to that extent, the point of the cross is where salvation would be. I don't know how you hear that, because if that's true in the centrifuge, you would immediately use the power of energy and you'd be gone from here. That's a true statement. So you make a Masonic cross out of it; you can do anything you want with the symbols. What I want you to see is

CHAPTER ELEVEN: Faith, Crop Circles And Chapter 17

in the crop circles you have a demonstration of universal harmony that cannot be explained in the limitation of your association because somewhere you want da-da-da-da, or you went da-ta-da-ta, or did something, where you began to express more harmony in the simplicity of your relationship rather than complicating it using the energy of your creator.

The joy you are experiencing is simply the loss of conflict of the barrier that you have set up in your own mind between you and your illusions. The solution has to be momentarily the admission of the entirety of the illusion of the association of temporal order. At least then you'll end up in more harmony with your circle, I hope. And obviously you have begun to be able to tell the difference in those who first of all have not even admitted to the problem. You would do absolutely nothing with that association. He's just trapped in his own mental incapacities. He doesn't hear you at all. As that expands, you find communication with people who are more harmonious in your efforts to seek each other and love each other. Finally that becomes a single whole purpose.

What am I doing up here demonstrating? I'll finish this up. I'll be very resentful if I miss the beginning of the Badger game. What did I just say? If I miss the beginning of the Wisconsin game, I'm going to be very resentful. Will you forgive me for the resentment? Or must I forgive myself? Must I forgive you for causing me to miss the game? That being expressed, what time is it? Ah, time flies when we're in love.

I just want you to know those next few pages are something. This is before all the lovely stuff. This is Chapter 17 that I was reading. Somewhere there is faith in love. But my certainty of my faith in you did not evolve from my measurement of you, nor of myself, in our relationship. Measured faith is not what faith is. I'm sorry, that's just the fact. You can put all the energy in measurement that you choose. Do you understand? Metes and bounds can be contained, and they can demonstrate angles of harmony in resistance, but they cannot create. And until you begin to see that with me, you will remain in a harmonious association of the correspondence of your circle and your line. That's true because it's true, not because I say so. I've stayed out of the Great Rays, the harmonious associations of music and the diatonic scale, the involvement of your emotion in with the apparent condition of your objective reality. I don't know how you do that in your own mind, and you may not do it at all. All I can really offer you is the simplicity of your escape from hell. The more you are willing to admit to me that you are in a condition that is not acceptable to you, the more I can offer you the solution. I'm at the crux of this teaching. If I have that situation sitting right there that really doesn't want the solution to the problem, there's nothing I can do. Do you hear me? Is there anyone who doesn't hear this? This is the whole teaching of the *Course*. If you are addicted and don't want the solution or believe that you can solve it within your own mind, I can't help you because you are the condition of that solution.

The whole first obstacle to Atonement is the non-necessity for it. The reason you're too early is the world doesn't need you. Can you hear that? You're making an offering to the world that it doesn't need. It doesn't have to hear you at all, and it doesn't. It didn't even have to crucify you. It couldn't hear you at all. Suddenly you're bringing it out into the world – now you're going to have to be crucified. That's good news! This is the whole *Course In Miracles*. Good news now because they're going to have to listen to what it says in order to kill it. Listening to what it says will begin a process of reason in your own mind because what we're offering you is reasonable. You are in a totally unreasonable association. As long as you give it reason, it will have reason. Why? You gave it to it.

Do you understand me? We have to share the pain before we can share the solution. I'm not trying to take your pain away from you. I'm telling you that if you'll release it, God will solve

CHAPTER ELEVEN: Faith, Crop Circles And Chapter 17

it for you. You don't like that. Why? You solved it! Don't tell me you haven't or you wouldn't be here. How have you solved it? Through pain! Through the acceptance of your condition and the admission you can't do anything about it, you simply retain the pain. And all things around you die and get old. And the children die, and your mother dies, and you're sick and I don't like you. I don't like you because you pretend to be loving and actually you're killing everything around you. That's a fact. I don't pay any attention to you personally and individually, but if you direct my attention to it, I'll pay attention to you because I'm offering you a solution that's not acceptable to you because it's not of this world. Do you hear me? Now, if I can get you to stay within your own mind, you won't have a problem. But very probably you won't. You'll immediately seek the revenge against me that you found by being here, so that you can quick go out and make a phone call "he's saying..." Who the hell are you talking to? Answer me. You're only talking to the momentary associations of your own mind. That's how complete my solution to your problem is. Everyone you address here shares your problem of the denial of what I'm offering you. You nod your head at me. Now at least you can feel the conflict when you go to the phone and say, "I've never heard anything like this, I'm never going to..." He'll say, "What are you doing? How dare you leave us?" And you're saying, "Well, I've looked at your dung and I don't want it anymore." "You always wanted it before." Yes or no? This is the whole lesson.

I'm not showing you that conflict is an illusion. I am showing you that conflict is real. At least you have it where it can be solved. What you're doing is outrageous. It's ridiculous. It's absolutely not acceptable. It's called *A Course In Miracles*. But you don't want the miracle. Then you look at other people and say to them, "Well, if you would have had the same situation I had, you wouldn't be able to solve it either." "I can see that your situation was not like mine." And that will include their situation being worse than yours, because I'm offering a worsening instead of a solution. They'll look at you and say, "If I had had the bottom you had, I could see how you got this." It's just another way of saying "I haven't suffered enough." Which is another way of saying, "I've escaped the pain that's inevitable in my own life." Do you hear that?

My mind is actually not concerned about the expression of this at all. It's only concerned about your acceptance of it. Do you see that? I'm talking to you. You appear to be weak; you don't look weak to me. I don't care how you're expressing yourself. All you've got to do is accept it and the power is there. If you reject it, the manner in which you demonstrate it, I'm indifferent to. You can kill me, go to the monastery, stand there and go like that. What do I care? This is not a real place. There isn't any such place as this. You're going to have to do that conversion in your mind. But the manner that you do it, what do I care? It will be manifested in an infinite number of ways. Quite literally. Any combination will work if you let it. And if you have to come at it obtusely, come at it! If you're afraid to look at it directly momentarily and you resolve other problems, other problems resolved will enter into spatial references of solutions of past and future references. Could you hear that? Could you get that? No.

I don't care what angle you set up to correspond energy in the association within the expanding pattern as long as it generates energy itself. Do you see that? There's no time limit in the game of baseball, which is nothing but a diamond, or a square, or a definition of a circle where you run in continuing expansions of the association. Whether you play the game or the manner in which you play it doesn't concern me. That is, if there's nothing outside of you, somebody's got to watch the game. I don't care what part you play in the production, but you have to get into the circle.

When the Old Man's a short-timer, you'd better look out. Do you understand you think your way out of this. This is just

CHAPTER ELEVEN: Faith, Crop Circles And Chapter 17

the truth of the matter. You are employing your own mind, setting up illusions; you actually think your way to Heaven because Heaven is an idea of your mind. You can't really be outside of Heaven, anyway. This is what, hopefully, you just read. See, I got to Chapter 18. It's just that little corner, and you're contained within that little corner. But you must see that first, in order to recognize your own Christhood. So I jumped into the hole first. Can you get this? But you knew perfectly well I was going in; it is impossible that you don't know that, because we are at the parameter of that association. And obviously there has to be a plan involved in this. Obviously I came to a part of your association in space/time where you do not recognize me. And just as obviously you know me perfectly well outside the well. You could not *not*. Every time I come to take you home and wake you from the dream, I say to you, "I came to take you home and wake you from your dream," and you say, "Who the hell are you?" Your denial of me must be an indication that you know me, otherwise why am I saying to you "I'm taking you out of your dream." You keep saying, "Who the hell are you?" At the minimum you say, "I'm not ready to hear you yet." This is a true statement. "I'm not ready to hear you now." Why not? "I'm doing okay." Boy is that individual. So you accumulate a lot of "I'm doing okays." And in case I come to you too much, you have a final resolution to deny me that you've always used before. What do we call that? Death. You live out that cycle and say, "Ha ha ha ha ha ha." But you didn't go anywhere. All you did was stay in your own association with yourself. That's your greatest fear – loss of death.

What I've actually done is cut off your escape. Escape is nothing but setting up a barrier of self- existence between me and what you are. As it gradually removes, it removes the old behind you that you used to fall back on, because you have projected it out in front of you as a defense of the association. Can you hear that? So when you go back and resolve it, the conflict that you were going to set up – that you're still setting up – in your own mind, you simply don't do anymore. It disappears because it's no longer a part of your old reference. See, you're rising above it. You're staying at that bottom all the time. If you stay there, it's always resolved. It's called turning your will and your life over to God. Do you see. And if you find yourself in a false bottom, the establishment of nothing and nothing, or your potential and the gratification of your potential within time, you could stay in time a very long time. That's the way it works. Your bottoms are so high, you are right next to your solution. You don't have to go down into the depths of despair anymore because they don't have any meaning to you. You've used up all of your despair. "Abandon hope all ye who enter here" means that if you'll abandon hope when you enter hell, you'll get out real quick because there *is* no hope where you're going. Stop trying to solve it in your relationships with each other.

Yesterday, hopefully, we had the philosophy. Today we have the psychology. Tomorrow we'll have the religion. It's finally all the same idea, because it's just ideas in your own mind. The lucidity of your new mind is exciting. Why wouldn't you be excited. You've been offered eternal life. You've been shown that happiness never leaves and all the other good stuff that goes with that, instead of insisting that I solve your meaningless problems for you. If you insist I solve your meaningless problems, it's nothing but your own mind projected from you insisting that the conflict must be retained in order that it can be resolved to justify yourself with yourself. It has no meaning whatsoever. This world was over a long time ago. I'd like that. Somewhere you can move into a new association where you'll see this one is gone.

Can you understand you are the product of a single mind that went astray? Can you hear that? You're the problem of one mind that for a moment heard something else. So you are both the problem and the solution. No matter how much he broke

CHAPTER ELEVEN: Faith, Crop Circles And Chapter 17

up his mind subsequently, which is what you did, he cannot escape the wholeness that he engenders in the entirety of him, so he has separate evil ones demonstrating his separation. So each one of them out there must contain the entirety of his solution, and that's what he's actually afraid of, because he knows perfectly well that his projections of his brother are actually Godly because they're all using the same power of his own mind. Isn't that nice? That's a true thing. Being the problem and the solution is causing you joy instead of pain because the admission of causation is what joy is because it allows you to exercise the power of God's mind rather than your own. Come on. It's so simple, don't you see? Did you see that? That's why you're so happy. It isn't that you can identify the problem and solve it, it's that you continue releasing the necessity for the resolution.

Okay, that's the end of Chapter 17. It deals with human relationships. I've always had problems with the sentence, "You've got to have faith." My perspective is always too wide in regard to the problem. I learned early that there were other solutions to the problem, which is a form of faith. Can you hear me? The action of my mind offered other solutions or creative associations that were not apparently contained within the problem. That, obviously, is an expression of faith outside of the realm of where the problem is. I was able to do that very well – until I discovered that no matter what I did, it couldn't be solved. So by not taking it too seriously, you are able to escape. And by suddenly realizing the whole thing is just a joke anyway – it's a cosmic joke. There is no real way that you could deteriorate and get old and rotten and die. It's totally senseless. It doesn't seem funny to you. Yet you make it up; you make horror up in your humanness. And you scare each other to life and death. I'm obviously trying to scare you to life. But you're afraid to look at the horror of the mask of you in its entirety or it would literally scare you to life. It could not *not* because you'd see the reflection is nothing but you in its entirety – that you had no conflict in your fear is what I just said. That's nice. The *Course In Miracles* frightens you to life, is a true statement. Jesus says that this is going to lead you directly into the fear of the horror of the one thing you didn't want to look at. That's what you've been offered. And that's what you've found. And you have the enjoyment now of the realization that it was nothing. Until you came into that situation in your mind, you could not know that. Now I'm back to: your readiness depends on you in the admission. From then on it's easy because you'll immediately begin to see the solution. The progress of your path or your program of enlightenment will be based on your willingness not to participate in the discovery of letting God be God. That's the end of this chapter. Obviously I'm teaching you that faith in God is the solution to your problems – not God as defined by your making, but God as he is in the entirety of the Universe. Boy is that nice. Thy will be done. I do not know who I am or what I'm doing, and I will not bring my old associations in here to solve it. That's not a perceptual something you should identify compared to something else. It's a statement of your condition in the relationship with yourself.

I want you to be happy with the music of the spheres and the harmony that is being offered to you. I don't want somebody to tell you that you have to specialize in something in order to demonstrate your limited creativity. It isn't that you may or may not be expert in something, but I want you to be free to love everybody else's expression without the necessity of the mechanics of how they obtained it. It is not that the discipline is not necessary – this is the great dilemma – but that you can enjoy the creative energy of that art of coming to God. And that's the fun of it. Do you see?

Isn't it fun? Out of the thousands of small towns in this country where dramatic classes put on Camelot, they just put it on in Baraboo, and there's always somebody in town who stars and somebody who directs and each community forms

CHAPTER ELEVEN: Faith, Crop Circles And Chapter 17

resolutions contained within their own locale, within their own limitation. This is exactly what is happening here on earth. What you're finally saying is, "I'm tired of playing in this production." Whoever produced this, it's not right. It's not working. I've got to get out of this little town. So you get out of the town and you go and you discover that everyone else is playing the same thing! They do it in different manners, but finally that's all it is. Not only that, but those that get the parts aren't as good as you are. They get the part on the basis of their résumé, rather than your talent. That's true. How elusive a thing real talent is. "Well, he doesn't sing as well, he doesn't act as well, but there's just something about him." That's what that is. That then becomes the new standard of association because it's more communicative and it's innovative in that it wasn't recognized in the other spheres of what constituted art or communication. Good for you.

But that doesn't mean if you turn on Mozart right now that you can't hear the entirety of Mozart. If you hear the entirety of Mozart, you will be hearing the entirety of yourself. It isn't that he doesn't give you a provision in his associations of the music of the spheres, of your capacity to define in the entirety of you the harmony and energy of love that he's trying to play. Put on a little Mozart. Now, there's no question there's more harmony in Mozart than Joe Schwartz. You say, "Is that really true?" It must be, because you can tell the difference.

The Weatherman

Once upon a time at a small TV station in a medium-sized town in the Mid-Western United States there was a weatherman. He was a competent meteorologist and after studying National Weather Bureau data and other local sources would appear nightly on television and, as accurately as most forecasters, predict the weather conditions.

One night, to his amazement, a miraculously beautiful spiritual vision overcame him. He was shown the total unity of purpose of man in his search for truth. He saw that God is - and through the revelation recognized that he had the power to make absolute and inevitably perfect predictions.

Deciding to test his newly-acquired talent, on the 6:00 weather the following night, he forthrightly made the incredible prediction that beginning at the end of his broadcast and for a 24-hour period, no precipitation of any kind would fall on the earth. Not rain, not snow, not sleet, not hail, not anything, not anywhere. And sure enough, the miracle happened. Hour after hour passed and as the deadline approached all reporting stations confirmed the total absence of moisture of any kind. The earth trembled at the prospect of perfection. Fortunately, at the last moment, a flock of high flying birds plopped on a Bulgarian wheat farmer. The weatherman immediately became the target of intense criticism, was attacked, derided and scorned and forced to resign from the station.

Three days later, rejected, despondent and friendless, he was run over by a taxi In downtown Cleveland and killed.

Following his death his near-perfect prediction became legend. And his martyrdom verified, he was proposed for Sainthood and canonized in record time.

He is known as the Soothsaying Saint and is venerated as the patron of Fortune Tellers, Clairvoyants, Religious Prophesiers, Economic advisers, Market Analyzers, Bookmakers and of course Weather persons.

(From The Spiritual Teacher's Notebook)

CHAPTER TWELVE

Christian Enlightenment

We are just sort of rambling here. The sun is shining. Tomorrow is Palm Sunday. And we have thought forms projected from us, don't we? Finally, in perceptual consciousness, thought becomes form inevitably. There are some lovely sentences from the Master Teacher Jesus in the *Course* that would indicate from certainty that nothing represents anything. The whole nature of the schism is the notation that Adam represents himself separately from his whole and must by necessity begin to what? Name the animals. The moment that he names anything he gives it a separate identity from his self-association, and it becomes part of his nomenclature of thought forms.

We get them started around here at 5:30, so those of you who come to God's Country Place must know. I'm up at 4:30 kneeling! Don't you believe that, it's later than that. It's 6:30. It's a thought form, do you see. See how your mind organizes time in relationship to the form that you are being presented with. We are faced, then, with the impossible dilemma of the perceptual mind in association with its own forms as directed by its memory.

Without getting into the basis of the Workbook, obviously, the consciousnesses doing the *Course In Miracles* are not doing the Workbook in the nature in which we would make a provision for it. The initial statement of the Workbook would simply be: You don't really know what anything is, but have given it a form in a space/time relationship in a comparison of your consciousness mind as you apparently have constructed yourself, since obviously the construction of yourself would be a denial of the absolute source from which the emanation of your thought protrudes. That being said, you are caught with these forms. I'm going to give you the forms. Why? I must give you the symbols of your own reality. There is a lovely sentence in the *Course* where Jesus says the Christ is not a body, yet is the Christ always with you. That means literally that every form that you have associated in your apparent symbiotic self-relationship must contain the bright light of the absolute, more-than replica of the single wholeness which is the Light of the Universe. It cannot be different than that. Do you see?

Now you say to me, "Master, is there value in giving correspondence to the relationship of my bodily functions with the Apocalypse of the New Testament?" Apocalypse, that means the awakening of the churches or the centers of your body in the esoteric definitions of Christianity. And I say, certainly! But remember that nothing symbolizes anything. There might be a great deal of value in the association of your pineal gland with the Philadelphia church or with the ajna chakra. I don't know. What value do you give to the certainty that finally you are only a conglomerate self-expression? But remember, my declaration to you is that the thyroid gland, or the pituitary, is an absolutely true association, not a symbolic representation. Can you see this? Then your assignment would be to connect, or expand your comparative consciousnesses in relationship with yourself.

CHAPTER TWELVE: Christian Enlightenment

Remember that you have mis-defined yourself. But you have defined yourself totally unto yourself. If the lion could hunt down wind, there wouldn't be any antelope. The lion has provisions for his lion-ness, over which bounds he will not step. If he did, obviously he would disrupt his previous association with himself. Do you see that? You can't teach the lion to hunt down wind. His lion-ness is based on blundering, finally, into the antelope so that they can smell him from a mile away. You have a tendency now, as man – split-mindedness, form identification – man very well can learn to hunt down wind. And did. And depreciated the antelope herd. Man then became responsible for his antelope association because he knew somewhere within his framework that the antelope was him. This is the nature god evolving. This is pantheism finally; that everything is a God unto itself in its own wholeness association. That's wonderful. What are you going to do with that in your own thought associations? At what point do you separate the lion from yourself, or, as Jesus says, the coat hanger. In the Workbook, He says God is in the coat hanger. He doesn't mean that the coat hanger is a piece of God; he means that the coat hanger is God. And that's quite a step, isn't it? The admission that the thought forms of you in space time, in your own association can be brought together and must be brought together in the wholeness of your own mind. So Adam named an animal. Wow. From then on he was caught with naming, because if one thing has a name, everything must have one. And he'll live within that framework of the thought forms of his own creative mechanisms.

That's what we're faced with here. You are using this power of singleness of consciousness and identifying it separately from you. If you used Master Jesus, you'd say there are no separate thoughts. There is no such thing as a separate thought. Everything must be only your thought about it. You can do anything you want with that relationship, but you will not make it not so. The difficulty of identification or the impossibility of identification with the awakened mind is that it's perfectly clear to me that the candle there on the table is whole, not only unto itself, but unto me, and I have no relationship with it that is symbolic, although I may, in my perception, identify it and perform the ritual of the symbolism of subtracting the distance between that candle and my mind process. You would call that, perhaps, the mass. I can remember when somebody said to me that in Catholicism, in the Catholic mass, that the wine becomes the blood and the wafer is the symbol of the body. And I'm perfectly aware that in reality that's exactly what they do become – the body and blood. This is the statement of resurrection, transfiguration. This is the statement of transmutation. Finally this is the declaration that you are whole each moment, and as these symbols come together you'll see the incredible allegory of the passion of your reality. Isn't that nice to know. Do you want to do that? Or would you prefer to continue to assemble the annihilation forms, the temporal forms that you see come and go and fade. Your attempts to find a true frame of reference with the symbols that you have constructed is finally impossible because the mind in self-identification requires the conflict of the separation of disassociation. And this is where your problem lies.

We're laughing. We laugh at my so-called esoteric teaching. I didn't know there was a connection between the chakras of the Eastern tradition and the Revelation. The declarations, the admonitions of the vision to the pineal gland, which you term the Holy Spirit, are very lovely. If you'd like to read Revelation sometime, you could see. There's a dialogue that goes on with Spirit concerning the churches which are the centers of the body. When it gets to the pineal, which is the Philadelphia, which we call the church of Brotherly Love, he says, listen, I'll read this from Revelation, this is kind of fun: *And to the angel of the church in Philadelphia write: These things saith he that is holy, he that is true, he that hath the key of David, he that openeth, and no man shutteth; and shutteth, and no man openeth; I know thy works: behold, I have set before thee an open door, and no man can shut it; for thou hast a little*

CHAPTER TWELVE: *Christian Enlightenment*

strength, and hast kept my word, and hast not denied my name. This is very familiar to you. *Behold, I will make them of the synagogue of Satan, which say they are Jews, and are not, but do lie; behold, I will make them to come and worship before thy feet, and to know that I have loved thee.* The awakening of the Christ. *Because thou hast kept the word of my patience, I also will keep thee from the hour of temptation, which shall come upon all the world, to try them that dwell upon the earth. Behold, I come quickly; hold that fast which thou hast, that no man take thy crown. Him that overcometh will I make a pillar in the temple of my God, and he shall go no more out; and I will write upon him the name of my God, and the name of the city of my God, which is new Jerusalem, which cometh down out of heaven from my God: and I will write upon him my new name. He that hath an ear, let him hear what the Spirit saith unto the churches.* (Revelation 3:7-13)

Isn't that lovely? The expression of the New Jerusalem, of the awakening of your crown chakra, you like to call it; the indications of your awakening as manifest symbolically in Revelation. It's interesting that when He gets to the pituitary, the final so-called church, He's a little cool to it because there is a tendency for the so-called awakened mind to become lukewarm in its associations. And He rebukes it and directs it to be heart-felt. It's lovely. I don't know what you do with this as far as the teachings go, but I declare to you that all of this will be of immense value to you if you will do a direct association with the transformation of your so-called body/mind to the awakening, to the new covenant, to the directions to New Jerusalem emanating from your Bethlehem. This is what you would term esoteric Christianity.

If there is one thing that Master Jesus was, and only one thing, it was mystical. Anything else that you add to the simple statement of the transformation of man to become God, or to know that he is God, that is, as to the doctrinal dictation, the catechisms, don't really have any meaning at this point for you, do they? Not if you're going to teach the *Course In Miracles;* not if you're going to take the scripture of Jesus Christ resurrected, man become God, and make application to your body/mind, which indeed you did and have risen, and are on the right hand of the Father, aren't you? How lovely.

Now the problem that we have in the direction that this attempted correspondence with split mind takes is to the observation that all action means nothing and is simply the distance between the thought forms, and that your continued motivation to direct your thoughts in future frames of reference are what keep you in the time-sequential relationships. So we end up saying, "Do nothing," which to you is a form of action, so you sit in your apparent nothingness, and now the application of the discipline of these talks will become important to you because with the allowance for the continuing subtraction of your perceptual associations you will undergo the transformation. This is the initiation teaching. This is the bringing together of the thought forms of your mind and the opening of the tomb, the splitting of the temple, the Easter of your remembrance. That is what you are undergoing now.

Does this give you happiness and peace? Or does this cause you consternation as your value systems shift and you suddenly have to look at the things that have been occurring around you that you have previously been willing to tolerate that are no longer tolerable to you. You are what? Seeing a view of hell, as Master Jesus would say. You see that by the guilt of your associate thoughts you have literally constructed a falsity of a dimension heretofore unknown to you by the determination of you to subtract yourself from your own reality. This, then, is *A Course In Miracles,* a course in the coming together of your mind, the wholeness of you in the absolute universal association which

CHAPTER TWELVE: Christian Enlightenment

we call Heaven, a Heaven which you couldn't possibly have left since disassociation from everything is impossible.

The teaching that this is a process of symbolizing at a new level can be very valuable to you, that the passion of your union with God is the single occurrence of value here, the only thing that really matters. In that sense, when Jesus says in the *Course*, "This is a required course," that is literally true because anything that is not in Heaven is not real and is no thing. You keep a gap in your visions, don't you, a gap in your dream, in your thought forms, and continue to construct this adversary, this Adam, and attest to his reality. But it's a dream. And whole consciousness knows not of it; yet you use the power of your whole mind to make that false determination.

What is occurring to many of you now as this road reaches its final manifestation, its final assertion, is that all of these forms that were in your mind can be, and must be, brought together in this single assertion so you don't subtract anything in your mind. That's a real occurrence in your perception. That's a lighting up of the caverns of darkness that you have constructed. Literally the dark knows not of the Light. You become Light and know not of the dark. This is gone and never was. It is simply passed away. Jesus says that the time will come, and has come, when you won't remember this at all. You retain just a momentary remembrance of it now in order to reenact your Christhood, teacher. That's your assignment. For a moment we would appreciate it, while you can remember this, although you're not required to, that you would aid us in this circle of atonement. Obviously we are providing you with the mechanisms of teaching, and it must be that you taught; that somewhere along the line you signed up for this assignment. Otherwise what? You'll simply spring into Heaven and be gone.

There's a rather ambiguous, ambivalent statement in the Teacher's Manual where the young perpetrator declares that your job is to become enlightened, but not to get there, or something to that effect. Obviously my whole mind isn't here. The corruption of my capacities to assume the momentary guilt of my own relationships make me the Christ. But I am perfectly aware that I have constructed this in my mind; that when I am gone all of the apparent separations have no reality. That's what makes me a savior, isn't it? But my direction must be that since mind is singular, that you must be the disassociation as well as the reassociation. As you construct me in your perception, I will become. But I assure you that your separate associations, that is the symbolism of your perceptual mind, have absolutely no meaning to me. I see that you have them, and that qualifies me then to be a savior. But the idea of giving personal, individual value to my saviorship is absurd. I had nothing to do with my own awakening.

I teach you that you have everything to do with it until you see that you have nothing to do with it. Why would I ever take credit for what I had nothing to do with? Something that is unreal can't come to reality. But I can't know that from my unreal status. So I underwent the purgation of the relationship of myself with myself and awoke to my own truth. These statements have been made by every awakening mind and have always meant the same thing to the unawakened mind, but that does not make them not true. I am a perfect representation of an awakened mind in my capacity to assimilate thought forms into expressions to communicate to the chaos. And I am teaching you to become and do that as Master Jesus directs you in the *Course*. And you will do it because you did do it. When you do it in time is of no concern to me because my time is now and will be now whenever you make your own determination. Obviously you are afraid that this might be true, and I direct to you that you should be happy and joyous that it is true, shouldn't you? Does that require the acceptance of these words now that have come into your associations of death? Sure. What's wrong with that? Shouldn't we do that, then, and wake up together in the mandala of the reality of the bright golden arc, as Master Jesus says, as your mind transforms out of this dark period.

CHAPTER TWELVE: *Christian Enlightenment*

This is the transformation of your mind, then, that we teach. Has this all gone before? Certainly! Is this really all over? Of course! Did we all really gather at the point of debarkation and ascend together to Heaven? Of course! What's wrong with that? Somehow you want to have something to say about it, but the idea of absolute determinism will be of infinite value to you. Why? It will allow you simply to let go, to relinquish your symbol associations and become whole. That's the direction we lead you with the assertion that we are in your future. We share together this moment of schism now, but it has no reality. So let's step out of time together and be in eternity. We are at God's Country Place which is every place that there is or could be. And each moment you determine in your mind where you will be in this space/time ratio of your configuration. We would direct you now to shorten time and awaken to that moment of glory that came about the moment that the idea of the separation occurred. It has been long coming, but what difference how long, now that they have come, now that we are here, whether a moment or a million years. So we say to you, welcome home. Happy Easter. He is risen! He is risen indeed.

Who's the greatest initiate that ever lived? The original great one? Jesus Christ of Nazareth! He underwent the apparent passion of the transfiguration of the body/mind. How lovely, then, these symbols, this allegory of the resurrection through the birth of Christ and the virgin female reality and its flight into Egypt and its escaping the Pharaoh as this new Christ that is born in you ascends from your lower regions, from your glandular associations, on up to the Jerusalem or the Golgotha, the place of the skull, where you are crucified and transformed. Isn't that lovely? This can be a lovely initiatory statement that you are born in Bethlehem, seven miles from Jerusalem, in the cradle, with the association of the beast, in the manger of your potential, in the cave. And it never really stops. Most particularly, as Jesus says in the *Course*, it includes the week of the passion, the Holy Week. In the *Course*, in Chapter 20 of the text, He says this contains all of the elements of the necessity for your undergoing of this passion of the awakening of your own mind, of the springing open of the tomb.

How much Gethsemane does it include? How much apparent abandonment of the thought forms that you had established to give you solace within the framework of your own awakening? I don't know. Master Jesus says to the disciples, "Can't you even stay awake long enough to see what's happening to me?" Wow. Then He turns to the Father in His silent prayer, and says, "Father, I'd appreciate it if you would remove this cup of sacrifice from me," speaking as a man, of course. (Matthew 26:39-40) There's no answer, is there. Then the incredible words that nobody really wants to hear on the cross of, "My God, why hast thou forsaken me?" which is followed almost immediately by, "Into thy hands I commend my spirit" and, "It is accomplished." This is literally the process that you are undergoing as an initiate coming to your own truth. Is that okay for you to hear? Why shouldn't you hear it? Look at the value of Christianity in the statements of Christ. Why? Because following "into thy hands I commend my spirit" He is reconfigurated in the body/mind association to give you the absolute direction of the impossibility of death.

We don't die to prove there is no death in the sense of physical death but rather declare to you that "he that believeth unto me will never die" and will see immediately that totalness of his dedication to the reality of the Christ form brings him instantly into an awakened vocabulary of expression in the extension of his own mind. This is called speaking in the spirit. That is what I am doing now. That's what you will do. That's what Jesus commanded His disciples to do when He said go out into the villages, and don't take sides, just open your mouth and let the spirit speak. He sent out 60 or 80 of them and 12 came back, and they weren't all too sure what they were doing. That's okay. What does He say? If you're not being heard in the village, put dust to your heels. Meanwhile the lovely miracles are occurring all about them.

CHAPTER TWELVE: Christian Enlightenment

You must remember this: It is only the residual of the resurrection that remains here. If you are going to make that statement, you are going to have to look at the certainty that you were the residual, that you were the rejecter of the resurrection. For indeed do you make the proclamation through propitiation that the Christ is risen, you are no longer here and the earth is gone. This directs you to the absurdity of the continuing establishment of the mind in the limitation. Since if the Christ is real, indeed He is you and you are risen with Him. This is the new teaching. This is the direction of the later day Masters. The later day teachers through the *Course In Miracles* will make these declarations to you, and you did use them, and you did come to know this in the fabric of the continuum of space/time that you have constructed.

For me it's a little bit like stepping out of time and I view the fabric, sort of like a honeycomb of the reality relationship of space/time, and I can detect the bright spot of the insertion of *A Course In Miracles*. And we step out and then step back in to manifest in the certainty of the communicative devices of ourselves with ourselves. Jesus says if you'd look at it that we're all together out of time reminiscing about this, it would be of value to you. I assure you that's true and that the great Master Jesus sits with us now as He sits with us out of time. Is this an indication of another level of associate consciousness? Sure. What's wrong with that? Up from the grave you arose and became that new Light body. That's what we're teaching. This can be heard by people at various levels of their own maturation, and that's all right. But I direct to you that the power of God is you, is not more or less than that. When Jesus says that you are the only living Son of God, that is a statement of your whole mind in association with the creative forces of single reality. It cannot *not* be so, teacher. And if you'll look at it now, you will come more and more to that determination.

We're all laughing at esoteric Christianity. Of course when the Christ is born in Bethlehem, He is pursued by Herod which is the middle ranges of the human energy as the Christ progresses from Bethlehem to Jerusalem, and He hides in Egypt. So the parting of the Red Sea, the crossing of the Jordan, is the movement of the Christ child who is born, up to His full kingship. There are some lovely passages in the *Course* where Jesus says take care of this lovely little Christ child that is born in you now, and we might say this to you, you've got this Christ child born in you. You've reached a point of perfection in your own virginity where momentarily you had this union or this impregnation of spirit. And you want to tender full recognition to this Christmas Christ. The idea that you would remain in Egypt and teach the first covenant, the covenant of reciprocity or exchange, which was the law given to the ego – to Abraham, first man by true force – the process of moving from awareness, that is the naming of the animals to the statement of the New Covenant that you are the creator and only Love. So we're not going to leave you in Egypt. What about the forty years in the wilderness where you've been for some time in your hopes to find this truth. Indeed, we did hide Moses in the bulrushes. And Moses did begin the leading. But remember he never reached the Holy Land. He never reached New Jerusalem. But you are, and you did, because you rode into the Holy City and that will be celebrated on Palm Sunday. You had a room prepared, an upper room, and you admonished the foretellers of this, those who went before, to look for a man with a water jug, which is the dawning of the age of Aquarius in you. You sought out the upper room, the twelve of you. This is the reenactment of the Last Supper, isn't it? "Do this in remembrance of me" and the washing of the feet or the perfection of man in his momentary relationship with the falsity. And on and on. It's lovely to take the gospel of John and to read the Last Supper story. The determination of the disciples to hold the Master Teacher in the limitations of his own mind, and how He overcame and became whole.

 Are we teaching this within the Christian tradition? Hey! We are genetically, in a memory standpoint, directly connected to 2000 years of this tradition. Is there more value, then, in this

CHAPTER TWELVE: *Christian Enlightenment*

symbol relationship of Christianity, perhaps than with other traditions, Eastern traditions? I would direct you to this: To the extent that you subtract anything from your mind, you're not going to succeed in this endeavor. The happy surprise that will come as your mind undergoes this process of initiation, is you will literally begin to see differently. And suddenly a passage of a parable of Jesus that was obscure to you will light up brightly in your mind, and you will see the direct connection of your association in your mind with this. It's a wonderful experience! This is what's happening to you, isn't it? In that sense, and in a true sense, you are undergoing this awakening, this resurrection of your mind. Indeed, the dove did land on your head, didn't he? And the Heavens did open up, and this was the awakening as represented in the caduceus, perhaps, the yin and the yang, the intertwining serpents that became the dove. The twelve tribes of Israel, that represent the nervous system in your body. Would you like to do it that way? Teacher of God, it matters not how you do it, the necessity is for the realization of the connection of your mind with the wholeness of consciousness of God. That's the exciting part of it. Include it, brother.

Does that involve the forgiveness of your previous thoughts? Of course. So what? Why not? What a lovely adventure if you will become, through non-judgment, more inclusive of these thought forms that you have projected from yourself. That's the fun part about it. And that's what many of you are undergoing. We will see you soon in this continuing wider and wider circle of atonement.

Listen to me. It's certainly not my intention in the teaching of the awakening in the Christian vernacular to in any way subtract my certainty of the master teachers of Eastern philosophy, for goodness sake. We'll take some fundamental declarations if you would like to. For those of you who are not familiar with Shankara, if you'd like to read the *Course In Miracles*, or certainly Meher Baba, and it goes on and on. We're not going to do it. But if you ask any master teacher of the Eastern direction how to awaken the kundalini, he will respond "serve." This is exactly the admonition of Master Jesus when you say, "How do I accomplish this?" Serve! Forgive! Give! Give away! Relinquish! There is a certain abstraction in an Eastern teaching of transcendentalism that made allowances for meditation that are not particularly in the exoteric Christian tradition. They are contained, but only in monasteries, aren't they? And convents, where mystical Christianity was forced to find itself through the persecution that emanated from conceptual mind. But you remember this, Eastern philosophers made no attempt. They automatically went to Tibet. They put on the orange robes and banged the gongs in their determination to bring about their own physical awakenings. Master Jesus teaches that you confront, and this is the spread of Western civilization for goodness sake. The crusades and on to the industrial revolution – all the things that occurred through Master Jesus' insertion of energy with the declaration of the wholeness of earth in association with Heaven. Obviously this is conflictual. But finally you must come to know that you have been in conflict only with yourself. This is the statement of what you would call Existentialism; what you would term individual subjective reality which is the certainty of my whole mind as I direct it now to you in your awakening process.

How lovely, then, to incorporate all of the associations of your mind in this process and see that in fact the teachings of a true Zen master would be simply to take your perceptual mind and try to stop it through a koan, for example, from continuing to associate with a limited form of linear time, to force it into an inclusion of itself for just a moment, to disrupt it from its track of time to obliviation. The greatest Zen master there could be is the *Course In Miracles*. The Workbook is a perfect example of an attempt to dislodge you from your time associations. Isn't this lovely? Of course. So you be whole in your thinking and

CHAPTER TWELVE: Christian Enlightenment

stop doing all of these linear doctrinal comparisons. They have no meaning if the symbols have no meaning to begin with. Through this relinquishment of the necessity for opinion, judgment and self-identity, you will discover through this process of transformation the glory of the wholeness of you. Not as directed by you, but rather as determined by the absolute certainty of Universal Consciousness. Let go and let God!

To many of you now, the prospects of this individual awakening in you is becoming very exciting and very momentous and we encourage you now to become even more one-eyed as you direct yourself toward this full endeavor. Let's share just a moment now the certainty of our capacity to unite with this new energy and to be with God. We'll share these moments together. We hope we see you soon. We have never been apart.

The stone was rolled back. He had departed. The cave was empty. You are risen, then, aren't you? You are risen indeed!

Happy Easter!

Rachael Williams
Willow Valley Retirement Home
Manor North
8ᵗʰ 312.   what is last Jugement
3ʳᵈ 307.
Tel # 484-889-9380